Mistakes Were Made

(some in French)

Fiona Lewis

Regan Arts.

New York

All photos courtesy the author, except:

Courtesy AF archive/Alamy Stock: Pictoral Press, 97; Eva Sereny for *The London Sunday Times Magazine,* 101 (left); Norman Eales for *Harpers Queen* magazine, 101 (top and bottom); Courtesy Photofest, 121; Courtesy John Burnham, 133; Michael Ochs Archive/Getty Images, 144; Photo by Loomis Dean, the LIFE pictures collection/Getty Images, 149; Photo by Kathryn Ireland, 197 (left); Photo by Mikki Vang, 197 (right); Courtesy AF archive/Alamy Stock, 209; Photo by Guy Webster, 244; Courtesy Peter Fonda archive, 251.

Regan Arts.

65 Bleecker Street
New York, NY 10012

First Regan Arts hardcover edition, May 2017

Library of Congress Control Number: 2017937174

ISBN 978-1-68245-082-6

Interior design by Nancy Singer
Cover design by Richard Ljoenes

Printed in the United States of America

10 9 8 7 6 5 4 3 2 1

For my parents, my brother and sister, and most of all for Art.

contents

one
Los Angeles 2004.

One day, about a year ago, I felt myself coming completely undone, as if I were going off the rails. I developed strange allergies. I felt exhausted all the time, but couldn't sleep. And in the middle of the night, during those punishingly lucid hours, I would ask myself the same question: *Is this it? Is this the life I meant myself to have?* Because one thing was painfully obvious: if I hadn't accomplished nearly as much as I'd set out to achieve some twenty, or even thirty years before, it was almost certain now, in my fifties, I never would. A frightening thought. It was no longer realistic to focus on my own potential, because everything that was going to happen had happened to me already. I didn't know what to do with these feelings of worthlessness. In the past, I'd been able to ground myself in some kind of logic, to say, *Push on, start again!* Now I felt as if I were slipping backward over the edge of a ravine, abandoned not only by my old self but by that reliable standby, *optimism*.

I didn't mention this to anyone. How could I? After all, my life was privileged, enviable. I was living in Los Angeles, married to a successful man, the sun shone, nothing had changed—except I couldn't get out of bed in the morning. "What's the matter?" my husband asked repeatedly. "Nothing," I said, on cue. "Well, there must be *something*." Yes, there was.

There was fear and rage. A lot of rage—suppressed, naturally, or indiscriminately directed at a stranger, some foot-dragging check-out girl at the market. The fear was more pervasive. There were nights driving back on Sunset Boulevard when confronted by a blaze of oncoming headlights, I was tempted to flip the wheel and embrace the end. *I'm done.* Laughable, really. The self-pity. The drama. Not brave enough. And no, I did not really want to be erased.

What I wanted was freedom. I wanted part of *myself* back. Which part? Well, that was the quandary. The unsolvable question. Did I want my freedom enough to leave my husband? Did I want a divorce after almost twenty years? Was I paying too much emotionally for safety and understanding? "How can you even love me like this?" I would ask with exasperation, cowardly about what I obviously needed so badly. On the other hand, did I really want to be one of those aging single women taking late-night spinning classes or going on a scary sex date from Match.com? The anonymous fuck—that longed-for nonemotional thrill. God help me. I tried to imagine it: standing next to some stranger in the elevator with the scary overhead lighting. Then the undressing, the getting naked part, the *old* skin. What Saul Bellow once described, referring to a woman of a certain age, as "washed but not ironed." When exactly did *that* happen? Overnight, it seems. Ten years ago, I could still get a few morale-boosting looks from younger men. The kids at the gas station, California boys in surfing shorts and flip-flops, filling their beat-up coupes, would give me a stoner's wink. Now it's *ma'am.* "Excuse me, ma'am," they say, looking a little scared. Well, I did look scary. "Is it hormonal?" my husband asks, with far more affection than I deserve. "Possibly." Yes, of course it is. That and more. Some mysterious chemical imbalance, as yet unknown. To be discovered soon, I hope, along with a suitable drug to counteract the dread of aging, the burden of contemplation, of being *invisible.*

What is the definition of success anyway? And from whose point of view? Your family's, your competitor's—or from an inflated idea of your own worth? Is ambition the great self-motivator, or is it just a constant solicitation for love?

"You've had a good career," my husband likes to say. "Look what you've done."

Yes, I've done a few things. Way back in the glorious '60s, I started out as a model and an actress. Those innocent days when men could jokingly refer to us hyphenates as "mattresses" and get away with it. What did we know? I starred in many movies—albeit at the end as a horror heroine. I married the son of royalty, the Hollywood kind; I had affairs with famous men (is this still a career?), discarded them, not guiltlessly, but furiously, wanting *more*. I became a writer. I was a writer down to my bones—that was real passion: journalism, screenplays, a book, but then something happened. Or rather, nothing happened. It was a slow decline, like health, like aging. I was semi-famous; I *had* been something, but as one worthy critic remarked: *past laurels fade fast*.

What to do? Years ago, I would simply get on a plane. Leave. Reinvent myself. Coming out of an airport into a strange city with its sharp smells and foreign voices, time was suspended, the inevitable postponed. But even that stopped working. Suddenly hotel rooms were too confining, the beds too hard, and like some invalid I had to travel with my own feather pillow. I also needed a balcony, to get out, or at least to keep sight of the horizon. And however beautiful the view—some tree-lined avenue I'd longed for—as soon as I got there, I would start thinking about being somewhere else. No matter what city I landed in, I felt like a displaced person. In London I missed the weather in California, and in California I would start thinking about France—or more specifically, the South of France of my childhood.

The truth is, after more than two decades living in America, I still feel like an alien. "You've been living in L.A. for *half* your life," my husband reminds me. "I know. But I'm English" I say, as though I've finally pinpointed my particularly crippling disease.

"Try to be positive. Live in the present."

But I can't. Because I don't know what I'm doing here anymore. All I can think about is the past.

two
England. The 1950s.

Uncle Mike, a debonair man from the old school who favored handmade shoes and the cardsharp's mustache, once gave me some advice. "Remember," he said, "a woman has a choice in life. You can either spend it on your knees scrubbing the kitchen floor, or you can spend it lying on the deck of a yacht in the South of France. Yours to decide."

I was seven years old at the time, but something must have sunk in: a life beyond suburban England.

To be honest, for as long as I can remember, I wanted to escape. From danger, from boredom—from myself mostly, though of course I didn't know it. In the early years this vague impulse was confined to my immediate area: the space under the stairs or the back of the airing cupboard where, curled up on a shelf against the boiler, I was lulled by the comforting smell of singed sheets. Certain places I claimed as my own. Our bathroom, for instance, with its black and green tiles and a black tub, deemed by one of my mother's friends as *ultra* modern, interested me no end. There were things, too, that I took possession of: my father's medals, books with intriguing names like *West with the Night,* and a souvenir ashtray from Egypt in the shape of a camel. There was our solid oak front door with its outside striped awning—portal to future adventure. And then, in the dining room, a pair of stained-glass windows I was particularly fascinated by, brilliantly lit up by the afternoon sun, and that merely a decade later struck me as horribly suburban. In warmer weather, there was the garden, our rectangle of grass bordered by brown fencing. Sometime in the early '50s, my father bought the plot next door from a tea merchant. An old orchard, it was a mysterious place with an abandoned greenhouse, espaliered peach trees, and mulberries. But there I went. At first, escape was not a concrete idea; it was more a nervous reaction to my being a nuisance. Housework consumed my mother. Cleanliness and order were her way of organizing life, to make it endurable. I recognized her struggle early on—or at least I recognized that *I alone* of the children saw this; that, moreover, I contributed to it, and at the sound of the Hoover, that first disturbing roar, I fled outside.

Westcliff-on-Sea was a quiet suburban town, a seaside resort on the Thames Estuary, an hour east by train from London. In 1951, only a few years after the war, knots of barbed wire still littered the beaches, and everything was in short supply. We had ration books for meat and sweets, and no phone, the one allotted to my father as a naval officer having recently been moved to his law office in the High Street.

To get to the shops in the morning, my mother rode her bicycle, and occasionally I was allowed to go with her. (When I wasn't making myself scarce, I cherished our moments together because I was trying hard to become her favorite.) I was lowered into a small metal basket on the back and secured with a leather strap. Then my mother would hitch up her skirt and we'd take off. The thrill was enormous. The wind in my face, the rhythmic click of the chain, the smell of oil and asphalt and trees. At the top of Seymour Road, we turned left onto Imperial Avenue, a wider street with imposing Victorian brick houses. One in particular had a low wall banked by large blue bushes (later discovered to be hydrangeas). As she turned the corner fast, swerving in front of the house, and my thighs jammed against the metal sides of my little cage and my Kangol beret dipped sideways, I longed for the thin strap to break, to be hurled into the air and to land among those giant blue bushes. Far from being terrified, the idea thrilled me. I was secretly disappointed when we made it to the butcher shop and back unharmed. As far as I was concerned, we never traveled far enough.

I had to wait a few years, but finally the great escape came: we started going to the French Riviera for our summer holidays. In those days, my father was in partnership with Uncle Mike. Mike owned Bristol Freighters, big-nosed planes with room enough for two or three cars, and ran a service from nearby Southend Airport across the channel to Calais. Of course, he wasn't our real uncle. Smooth and disarming, he bore none of the reticence that prevented most well-brought-up Englishmen from making a fortune. He had flown supplies to Berlin when it was still a closed zone. Later he would pilot old Dakotas to Biafra, delivering arms to East African rebels, annoyed, he would say, because despite the Red Cross markings on the wings, he was continually shot at. Naturally, this was exactly the kind of man I planned to marry later on.

From Calais we took the Route nationale 7, my father at the wheel of our old Austin Atlantic, my mother next to him with my brother, the Michelin map spread across their knees. I was crammed in the back with my sister and Sylvia. There had been a series of au pairs by then, but I loved Sylvia the best. I loved her big, soft arms and her flowery dresses. My father teasingly called her "old Syl," though I often heard him complain to my mother that she stole his razor blades to shave her mustache. But I adored her. When she left the following year, to get married, I hung on to those big arms, sank to my knees, and wept.

It took three days to get to the South of France. We played games of I spy and capital cities, and had cloud formation competitions. There were improvised picnics by rushing streams and torturous forays into the undergrowth with a toilet roll. It was often cold or raining, but by the third day, the color of the hills changed. The earth went from brown to red, it was suddenly blazing hot, and by the time we got to Fréjus our legs stuck to the seats and we were groaning with boredom. Then we saw it:

A glimpse of blue. A cool inviting rectangle that appeared briefly, only to vanish as we made our winding descent. There were more sightings as my father navigated the murderous curves of the Corniche, flashes of bluish-green through the trees, and then, as we joined the traffic near Sainte-Maxime, the sky opened up and there it was: the Mediterranean. The curved bay, the fizzing pines, the rows of pink rooftops spilling down to that vast stretch of turquoise against a deep blue sky. It was shockingly beautiful, and it took our breath away.

After that, everything was hypnotic. Driving through Saint-Tropez, I tried to absorb the colors, the bright shops with postcards, beach balls, racks of espadrilles, the pots of geraniums, and the shock of pink bougainvillea climbing the walls of the Hôtel Les Palmiers. An old turn-of-the-century house in Place des Lyces, it was now a brightly whitewashed *pension de luxe*. There was a terrace and a garden, home to a few burnt palm trees, and beyond that a new annex where we had our three rooms. It was the garden, however, that made such an impression on me.

My brother, my sister, and me boarding the
plane to Calais.

. . .

At nine and three-quarters I am thin, gangly, with short, unruly brown hair. I like boys' clothes, boys' things. I am interested in being cool, and have already informed my father that I want a drum kit for Christmas. My thoughts about escaping are still vague, some woolly notion that never goes beyond the superficial. In other words, without my family, I barely exist.

But one morning this awakening did take place. It was around nine o'clock. My parents were still asleep, my brother and sister had gone somewhere with Sylvia, and I was sitting outside at one of the hotel's metal tables. The terrace was empty, everything was quiet, except for the rustle of palm leaves and a radio playing somewhere. Time had slowed down; I felt relaxed—that is, I was conscious of *being* relaxed. A few minutes later, I heard feet crunching across the gravel—the owner of the hotel coming from the kitchen. So far, I hadn't met any foreign women, but Mme. Guerin seemed the perfect picture of Frenchness to me, and about as exotic as a circus performer. She wore a semitransparent peasant blouse, a tight black skirt, and black heels. Her skin was nut brown, her dark curls had been licked into place, and her orange lipstick, applied along some forgotten path, rose temptingly close to her nostrils. Sashaying over, she bent down to deposit a *café crème* and a warm *pain au chocolat* on the table. Her face was close to mine; she smelled of roses and damp earth. "*Mignon*," she said, touching my cheek, then added a remark about the whiteness of my skin, "*Trop blanc!*" The intimacy of the moment was thrilling, unimaginably seductive. And in that instant something happened. I saw myself objectively, as a separate being. Sitting in a foreign country, in the hot morning sun, drinking real coffee (that tart, muddy smell), I was suddenly transported. I had escaped the damp wastes of Essex; my life had begun.

And it went on like that. We would drive through fields of vines, then down a mud track to get to Tahiti Plage. Almost empty in those days, a strip of white sand curving away like a desert island, there were only a few umbrellas and a makeshift bar, a bamboo shack with fake totem poles holding up the roof. But the heat was fantastic, the ocean transparent with schools of tiny yellow fish we could catch with our hands. In the afternoon, I would take a walk with Sylvia beyond Pampelonne to the nude beach. Nonchalantly we strolled, pretending to stare out to sea, while behind us, bodies emerged from little dug-out pits like roasted seals. I'd been told the police often raided these holes, barely screened by a few dried palm fronds. But I was more interested to see that naked breasts—breasts of any size—seemed far less attractive than those partially covered up. My mother's, for instance. Wrapped in her white sharkskin bathing suit, a homemade one-piece, her arms and legs slick with Ambre Solaire, she looked far more appealing, more mysterious, and, yes, compared with the harassed mother I knew in Westcliff-on-Sea, sleekly transformed. This aesthetic awakening, the idea of bodies and how they related to clothes, how one person's shape could attract the attention of another—in other words, how sex might work, although I didn't have the capability to pursue the thought that far—was also a revelation.

After the beach we went to Senequier, the most fashionable café on the port. By seven o'clock the terrace was packed, the streets swarming. There were sports cars roaring back and forth, rich boys in their open Lamborghinis and Fiats, who revved their engines and tried to pick up girls. Girls, by the way, who seemed unimaginably beautiful to me. Long-legged, olive-skinned creatures in short shorts and ballet slippers, who glided in and out of the cafés, arm in arm, with their heads thrown back. Even the older women looked impeccably *soigné*—sun-bronzed, wearing gold lamé trousers, and carrying little dogs. And then the local boys, the wet-lipped gigolos, who whistled and shouted over the noise— the staccato pop-pop of velosolexes, cars honking, and motorcycles in full roar—*Hellooo . . . eh, minou, tres belle.* I was mesmerized. I'd never seen anything like it. On the pretext of having to make a desperate run for the toilets, I would duck inside the café, then come out by a different door so I could watch the action on my own. I wanted to mingle with the crowd, absorb the sounds and smells, commit the scene to memory. By now, I was afraid that something might happen, that due to some

Left: My father, Aunt Olive, and my mother on Pampelonne beach.
Right: My brother and me, Saint-Tropez's port.

unforeseen circumstance—my own death, perhaps—I would be prevented from coming back.

In England, things returned to normal. A world of Birds custard,
Tizer lemonade, Wall's pork sausages, and rain. I can see my father
standing at our kitchen window remarking optimistically, "Yes, I think
it's clearing," when there was nothing up there but a sodden blanket of
gray.

There wasn't much to do for the rest of the summer. On weekdays, I
would wander down the High Street, then aimlessly drag myself around
Woolworth's, one elbow skimming the counters. Or in my wet sandals,
my thin cotton dress stuck to my knees, I would queue outside the Rivoli
with my friend Leslie to see a matinee: *The Ladykillers* or, later, something with Dirk Bogarde, who had replaced Uncle Mike as my future
husband. What I really wanted to do was play the slot machines at the
Kursaal, the big amusement park on the seafront. But this was forbidden
territory. Apparently, the risk of coming into contact with the local spivs,
the Brylcreemed teddy boys with their pointy shoes (known seducers of
gawky-looking ten-year-olds), was too great. We were also not allowed
near the public swimming pool in Westcliff, a place where any contact
with the water meant instant polio, or at the very least, a creeping foot
fungus called verrucas.

. . .

My father bought a beach hut a few miles down the coast at Thorpe Bay, a more fashionable part of town that had a bowling green and large gabled houses. These huts were simple wooden structures, dank sheds with no electricity or plumbing, but with fanciful names such as Skylark or Mon Repos. We went there every weekend in summer, despite the rain. There were occasional hot days, of course. Days when the hard stones burnt your feet, when horseflies roamed across the ham salad, and you might see, bobbing in the murky green water, a string of turds making their way out to the North Sea. But on most afternoons we just lay there shivering under a blanket, or played Monopoly inside the hut while my mother heated up baked beans on a Primus stove.

Like many women of her generation, my mother was cleverer than she let on. But at a certain point she had thrown herself into the business of housework and children. I'm convinced now that none of this came naturally to her; it had simply grown out of a determination to do the job at hand. Slim-hipped, Britishly blue-eyed and blond, she embodied those most lauded of talents: putting on a good face and getting on with it— cooking, washing, cleaning, and vacuuming—albeit with an air of quiet desperation, as if she were up against some mysterious deadline. Having survived World War II, she still lived in a world of efficiency and thriftiness. Nothing was thrown away. There were drawers for used brown paper and bottle tops. In the pantry were several rusting tins, minus their labels, that she couldn't bear to get rid of, "just in case." Disasters were anticipated, and a feeling that something was about to go wrong permeated the house. Still, the house was her domain. And part of her power was her ability to do everything. She ran up curtains and bedspreads on the old Singer. She made tweed suits and cocktail dresses, sketching the designs herself, cutting the patterns out of newspaper. On the odd occasion, I heard her lay claim to her lost independence; she'd say she always wanted to be a dress designer. "But I couldn't *draw*." At least she thought she couldn't, and so as a girl in her early twenties there had been no point in looking any further. Unqualified, she had marched straight into marriage and the kitchen.

. . .

My father was different. First of all, he was very handsome, and he knew it. Good looks were something that sustained him. My mother referred to him as "the peacock," which he took as a compliment. He also seemed impervious to what was going on in the house, the domestic crises taking place beyond the sitting room door. Parked in an armchair, listening to his Art Tatum or Duke Ellington records, the newspapers fanned around his feet, he would say with a laugh, "Your mother is on the rampage again!" But later their shouting came through the walls. These arguments—usually about some minor domestic issue—were nevertheless played out with alarming ferocity, doors slamming. I remember my mother saying to me when I was very young, "As soon as I'd married your father, I realized I'd chosen the wrong man." Yet every day around six, she would tear upstairs to put on her lipstick (Helena Rubinstein scarlet) before he got back from the office. Though the world of adults didn't seem so secret to me, there were clearly some things I didn't understand. Down on my lower rung of life, I had a narrow view.

And there were nights when my mother could transform herself, when she became (in my eyes) Betty Grable, or some stylish woman who had never willingly plunged her hands into soapy dishwater. In one of her homemade beaded evening gowns and elbow-length kid gloves, her hair swept up, she and my father would drive up to London for a Law Society affair. Or coming back from a yacht club lunch after a few soothing gin and tonics, they would pitch through the front door, arm in arm, drunk and happy. Then my father would sit at the piano and bang out "Yes! We Have No Bananas" or the "Hokey Cokey," and egg her on to give us a rousing interpretation, which she did.

But the rest exhausted her. She had headaches and problems with her kidneys, mysterious pains that in her opinion no doctor was sufficiently qualified to treat. "Run upstairs and get me a codeine, dear," she would say, sitting at the kitchen table, stirring a cup of murky-looking Nescafé and lighting another Player's Navy Cut.

My mother and father at a Law Society Ball.

My elder sister was often the cause of these headaches. I remember one afternoon having to run down to the bottom of Seymour Road to the phone booth to get my father out of court because she was chasing my mother across the kitchen with a carving knife, promising to kill her. He was in the middle of defending someone, but it was either that or call the police. She was about twelve years old then. There were grease stains on the dining room wall where she'd thrown a jar of mustard pickles. Scissors had to be hidden. My father said she was "difficult" because she was born during the war. As an officer's wife, my mother had gone to London's Queen Charlotte's Hospital to give birth, and he thought the trauma of the nightly bombing raids had affected her inside the womb.

Dr. Emery came to see my sister first. A general practitioner, he diagnosed her as schizophrenic, a word that was suddenly becoming popular. Next it was Dr. Bevan Jones, a psychiatrist, the only one in the Westcliff area, and whom my father disdainfully referred to as "a madman himself." He asked my parents if sending my sister to boarding school at eight had been done as a punishment. "Yes," my father said, as he was accustomed to speaking the truth. Rather than proclaim her mentally unbalanced, Jones's verdict was "highly strung." No medication was prescribed, and no one remarked on her condition. But after that, to prevent any possible eruptions, we tiptoed around her. She never had to make her bed or do the washing up again—which only made her more aware of her power. I was particularly envious of this, as was my younger brother. When he was about eight he tried to burn down the house. We were out one Saturday morning, and he'd come back early from his prep school to find the doors locked. He took bundles of newspapers, kept in the garden shed, then placed them at strategic points along the walls and set fire to them. As we pulled into the driveway, he was busy fanning the flames, though by then only one stack was alight, plus a few flying embers. "I can't get it going," he shouted furiously. "The papers are too bloody damp to stay alight!"

I could hardly compete. Besides, it wasn't in my nature to draw attention to myself—at least not yet. I watched these family dramas from the sidelines, saying nothing. I *learned* to say nothing. Or I escaped to the orchard, where I'd crawl under one of the big red currant bushes and stay there, deaf to Sylvia's calls. When my brother and sister fought, which they did constantly, I would hear my mother shout, exasperated, "Fiona's the easy one, the *good* one!"

But I didn't want to be good. Most of the time, I was simply toeing the line to get my mother's attention. I never did get it. Goodness is rarely a big lure. And finally this must have sunk in. Because by the time I was seventeen, I had thoroughly disgraced myself.

three
Los Angeles 2004.

Communication, understanding, compromise. Love. "You want to be adored. But that's never going to make you happy," my husband likes to tell me. All my life I've been looking to be loved, he says, without realizing that what's more important is who *I* love. Not what a man thinks of me but how I feel about *him*. He is sitting at the breakfast table, drinking his coffee, his thick Guatemalan brew, and in between appreciative sips and swallows, he imparts these words of wisdom. "You see, women always get this wrong."

"Oh, really, *women*?" But he's often right. Annoyingly so. I'm tired, sluggish in the morning; he is full of caffeine and energy. "Look at your life; it's fantastic," he says. "Come on, let's walk to the cliffs and see the ocean." The beautiful Santa Monica cliffs. The Bay. I am still in my pajamas, in the unflattering men's bathrobe he hates. But I smile at the suggestion and nod. Yes, an affirmative stroll. Exactly what I need. I go on smiling as he brews a second cup, showing me the thick *cremora*, proof of its caffeine richness.

His big enthusiasm for life makes me want to scream. Can't he see how far I've slipped down the pole? Of course, he's not big on pity. No future in that, not in Hollywood. He also knows I'm a sucker for drama, my way of generating a little action. I still suffer from the English habit of not saying what I mean—lately not even *knowing* what I mean. And my anxiety, normally diffused in order to get through the day, now hovers around me like a poisonous haze. "Try to be *positive*," he says repeatedly. Positive? As if I can just slip it on like an old sweater. An hour later, he's gone, over the hill to Burbank, for a meeting at Warner Brothers. The house is quiet. I walk into the garden, our luxury square of green in the desert, to stand barefoot under the old palm tree. Immense, it was planted a hundred years ago. Rats live in the dense fronds.

At 9:15 it's already boiling outside. Only a slight breeze. I can't help thinking as I do *all the time* now about our early days together, about one of our first clandestine meetings, when we were both married to other people. The day we finally decided to screw our brains out. It was August, scorching then too, the air full of exhaust and the smell of asphalt. We had borrowed someone's apartment in Malibu, a split-level concrete block with knotty wood floors. We didn't care. We lay there naked, the waves crashing outside, *La Traviata* playing—God, we loved *that* drama—laughing like idiots after polishing off almost a full bottle of Absolut. There were warnings of brush fires in the hills that day. We took no notice. Ravenously, we slithered across each other's bodies while the plate-glass window generated enough heat to send us to hell. Then we heard banging on the door, someone threatening to break it down. And they did. Two firemen rushed in. They were shouting. Then, ignoring our nakedness, they shouted louder. We were weak from sex, but finally got it. The hills were on fire. The beach was being evacuated. We ran out half-dressed. Then we drove back through the black smoke, through the police barricades, laughing foolishly, linked irrevocably by our escape from death.

That was almost twenty years ago. We left our spouses (I was already separated), still giddy with love but cynical about the institution of marriage. It took nine years before we finally made the leap. There was no formal wedding; we stood on a beach in Kauai, facing a local judge and backed by a ukulele player. Corny, and utterly romantic. Now, alone outside, listening to the palm fronds rustle quietly, I am dizzy with emptiness and remorse. How do you discuss the boredom, the lack of mystery, after two decades? How to explain my ambivalent need for solitude, my fear of being alone? Marriage is difficult, or I am difficult—the difficult woman.

And I'm still angry. Because he refuses to talk about France.

The writer Cyril Connolly spent a lot of his life dreaming about a house in France. The self-proclaimed hedonist, the (albeit guilty) lover of travel, food, and pleasure, he longed for Paris, the Mediterranean, and various points in between. In his slim volume *The Unquiet Grave*, advertised as "an experiment in self-dismantling" (published in 1945), he includes, on page 29, a map of the French countryside. Or, rather, a section of the Southwest, a circle drawn around his favorite part. Inside this "magic circle," as he wistfully calls it, between Périgord to the north and Toulouse to the south, he planned to buy a house: "a golden classic house, three stories high, with œil-de-boeuf attic windows." His haven from madness, he said, and from the *permanent disappointment of life*.

Well, there was something I could relate to. I'd come across the book a few months before when I was wandering aimlessly from room to room, pulling out boxes of old letters and photographs, looking for something to justify my wallowing, or to miraculously lift me out of it. The cover was tattered; inside there were pages turned down, many of the sentences underlined. *It is a mistake to consider happiness as a positive state*, for example—words of wisdom I had no doubt taken too literally. There were also pencil marks against Connolly's descriptions of France, including the now-famous: *sizzling down the long black liquid reaches of the National sept, the plane trees going sha-sha-sha* . . . but somehow I'd never noticed the map before. I knew nothing about that area of France, the Southwest. In the old days, despite our deviations driving down to Saint-Tropez, it would have been too far west.

Coincidentally (or fatefully), a few weeks after rediscovering the book, I was invited to stay with a friend of mine, Kathryn Ireland, an

English designer who had bought a house in that area of France fifteen years earlier. My husband encouraged me to go. "It might cheer you up," he said. Or perhaps he needed the break. Of course, I wasn't in the habit of traveling anymore. Not on my own. And there was a panicked moment during packing when I stood looking at handbags and cocktail dresses, wondering if I might need them. Really? In June, in the countryside? Marriage had turned me—willingly, so it seemed—into a complete idiot.

Fortunately, Kathryn was more evolved. An eccentric *femme liberée*, devoid of anxiety or guilt, or some maudlin preoccupation with the past, she managed to waltz through her days effortlessly. Dogs and chickens roamed the halls of her old stone farmhouse, guests were encouraged to run wild, and as far as I could tell she had yet to encounter a malaise that a bottle of rosé couldn't solve. It was a long time since I'd been in the French countryside. The relief I felt was overwhelming. Seeing the village shops with their colored awnings, the quiet cobbled streets, the bastides perched on hilltops, I was suddenly back in my childhood. Admittedly, there was no Mediterranean, no seductive stretch of blue, but the rest was soothingly familiar.

"Want to go and see a house?" It was the second day. I was sitting in her kitchen (the converted cow barn), still bleary-eyed from jet lag, and she was standing in the doorway. Tanned and barefoot, wearing nothing but a slip, she looked like one of Fellini's Italian mamas. "I hear there's a nice one for sale over the hill"—a reliable piece of information, she assured me, extracted from the local butcher. "It's only a kilometer away. Let's cycle over." Cycle over? Off we went, over the hill, past the wheat fields and poppies, down a sloping driveway, then through a long tunnel of trees. And there it was: an imposing manor house, a *maison de maître* set on a knoll. A man was standing outside, next to a tractor. Handsome, with a nut-brown face, he greeted us with a wary smile. The owner, we presumed. "You've been misinformed," he said, "Château de la Vinouse is not for sale." Not yet, that is, he added, because his elderly mother was still living there.

"But couldn't we just take a look inside?" Kathryn asked. *"Cinq minutes?"*

She was leaning persuasively over the handlebars, her skirt hiked up, showing an attractive foot or so of tanned thigh. If M. Moulin was hesitant at first, French civility now obliged him to concede. *"D'accord,"* he said. Okay. "But only for a minute. My mother will be back soon."

Still called a château, the house had been built on the ruins of the original, burnt to the ground during the French Revolution. Even so, it showed signs of serious neglect: large chunks of the *crépi* had fallen away, and several of the shutters—half closed against the midday sun—were hanging off their hinges. It was dark inside. We could make out a central corridor with a pair of high doors at the other end and rooms leading off. One, a paneled salon divided by makeshift partitions, contained a small bed, a chair, and a wardrobe. Farther down, behind another door, was an unused staircase. We made our way up. Cobwebs and old water leaks stained the walls, but the rooms here were just as large, with high ceilings and marble fireplaces. There was no electricity to speak of, however, just a couple of bare bulbs hanging down, and no evidence of a bathroom. Apart from the linoleum—a stretch of lurid green that covered the entire downstairs—a 1950s' modular sink, and an odd three-legged tin tub stuck in a corner of what passed for a kitchen, no one seemed to have touched the place for decades.

It was, in other words, perfect. Unspoiled. Or it would have been if I'd wanted to buy it. But how could I? I didn't have the money, it was practically a ruin, and I lived in Los Angeles. Also, I couldn't remember thinking I *wanted* to buy a house in France. Or perhaps I'd been thinking about it all my life. I felt suddenly light-headed, and walking back into the sunlight I heard myself say: "So when would it be available?"

"Bientôt," said M. Moulin.

"Soon?"

Yes, he said, adding some nonspecific arm-waving. As there was obviously no way of knowing how soon bientôt might be, I told him I was seriously interested, then went back to L.A.

I didn't mention the château, but my husband couldn't help noticing my sunny demeanor. I was bright-eyed, interested suddenly in the mundane: a trip to the supermarket, the cleaners. I pored over travel magazines. I went on enthusiastically about the French countryside, the food, the unpolluted air. Finally, I told him.

"What? You want to *live* in France?"

"No. I want to buy a house there. A summer house."

We were in the kitchen. He was going through his morning ritual, coffee grounds, cup placed just so, machine hissing. "Since when?" he asked. It was as if I'd woken up that morning and announced a sudden burning desire to move to Kansas. He looked bewildered. And I could hardly blame him. After all, he hadn't spent his teenage years wandering the hills above Pampelonne beach, or dreaming nostalgically about a memorable *soupe de poisson* in some backstreet bistro. He'd grown up in the Knickerbocker Hotel, a semi-luxurious establishment on Hollywood Boulevard whose clientele included movie stars—some on their way down, admittedly, but movie stars nevertheless. His father, a native of Chicago, spent his afternoons playing cards on the rooftop, the bellhop was his best friend, and George Raft was in the elevator. His idea of an excursion was to ride the streetcar to the Magic Shop or to the Egyptian Theatre to see a matinee, or to have kishke with his Aunt Pearl on Babcock Street, "a new area in North Hollywood that was already a bad area," he liked to joke. As soon as he could drive, he headed for the beach—yes, the one right here below the cliffs. He loved living in Santa Monica; life was good. He'd been a successful movie producer and writer for decades. "This is paradise. You've got to admit, it even *looks* like the South of France."

"But it isn't," I said, sounding altogether too desperate.

"How much?"

"About $300,000."

"That's still a lot of money," he sighed, looking relieved it wasn't more. "How many bathrooms?"

"None, so far."

"*None?*"

Four months later, he still refuses to take it seriously. My little fantasy, my refusal to come to grips with life, he says. But then again, I've still heard nothing from M. Moulin. I call every two weeks. He's rarely home, so I leave pleading messages with his wife, Eliane. *Don't forget me . . .* Meanwhile, I sink back into my dark cave, my alien self. I try to work. I have been working on my "book" for several years. I sit in my office writing— or, rather, *not* writing, thinking I might as well go somewhere else and not write, because I can't concentrate. All I think about is France. I am obsessed. The photographs of Château de la Vinouse, and Connolly's dream map of his "magic circle," pinned to my noticeboard, are now faded and curling at the edges.

Then, miraculously, three weeks later, M. Moulin calls. He's ready to sell. Am I still interested?

"You're actually going to *buy* it?"

My husband thinks I'm deranged. He is more furious than I ever could have imagined. "You've completely lost your mind! I'll never go!" I can feel all the old insecurities welling up: the sense of suffocation, of longing tinged with grief. How could he not understand how important this is to me? "It's as if you've never noticed who I *am*," I shout miserably to the person who has loved me more than any man, who over the years has dragged me out of the shitty depths. But I can barely explain my desperation to myself, let alone him. And he's a generous man. When my allergies and headaches get worse; when, morosely, I start looking through the old black-and-white snaps of those childhood summers and he's ready to strangle me (and who could blame him?), he agrees to give me the money. Perhaps for his own sanity. I have $130,000, an inheritance from my mother. He says he'll make up the rest. I am in tears.

"Thank you," I say over and over, feeling guilty for getting what I want. He shakes his head. He knows I have a problem about being grateful. He's also aware of the possible consequences. "You'll see. It'll be the end of us."

"No, it won't," I say, protesting loudly enough for both of us. "It'll be *good* for us. And I'll be a better person. Nicer, I promise."

But he's often right about these things.

four
England 1950–1963.

We weren't Catholic, or even religious, but my mother was educated in convents and she liked St. Teresa's in Effingham, Surrey. I was shown a set of the school photographs: the imposing Georgian manor, the tennis courts, the swimming pool, the chapel, the stables, and the elegant sloping lawns—an establishment that, according to the brochure, prided itself on turning out "young ladies." My sister had enrolled there the year before, and when my turn came a few weeks before my eleventh birthday, my mother, my sister, and I took the train to London to buy the uniform from Gamages: an assortment of tweeds, a boater, a pair of Clarks Rosalynd shoes, a white satin dress for saints' days, a gabardine raincoat with the usual unworkable belt buckle, and four pairs of regulation lisle stockings.

One of the reasons my mother preferred convents was that she thought the food was better. In fact, it was terrible. And it seemed all the more frugal sitting in the formal dining room with its trompe l'oeil marble pillars and oak-paneled walls. We were allowed one egg a week for breakfast, and tea was often just bread and jam. I can see the white loaves standing upright in their greaseproof wrappers, next to the brick-sized slabs of margarine. On saints' days we might get pilchards in tomato sauce as a treat.

Two things are memorable: I was permanently hungry, and I always felt cold, particularly on winter mornings when we had to get up at six for Mass. I wasn't sure what I felt about God. My father said it was hard to believe He existed when He had allowed so many men to die in World War II. But I grew to love the ceremony, the formality of Mass, the holy water, the heavy smell of incense, and chanting Kyrie Eleison in reply to the priest. I bought imitation pearl rosary beads. I made the stations of the cross and prayed fervently for my own salvation. I took on the drama and seriousness of it without really thinking about what it meant, because in those days I felt secretly emotional about everything. I also wanted to be good because I had such a track record of goodness at home. But the nuns saw through me. In fact they were waiting for me to misbehave because of my sister's disreputable behavior. Having been expelled from her last boarding school the year before, she'd recently led St. Teresa's fifth form out on strike. There were sit-downs on the lawn and words scrawled on pillowcases in protest of the bad food, in particular, she claimed, some green-looking fish that had been served up the previous Friday.

As a rebel, she had many followers, and though I admired her from afar, I was still scared of her. She was physically strong and quite beautiful, with a box-shaped jaw and startling blue eyes. The day I arrived, she instructed the fifth form and her "swains"—as her admirers were called—to "send me to Coventry," which meant no one was allowed to speak to me. And no one did, not even the daygirls, who were considered second-class citizens. I spent my first weekend alone, squatting on the floor of an empty classroom, my back pressed against a lukewarm radiator.

At home I would have sunk under her punishments, but I was determined to fight back. In that way my sister did help me to stand up for myself. I decided I had to be either clever or funny, or at least "interesting." So I became a show-off. This consisted of making rather lame remarks about teachers behind their backs, or corralling some startled sixth-former coming out of chapel: "I'm so *bored* here. How about you?" Anything to get attention. For our class outing we were taken by bus to

London to see a production of *Romeo and Juliet* at the Old Vic. The next day at school I stood in the stable courtyard and read aloud a "witty" note I'd composed for Mr. John Stride (Romeo). Watching him scamper up the tree to Juliet's balcony (Juliet played by a young Judi Dench), his "ardor" had been so convincing, I said, that surely there had to be some secret romance taking place beyond the confines of the stage. I was full of myself, and became even more so after my audience erupted with applause and laughter.

But Reverend Mother found me less amusing. I was called to her office one morning, a tiny cubicle of self-imposed claustrophobia lodged under the back stairs. A large woman, she almost filled it. She had small, watery eyes and flaming red skin—some kind of rosacea, I imagined, which looked all the more frightening against the starched white gimp of her veil. The torturer's flush. "Do you know why you're here?" she asked, her high-pitched voice already laced with displeasure. "No, I don't," I said, though I thought I might. "Because it's *forbidden* to wear makeup in class." "You're wrong," I replied. With my new self-confidence, I explained that the mauve on my eyelid—and it was only *one* eyelid, I pointed out—was actually a bruise from a stray ball during hockey practice. However, when I invited her to come over to try to wipe it off, she called me impertinent and said, "I can see you're turning out just like your sister. Hold out your hand."

So I did—as I would do many times after that—waiting to receive the punishing whacks of her ruler.

On Monday afternoons we took deportment lessons from Mme. Vacani, who claimed to have once taught the royal children. "When I was at the palace . . ." she would say as we walked up and down the front hall's creaking parquet floors, books balanced on our heads. We learned to enter a room correctly and how to slide gracefully into a car—certainly not a Ford Zephyr with red vinyl seats, the car my father was driving at that time; presumably our young behinds were destined for the more lush interior of a chauffeured Rolls.

In those days it was considered perfectly acceptable that a girl be sent out into the world having mastered nothing more than the art of riding sidesaddle and how to curtsy to the queen. We were being groomed to be debutantes and, beyond that, perfect wives. Education was of minor importance. I wasn't a good student, anyway. I was more interested in the social hierarchy and relationships between the girls—in swimming, in being popular, or performing in the school play. Being thin and reasonably tall, I usually got the boys' parts. Algernon in *The Importance of Being Earnest*, or Lysander in *A Midsummer's Night's Dream*. I said *"quis"* and *"ego"* in class without understanding what they meant. I had sycophantic friendships with bouncy horse-loving girls, and we exchanged holy pictures with poignant notes on the back to commemorate a birthday or a gymkhana. I went to the matron's room for my dose of fortifying Virol after a bad bout of pneumonia. I was sentimental. I was interested in poetry because it spoke to that other part of me, the part I never mentioned. But I failed at math and science and French.

Above everything, I had boys on my mind.

I was friends with two girls in my class from Trinidad—Karen de Lima and Suzette Herrera—who were light-years ahead of me and who reeked of sexuality. Their families were well-off, in the sugar trade, I think, or perhaps it was gold. Karen had the soft, moist look of a young Elizabeth Taylor, with olive skin and black hair. Suzette was a tall, shoulders-back blond. English girls were sickly looking by comparison, myself included, with our chilblains, our gray, wintry complexions, and our mouse-colored hair. But we were all desperate to transform ourselves. We altered our uniforms, the prickly, blanket-like tweed skirts, sewing up the sides and shortening them. Somehow Karen's and Suzette's were tighter and shorter, and their bodies moved in mysterious and seductive ways.

At the age of eleven, I didn't know any men, except for a small group at home in Westcliff, in Miss Bellelock's dancing class, where my knees would go weak from the thrill of some spotty boy's hand on my back as he wheeled me around the floor for a quick step. But by thirteen, I had experienced a few hot gropes. There was a terrible urgency to have contact with the opposite sex then, particularly as any success in this area came with the additional thrill of possibly qualifying as a mortal sin. One night during the Christmas holidays, after a square dance in the local church hall (twirling in my calico-fringed cowboy skirt), I stepped out into the freezing night air to find myself being pushed into the bushes by some boy I barely knew. I remember a frantic five minutes of hard kissing, my knickers riding up into my groin, my mouth raw, my barely formed breasts aching because he couldn't get my bra off. It was only when I felt the erection through his trousers that I pulled away—not in fright but with a feverish dread of capitulating to the thrill. We hadn't said a word. I walked home dizzy, sweating, thoroughly ashamed, but still longing for it, not even sure what *it* was.

There was no real sex in films in England in 1959, nor was it on television; what we were exposed to was either the British comedy/love story, which included pratfalls and loose women in corsets, usually French or Italian, or a kind of sanctified, idealized "love." And I suppose that's what I was hoping for—or, rather, I had some glorified idea of *being loved*, which I presumed would automatically follow right after penetration. But the Trinidadians were focused on doing it as soon as they could. Island life had made them unashamed of their bodies. They showed me photographs of themselves in Port of Spain during Carnivàle, standing on a parade float, fully made up and wearing low-cut satin evening gowns. They had deckle-edged snapshots in their blazer pockets of boys with big, white teeth and slicked-back hair the color of coal, grinning like young Elvis Presleys—a future boyfriend, or some cousin they had designs on. They were foreign, glamorous, and their friendship was important to me. Given so generously, I could return it without cynicism. With everyone else I was still trying to be amusing or sarcastic: "Put that in your pipe and smoke it, Ward-Smith," I would say, or, "Dry up, Monica; you're such a drip!" and walk away triumphantly. Then an hour later, I'd be wandering aimlessly around the back lawn plagued with guilt.

At the end of the day, we would change into mufti, our own clothes.

In those days, girls didn't have much. I had a Black Watch tartan skirt my mother had run up for me, some Marks and Spencer pullovers, and my school shoes. I used to dream about shoes. I was saving up for a pair I'd seen in the Southend High Street in Dolcis, pearlized green with Louis heels costing the then-unobtainable sum of twenty-nine shillings and sixpence.

After supper, we played records in the gym. Karen and Suzette wore tight sweaters that showed the outline of their conical American bras, and often their nipples. We danced to "Rawhide" and "Cathy's Clown," acting out emotions we'd yet to experience, moaning and sighing and clinging to each other, pretending to be women, exaggerating every move to cover up our naïveté. Under Karen's tutelage, I loosened up. She would hold up a hockey stick, and then with my back arched, my feet shuffling forward to the beat of "Limbo Like Me," I had to slither underneath. Each time she would lower the stick a few inches more until, bent almost double, we both fell to the floor, screaming with laughter. This was Mother Clare's cue to appear, the Reverend Mother's young emissary. Tall and quivering, with a big moon face and thick eyebrows, she loped down the corridors wearing that uncertain look of the recently ordained. Any activity to do with the outside was considered a threat, and so seeing us on the gym floor, rolling around "like hooligans," she would clap her big hands and scream excitedly, "Up. Get *up*, both of you! And Fiona, pull that skirt *down*." Then she would send us off to bed. Mother Clare also viewed me as the wicked successor to my sister, and what happened the following term would seal that fate.

I slept upstairs in the main house, off a long corridor that smelled of wax polish and mold. There were several rooms on either side, plainly decorated with whitewashed iron beds and housing four or five girls. It was my birthday, a cold September morning, and I woke up early. Excited, I slipped across the icy floorboards to climb into my friend Corby's bed. We were huddled together, laughing stupidly to keep out the chill, when the door opened. It was Mother Clare, who had come to wake us for Mass. Seeing us, her face turned white. We got a few seconds of her unblinking stare, then the door slammed shut. Later that day, I was called to the Reverend Mother's office. "Do you know why you're here?" I did not, I replied—and for once it was true. "Because you were in bed with another girl, and because your hands were *under the covers*," she said. Under, not over, thereby confirming my guilt. She carried on admonishing me, lips pursed, her cheeks ablaze. When I heard the fateful words "mortal sin," I felt a wave of hot disgrace creep up the back of my legs, though I hadn't a clue what "being a lesbian" meant. It didn't matter. I was banished to the pink dorm for the rest of the term, to sleep with the seven-year-olds. As an added penalty, I would have to go to Mass every day. That afternoon, having tea with my friends in the dining room, cutting the birthday cake my parents had sent me, I managed to laugh the whole thing off. But years later, if I saw a nun walking down the street, bent forward against the terrible temptations of the world, I would think of Reverend Mother and find myself smarting with shame.

To say I had no formal education would be an understatement, and when I left school that last summer term at fifteen (as soon as it was legally permitted), I knew I'd learned nothing, except that religion was a particularly effective method of torture.

five
France. November 2004.

I am in a bistro in the Place Nationale, an impressive seventeenth-century square flanked by pink-bricked arches, in the heart of Montauban (the town, incidentally, in the center of Connolly's map).

With two hours to kill before my meeting with Guy and Eliane Moulin, I order my third *café serré*. Jet-lagged, I feel nervous and exhilarated. I also feel stupidly overdressed in my fur-lined parka, as if I have mistakenly stopped off in this mildly damp southern French town on my way to Antarctica. The *notaire*, the local notary whom I'd visited an hour ago, had politely asked how the weather was in Los Angeles. "Still hot, I presume?" he said ruefully, taking my coat. It was years since I'd practiced my French, and the plump, rosy-faced M. Garrisson, like most professionals, seemed to speak almost exclusively in the subjunctive. But I managed to struggle through. I handed over my passport and driving license to secure the sale of the château (no mortgage available). I signed all outstanding documents, a lengthy procedure involving an avalanche of pages with indecipherable print, in accordance with the Napoleonic Code. Then, taking advantage of his expertise, I asked for his advice about the land. What did he think agricultural terrain might be going for these days? I wanted to buy a few more acres around the château, I told him, and Guy Moulin was asking for 7,000 euros per hectare. That gave M. Garrisson a good laugh. Readjusting his silk tie, he disdainfully waved the figure away. "Uppity farmers out to exploit the foreigner," he said, then added, *"Pas plus que cinq milles!"* He wanted to make sure I'd understood this, so he repeated it when we shook hands at the door: "No more than *five* thousand!"

Guy and Eliane Moulin live in a new bungalow at the corner of my lane, a few hundred yards or so from the château. We are in their dining room, a pleasant whitewashed space with dark furniture. The old château plans are rolled out across the table, our wine glasses holding down the corners. A pencil is at the ready. For the transaction, Guy has opened a local white from nearby Gaillac. He also brings out a bottle of violet liqueur as a chaser, a syrupy liquid that after one sip I realize is lethal. I'm already shaky from my afternoon shots of coffee, and now feel light-headed at the prospect of actually owning a house with *land.*

But we're in no hurry. Negotiations take time. We talk about the weather. We discuss French politics—terrible—then American politics: even worse with Bush and Iraq. *"L'idiot,"* says Eliane, a slim, no-nonsense brunette. *"Honteux!"* Disgraceful! And Guy nods in agreement. Still, he's fascinated by America. Fashionably low-key, dressed in 501 Levi's and a white pocket T, he says he dreams one day of living in the States. It's the classic fantasy: acres of wheat as far as the eye can see, streamlined supermarkets, prosperity, and fast cars. "How much does a new Porsche cost there?" he asks eagerly. I have no idea, I say, although having paid an exorbitant price for my small Peugeot rental, I tell him it's probably cheaper. He asks about Los Angeles. Yes, I admit, the weather is still good. "And have you ever met Robert De Niro?" Yes, I say, immediately wishing I hadn't. But he's excited by the thought and offers me another shot of liqueur, suggesting this time I try mixing it with the white wine. *"Allez, un soupcon,"* he says, and pours a slug in my glass.

A moment later, I am bent over the plans with the pencil, trying to work out if I should have more land at the bottom of the house or on the side. I feel awkward sitting with the Moulins, carving up the farm like this, but tomorrow we have to report back to M. Garrisson, who will then engage a geologist to officially pace off the land. I draw a rectangle around the château. Then I rub out the lines and draw it a little bigger. For the delicate discussion of money, Eliane leaves the room. Guy gets up to open another bottle of wine. I am a terrible negotiator, hopeless when jet-lagged. But I can tell Guy is nervous too. I offer him 5,500 euros per hectare, a little more than the notaire suggested. Guy nods and sits down. He looks disappointed. He says nothing. Embarrassed, I immediately go up to six. A pause. He sighs, then tells me he'll have to buy his son some land elsewhere, and it's expensive. (Although perhaps not as expensive as this, I think.) But I'm feeling a warm camaraderie toward the Moulins, not to mention a sensation of weightlessness from the third glass of wine, now a swirling purple. Guy is staring at his hands, tanned and weather-beaten. I think about the bad melon harvest, then offer him 7,000. At this point, Eliane, who has obviously been listening, flings open the door and says, "Oui." We shake hands. We make a toast to health and prosperity, and they promise to watch over the house when I'm gone.

Later I realize I've bought three hectares, about seven and a half acres, costing 21,000 euros. The money will have to come out of what's left of my savings. I can make it up later, I tell myself, by cutting costs during the renovation.

I am staying in Kathryn's empty farmhouse, five minutes from the château. And the next morning, the sun barely seeping through the trees, I drive over. This is the first time I've been inside in daylight. Does it feel strange that I've bought a house I've only seen once, and then in near darkness? No. Not yet, anyway.

I let myself in using one of the old, rusted six-inch keys. It's dark inside, musty. But surprisingly, the house seems bigger than I remember, particularly when I open the back shutters and light floods into the corridor. Of course, it also seems more dilapidated—shockingly so, with the old paintwork and torn wallpaper, the brown water stains circling the ceiling. Not to mention the runway of electric-green linoleum covering the ground floor. Oddly enough, this is what I remember most. Up at night in Santa Monica, I tried to imagine what might be underneath. Tiles? The original wood floors? Now I'm anxious to find out. I've brought one of Kathryn's kitchen knives with me and sitting on the icy floor, I start to dig in a corner by the front door. It's stiff and thick, but finally the old glue gives way. Underneath is another layer of linoleum, then another—green, pink, a bright, streaky blue. Then cement. *Cement?* A cold, dark slab that I tell myself must have been laid for repairs. It couldn't possibly cover the entire downstairs. Could it?

A rush of panic. I ignore it. I walk into the salon to see what needs to be done. I open the big shutters, and again the room fills with light, dust

Château de la Vinouse, 2005.

specks whirling up to the ceiling and across the top of the huge fireplace. The fireplace is beautiful, extraordinarily so: marble in a soft shade of gray, flecked with amber and red. But the inside has been bricked up, only a small opening left, stuffed with newspapers. And the chestnut wood paneling surrounding it, obviously salvaged from the original châ-teau, is water-damaged, blackened in spots, and stops short at the south wall, exposing more than a foot of crumbling plaster. Obviously I didn't notice this before, nor did I see the rising damp under the windows, or the crack in the north wall, widening near the ceiling like a small ravine.

I decide not to explore the upstairs and instead walk out to the front garden. A cold wind is blowing, but the sun is out, the air is crisp, win-try, and the view is magnificent: M. Moulin's fields falling away, then swooping up again as far as the horizon. To my left, under the ancient chestnuts, are some swirls of box hedge, the remains of the château's formal parterre. There are more clumps down behind the house, over-grown, rising to thirty feet, their original shape now unrecognizable be-hind the thick mass of the cedar. But up here the hedges have been kept up, clipped into perfect smooth shapes: two large circles, one sitting inside the other, with a few oblong lozenges around the perimeter. There seems to be no entrance, but then I find it. I slip inside and sit on an old sawn-off trunk. The silence envelops me like a giant tomb. The leaves, ankle-deep, smell of wood smoke, and above me, the tops of the chestnut branches give way to a square of brilliant blue. This, I tell myself, will be my "magic circle," the perfect setting for a *dejeuner sur l'herbe*. That is, as soon as I can get a kitchen built.

On my way back, I drive to the village. Past the Moulins', then down the hill and up again; there is a cluster of old houses, a church, some desolate-looking plane trees—the pollarded stumps now like big fists— and one local shop.

Though small, the *midi prix* sells everything from lightbulbs to lamb cutlets. Inside there are refrigerated bins, shelves packed to the ceiling, and a pungent odor of cigarettes. *"Bonjour,"* I say to Raymond, the owner, who stands behind the small counter, his thatch of silver hair illuminated by the recently installed strip lighting. By now it's eleven thirty, and I still have a hard time remembering that, like most small shopkeepers in France, Raymond closes for a two-hour lunch at noon.

Several locals are waiting to pay at the register, while others roam the narrow aisles. If love for a country also promotes affection for its inhabitants, then I'm already feeling very neighborly toward this odd assortment of faces—though obviously they have some reservations about me. A woman in a big apron and carpet slippers, sorting through a bin of oversized leeks, gives me a wary glance. I get a suspicious leer from a red-faced farmer with a wandering eye, most likely her husband. And another man in blue dungarees, clutching a can of *petits pois* like a hand grenade, turns his back on me, even though I have said "Bonjour" several times—admittedly once too many. I am too familiar. I'm also a stranger and a woman alone. Obviously nothing but trouble. Raymond, however, soft-spoken and courteous, sets a good example. He returns my bonjour and, unleashing a smile, asks, *"Comment ça va?"* How's it going? I say it's going fine, realizing he means the house. It's a small village. Finally, it's my turn. Raymond retrieves a fresh croissant, saved for me behind the counter—already a good sign that I qualify as a member of the community. He slices some ham. I buy butter, a baguette, and an expensive jar of the local foie gras. More evidence of foreigners run amok. But who can blame them? I'm an American (even if I think I'm not) from a place where people hug you on the first meeting, tell you all about themselves, and presume things will improve from then on. The French are cautious by nature. A country that has been occupied too many times, they wait to see what you're made of. *"Au revoir,"* I say to the glacial-faced crowd. I will win them over.

Across the small square is the beautiful red-brick church, its base medievally rounded, its steeple soaring. Despite my reservations about God, or perhaps because of them, I'm still awed by churches. I go in: a large empty room with a domed ceiling and an impressive configuration of high crossed wooden beams. It exudes a humbling stillness. This is the reward for believing, I think—not answered prayers but the architecture of hope. I sit on one of the rush-seated chairs lined up instead of pews. I want to *feel* godliness, to let Him in. Instead, I start thinking about Mother Clare. It was the end my last term at St. Teresa's. I was standing outside with Karen and Suzanne and the rest of the class, waiting to board the coaches to take us to the train station. Suddenly, Mother Clare walked over. Having failed to tame me for four years, she pulled me aside, her big face boiling. "You will become a bohemian," she blurted out. *"A bohemian!"* Damning me for eternity. I did become one later, of course, and worse: a burn-in-hell sinner. In those days (the mid-'60s) being a nonbeliever had its drawbacks. There wasn't much to fall back on. No enlightening sermons about faith versus the multiple orgasm. Nothing to save a girl but the divine possibility of self.

I'm still cynical. Though I want to be worthy now, or at least grateful. When I leave, I dip my finger in the font, cross myself, and pray I'll get a contractor soon.

My soul, as usual, will have to wait.

"So how are things going?"

"Great. The house is amazing."

Back at Kathryn's, I'm talking to my husband. At seven a.m. in Los Angeles, he is just getting out of the shower and, pre-caffeinated, finds it hard to hide his annoyance that I suddenly sound so relaxed here, as opposed to *back there* with him. I tell him about my meeting with the *notaire*, then describe the town of Montauban, going on enthusiastically about the beauty of the buildings, constructed of slender, pale pink Roman bricks, about the magnificent ramparts overlooking the wide river Tarn. "It used to be a famous Huguenot stronghold."

"Huguenot?"

"Yes, *Protestants*. You know, my family comes from a long line of French Protestants who were persecuted in the seventeenth century. They managed to escape to England. One ancestor, Jacques Chabot, was smuggled across the channel in a boat, hidden in a laundry basket."

"You never told me that."

"I did. You forgot. Anyway, in 1692 the Huguenots of Montauban held out for eighty-six days against Louis XIII and his army—" I can hear him walking with the phone to his office, then the unmistakable whoosh of an e-mail being sent. "You're not listening."

"No, I am. Sounds interesting."

But like a man under torture, he refuses to divulge a word of enthusiasm. "Look, Europe is *your* thing," he says, and not for the first time— as though part of his Americanness would evaporate if he liked it too much. I remember early on in our relationship, taking a trip with him to Paris. It was a perfect spring morning, and we were walking from the Tuileries Gardens to Saint Germain. Halfway across the Pont Royal, I had to stop. Seeing the Île de la Cité, the magnificent Notre Dame, and the Conciergerie soaring against a cloudless sky, I was ready to weep. "Oh my God," I murmured, "so beautiful." "Yes," he replied dryly, "a beautiful museum to be visited swiftly. Preferably before lunch." It was said for effect, of course. His humor is deadpan, alarmingly direct. A front for the anxious, clever boy from the Knickerbocker Hotel, and used regularly to detract from his accomplishments—his movie career—which he prefers his mother to brag about. He's had many successes, which he downplays. And when someone recognizes his name, a nurse, say, in the dentist's office, or a waiter—"Wow, *The Untouchables, Fight Club,* I'm such a huge fan!"—it always takes him by surprise. And he's just as cool about the flops. "Let's face it, Hollywood is brutal. You have to be good here just to *fail.*"

To be honest, it's his humor that's probably saved us. Saved our marriage or, more accurately, saved *me*, the serial bolter and complainer. And normally I'm grateful.

"I just don't understand why you want to *live* there," he goes on now.

"You keep *saying* that. I won't be living here. For most of the year, I'll be living with you."

"Who knows? You don't have a great track record. You've spent a lifetime running away from men."

"Well, you've spent a lifetime being married," I reply, "so how could you possibly know what it's like out there?" I'm laughing, but I can feel the old insecurities welling up. "Anyway, I'm not *running*. I'm just trying to build a house."

And this is what I tell myself. I am just building a house.

"Maybe it's more than that. Is it?"

"Why do you always think I'm hiding things from you?" I say, still amused.

"Because it's in your nature. You're a writer. You live in your head."

"Look, sometimes it just feels good to get away from Los Angeles."

"So why don't you say that. If you want to be on your own, to be happy, you should say it. Say what you mean. Just tell the *truth*."

Tell the truth and you will be forgiven. Maybe. These days, I could do with a few more lies. But truth is something he's been fixated on from the start, from our first lunch together. It was 1986, we'd met at an art gallery opening. Or rather, we spied each other across the room, and when I left, he followed me outside to my car. We arranged to meet, ostensibly about a job: he as the hiring producer, me as the writer. We had lunch at Le Dome, a fashionable restaurant on Sunset Boulevard. Several martinis had already been consumed and I was going on about the terrible ordeal of creating a good screenplay—as if he didn't know—trying to be provocative. At the same time, I was desperate to convey an air of seriousness, the soon-to-be-ex-actress, now budding writer, despite the fact that I was dressed more like a Vegas showgirl in thigh boots and a short leather skirt. My usual confusion about identity. And he knew it. "What are you saying?" he kept asking. "You're not being honest about yourself. Tell the *truth!*"

What truth? I didn't even realize I wasn't telling the truth. At that time, I was in the process of extricating myself from my first marriage to a charming but damaged man from an established Hollywood family (more on that later). And admittedly, during those seven years I'd regressed into my former self, the well-intentioned English girl, enamored of men with good manners, the door-openers and napkin-retrievers—the kind of cinematic suaveness that passed for romance. His knife-to-the-throat approach shocked me. No doubt I was ready to be shocked. "You're quite beautiful," he announced that day over the lobster salads, studying me in profile. "Although you're not really my type." But then he wasn't my type, either. A month later, when I'd finally left my husband and moved into a grim little apartment in Hollywood, I ran into him again—at a dinner party in Beverly Hills. I was unlike my mother except in one respect: as a guest I considered it my duty to charm the entire table, even flattering some people I didn't like. Halfway through this charade, he pulled me into the kitchen. "Look," he said, "manners are just a convenient way of *avoiding* the truth. To keep people at bay. You don't have to be so damn polite all the time. It's fake." How could I be attracted to a man like this? If he didn't like the dress I was wearing, he said so. If I complained about a bad day of writing, he would come back with, "Being a victim is just an excuse not to succeed. It's tough out there!" and if I tried to defend myself, saying I'd always been overly sensitive to criticism, his cool observation was, "But then you *punish* everyone for your sensitivity."

He liked to cut through the shit.

And of course I was attracted to him *because* he wasn't my type. He talked loudly; he wore a wide-shouldered, pinstripe zoot suit jacket over a Grateful Dead T-shirt (admittedly, he'd once been in the music business); his nose was too prominent; he had a receding hairline and a permanent three-day growth of beard. All of which was okay. I was happy to be with someone who was the opposite of the superficially refined-looking men I'd fallen for before. That said, when I finally introduced him to my family—in particular, my mother—the critical part of me couldn't help wishing he were taller, quieter, and more conventional-looking.

But to go with the scathing humor, there was an endearing schoolboy naïveté. And what he called truthfulness was often a way of baring of his soul. One minute he'd be going on about the ecstasy or agony of love—*what it felt like*—the next, he'd launch into a fury about what seemed to me inconsequential things: missed phone calls, traffic, temperature, food, or being shown to the wrong table in a restaurant. He would even hang up on his parents if they talked too long. I'd never seen life lived in such torment, the emotions pouring out. He loved me, or he didn't, or he was "trying not to" because it was "killing him." On the other hand, I was thrilled to be the shiksa goddess, the antidote to his overindulgent childhood, during which, according to him, everyone had to shout at the dinner table to be heard. But eventually I did fight back. Or rather, in a burst of outrage, I'd say, "Look, you talk too much. There's *no filter* between your brain and your mouth. You're uncivilized. A *barbarian!*" And he'd smile knowingly, or shrug, or make fun of my Englishness—the gardening, the white tablecloths, the cucumber sandwiches. "Oh, tea time," he'd announce, laughing, gently kissing my neck, as if he'd rescued a stray, some poor émigré still wallowing in Dickensian quaintness.

By that time, I was in love. So I told myself I didn't care if he was married.

My husband and me, 1988.

six

Westcliff.

My father's way was to make fun of things. He made fun of us all but particularly my mother, and in those days I didn't realize how wounding this
was for her. Or maybe I saw it and chose to ignore it. Her conventional
decorum was there to be challenged. "She married beneath her," he would
say, cheerily. Or he would rib her about her undying allegiance to the royal
family, whom he considered a disreputable bunch of bores. She absorbed
these cuts, but the silences were telling and the headaches came later.

My father—in his Hawes & Curtis pinstripe suits and stiff collars, with
his gray, wing-tipped hair and the faint aroma of Imperial Leather soap
drifting in his wake—exuded a very non-suburban glamour. He was charming and he disarmed me, as he did everyone else, with his bawdy music hall
jokes and his war anecdotes—stories that successfully kept the world from
penetrating that outer layer. He was also a bluffer and a teaser, and I became
his most adoring audience. "Did you know, when you were born, you had
a pointy head and looked like a turnip?" he would announce with mock
horror. "I said to the nurse, 'Christ, I hope that's not *mine!*'" And I would
fall about laughing. By that time, I was cultivating my unserious side partly
because I'd learned that by keeping things on the surface, by being amusing,
I could get people's attention—particularly his. I did cartwheels on the lawn,

imitations of Elvis and Gerry and the Pacemakers. I parroted back my father's old jokes: "Have you ever seen Helen Keller's dog? No? Well, neither has *she!*" And to reward me for the effort, he would throw back his head, guffawing, one hand banging the breakfast table. "Ha ha ha!"

As far as I was concerned, my father and I existed apart in the family. Our club of two. We were unique, we thought, in truly appreciating music and paintings. To compete with my mother's landscapes, her thrift store finds, he hung Toulouse-Lautrec prints in the hallway, declaring, "At least this is *art!*" We listened to his jazz records, lying together on the living room floor in order to "feel the rhythm": Lionel Hampton's *Vibe Boogie,* Jonah Jones's *Arrivederci Roma,* Ella Fitzgerald, and Miles Davis, who, admittedly, was way above my head.

At the beginning of the '50s, my father formed a trio with Uncle Mike and Charlie Bruce, a tall Scotsman, who was a friend of the family. By then, Uncle Mike had expanded the Rochford Airport beyond its few original Nissan huts. A lounge had been built, and a modern, low-ceilinged restaurant. There were tablecloths and elaborately decorated menus, designed by Mike's wife, Wendola, a former Pan Am stewardess, and on Saturday nights it became a minor hot spot with the shrimp cocktail and steak flambé crowd. The house band, Sid Uren and his Quartet, played until eleven, and then my father's trio might step in, particularly if a plane had been delayed and the passengers had to sleep over. By popular request, they finished with "Big Noise from Winnetka"—their best number, according to him. In fact, everything he said or did appealed to my naive idea of sophistication. At the airport, on a Saturday afternoon, I would sit with him and Ken Potter, the bartender, a friendly dome-headed man who fed me maraschino cherries. A millionaire at one time, heir to the famous Potter's Catarrh pills, he bore the distinction, so my father said, of having squandered his inheritance on "women and drink." This was another idea that played into the fantasy I was happily forming for myself—to be a woman for whom men ruined themselves.

Movies perpetuated this fantasy. My father loved movies and wanted me to love them too. He'd been going to the cinema religiously once a week since he was ten. "You have to understand the power films had on people," he said. "In the 1930's and '40s there was nothing else. When Bogart smoked a cigarette on-screen, the whole theater lit up too. When Clark Gable took off his shirt in *It Happened One Night,* and the audience saw he was bare-chested, the undershirt business was finished. Men stopped wearing them! Imagine!" I couldn't, of course, but was enthralled anyway. I had seen my first film with him when I was three years old, *The Red Shoes,* playing at our local Rivoli. The theater had me spellbound, a classic example of rococo chic, with gilded pillars, brass spittoons, and vast expanses of dripping red velvet. I remember nothing of the movie, however, except for the tears (my own) as Moira Shearer dances manically *en pointe,* and her scream when she leaps onto the train tracks to her death.

My sister, father, and me in the garden
on Seymour Road.

. . .

Still, my fascination with movies started there. Also, I believe (through my father's eyes), my early concept of women: the drama, certainly, and the fact that beautiful, troubled women had an irresistible allure to men. He loved Rita Hayworth in *Gilda* and the besieged Ingrid Bergman in *Notorious*. Several years later, on the day Marilyn Monroe died of an overdose, he walked around our living room close to tears. "Why didn't she call me? I would have saved her," he said, as if they'd been best friends. Clearly these desirable beings inhabited a different planet—one that did not require a woman serving her husband three meals a day or picking up his socks. I would obviously have to become something similar or be doomed to obscurity.

Being my father's favorite had its drawbacks. My mother said nothing, but her jealousy was apparent—at least to me. I noticed everything, as usual, my brain pinging away like a tuning fork. She had my younger brother, of course. Her darling boy, the tousled-haired blond with the toothy smile, whom I also adored and wanted to possess, perhaps in an attempt to extract a little of that charm that worked so well on her. But the intimacy my father shared with me was something else. My mother retreated even further into her domestic world, getting on with it, clearing up, cooking, moving furniture around with her martyr's strength. "Mind, dear," she'd say, sweeping past with a tray of dishes. "Can I help?" "No, it's too late *now*"—her irritation barely masked by her determined smile or some face-saving remark: "It's simply *boiling* in here, Fiona. Open a window and tell your father to come down for dinner *this minute!*"

She called me Fiona; he called me Fifi. I longed to take her aside and say, Talk to me, but I couldn't. Perhaps the distrust between us started there. And later it would haunt me: the affection my father gave me that I knew should have been hers. Not that he was unloving toward her. He applauded her for her talents. But he wasn't so sympathetic about the headaches and backaches, about her ongoing kidney problems, all of which baffled him and, compared to his own robust health, he couldn't help seeing as a kind of female weakness. She was begging for sympathy; he entered the house every evening as if it were a circus. "What's happening?" he'd shout, throwing off his overcoat, rubbing his hands as he marched through the front door. And I'd be there waiting. "You're just like your father," my mother would say. And I was. I joked about everything. I was absent-minded. I lost keys and money. As a teenager, I left a pale blue herringbone jacket she'd made for me on a bus. But there were no reprimands, just cool observations. About my lanky hair or my unfortunate, waiflike legs: "You've got mine, dear, I'm afraid." One summer, they came to St. Teresa's to see me play Lysander in *A Midsummer's Night's Dream*, the big end-of-term production. No doubt there was some praise from my father, but what registered was my mother's remark: "You know, Fiona, you have a rather *flat face* in profile." All the more stinging because it was true.

And so I stubbornly aligned myself with my father, as later I would align myself with other men. I'm not sure it was a conscious decision; I simply felt safer in their company.

There was no cachet in those days to being young; at fifteen, I was merely an unformed adult, precociously adrift, obsessed with boys, and after boarding school I had no idea what to do with myself. By this time, my brother was away at the Malvern School and my sister was working at my father's law office. Against all predictions, she'd turned out to be a very efficient clerk. A remarkable leap from her early teenage years when most of her holidays were spent in bored idleness, lying on the sofa, quietly smoldering at the TV.

In 1962, there were few options. A secretarial course, then the hope of finding a job in London at some insurance firm, although the idea of having to commute every day by train seemed like a death sentence. Then, by some miracle, my father decided I should be sent to France. He'd always wanted me to go to university, but as I'd insisted on leaving St. Teresa's before taking my A Levels, I didn't qualify for an English college. So he wrote to the French consulate. The Sorbonne was full, but by the end of that summer, I was enrolled at Grenoble for the Cours Etranger, a year's course to study literature and language.

"I can't believe I just dropped you off, a girl of sixteen, to live on your own in a *foreign* country," he said years later. I had no fear whatsoever. Nor do I have any doubt that going to France saved me—and not only from a dreary provincial life in Westcliff-on-Sea. It changed my life forever.

In October 1963, my parents drove me down to Grenoble—a large town at the foot of the French Alps—then delivered me for safekeeping to a Madame des Francs. She owned the top two floors of a rather grand house on Rue de Tilsitt, now falling into ruin, where she ran a pension for foreign students.

A maid let us in. We were led down a dim corridor, smelling of soup and damp washing, to a room at the far end. Even though it was only three in the afternoon it was dark inside—splashes of light filtering through the lace curtains—and Mme. des Francs was in bed. She lay propped up on pillows, a large woman with a big white face and skin like creased tissue paper. There was an old cardigan draped over her nightgown, and one of her legs, wrapped in some kind of surgical dressing—fibrositis, I later learned—lay like a frozen log on the counterpane. "Bonjour," she murmured to my parents, who had halted a respectable three feet from the bed. *"Enchanté,"* replied my father, and offered her a courteous bow. He then turned to introduce me, but Madame had no interest in her young charge hovering behind him in the gloom. Instead, waving a fleshy hand, she said, *"Reglez l'argent, s'il vous plaît, monsieur!"* She was only interested in the money, the fee for the first month's board and lodging. Obligingly, my father reached inside his jacket. However, barely did he have time to pull out his wallet or count the large banknotes (or even register his surprise), before Madame had heaved herself across the bed and grabbed them. She immediately shoved them into the folds of her décolletage—a deft sleight of hand peformed while her other arm lassoed a walking stick. She then rapped on the wall, and a few seconds later, the maid appeared to show me to my room.

The boarders were mainly English. There were three startled-looking young boys from minor public schools who, judging from their clothes—an assortment of fecal-colored tweeds and cavalry twills—had never been farther than the home counties. There was an English girl like me, and two older American girls, whom Madame simply referred to as *"les Américaines,"* respectful of their obvious wealth. It was true, they owned unimagined luxuries. Expensive winter coats hung in their room, and there were pairs of skis and real fur boots lined up against the wall. Cartons of Winstons sat on the twin beds, along with several jars of Hellmann's mayonnaise and tins of Folgers coffee—imported, presumably, on the assumption that by American culinary standards, France was bound to let them down. In those days, most people in Europe were still living in postwar conditions—not so much out of poverty but habit. I was allowed two pounds pocket money a week (the equivalent of fourteen francs, or almost three dollars); I'd brought a small transistor radio and a clock. My wardrobe included the usual homemade skirts, a kilt, some Shetland sweaters, and a thick brown duffle coat—none of it fashionable.

Because one of the students hadn't shown up, I managed to get a room of my own. It was on the top floor, down the hall from the Americans and our somewhat grim communal bathroom. There were two sizeable beds (one missing a leg), a chair, a cracked marble fireplace, and an ancient light fixture holding a single forty-watt bulb. In daylight the room was bright and airy. It was also spectacularly dirty. Dust balls floated like clouds across the floorboards, and a sooty film decorated the windows. After the cleanliness of Seymour Road, I was in awe. In fact, it represented everything I'd dared imagine about being a foreign student: a life of bohemian chic.

I immediately went to Galeries Lafayette and bought myself a shocking pink chiffon scarf for three francs. I enrolled at the Faculté des Lettres. I went to class every morning in the Rue du Vieux Temple and sat in a freezing room with enormous windows, but I couldn't concentrate. The endless drone of the teacher's voice, then hours staring at the deadly columns of verbs slayed me. So I just stopped going, or I turned up only sporadically. No one seemed to notice. Instead, I spent the day walking around the streets, or sitting lazily in cafés, and a lot of the other students were doing the same. In La Maison du Café, a modern glass emporium on Place Grenette, with lurid brass chandeliers suspended from the mezzanine, the foreigners sat grouped together. We huddled over our café crèmes, our *tartines,* bright-eyed, pretending to be part of the university crowd, but looking more like refugees and easily identifiable by our clothes. The Norwegians were dressed in big oiled wool sweaters and hiking boots; some of the Germans still wore lederhosen and little Alpine hats. And the English boys, careful not to look self-indulgent, clung resolutely to their old raincoats and their fathers' trilbies, though occasionally they would show off by ordering brandies and laughing loudly at their own jokes.

Back at the pension for dinner, we were politely restrained—in the beginning, that is. But after the first week, we managed to get past our tame hellos by drinking Madame's cheap red wine as fast as we could. The dining room was cream colored, with curved, flaking walls. There was also a concealed door—noticeable by a line of smudged finger marks—and used solely by the maid, who emerged from the kitchen at eight o'clock with the food. Madame herself always arrived late. We could hear her in the corridor, tap-tapping like a blind woman, her stick preceding her. Eventually the double doors would crash open and she'd appear, like a battleship, listing to one side as she favored her good leg. We were all terrified. Even the American girls went quiet. And no one dared complain about the meals, which were memorable only because they were so bad: overcooked spaghetti, macaroni pudding. There was hardly any meat, except on Thursdays, when we had sauerkraut. This consisted of a bowl of vinegary cabbage topped by a few lethal pork sausages, large and so pink that even the English boys considered them too scary-looking to be safe.

During that first week, one of them made a point of sitting next to me. About eighteen, Jeremy was tall, with a pale, unformed face and a thatch of springy ginger hair—a wedge of wooliness that defied the comb. He leaned over, one Harris Tweed elbow sliding my way, ink stains dotting the sleeve. "I'm from Wales," he announced. "Well, actually, my parents are. I'm frightful at languages. Can't speak a word of French. In fact, I'm not overly endowed in the brain department, either. That's why they sent me over here!" It was a cheery confession, his way of trying to open up to a girl. "Oh, really?" I said. I was staring at his white hands, folded together on the tablecloth and looking, I thought, like dead fish. "Well, I suppose we're all here trying to learn something. A little savoir faire!" I was haughty, anxious to sound sophisticated. I had recently cut my hair in a pixie bob, like Jean Seberg's in *À Bout de Souffle.* It was too short for my round face, and to compensate I'd wrapped the new pink chiffon scarf up to my ears. Every night, Jeremy sat next to me. I heard about his skin condition (nerves), his debutante sister, his mother's love of geraniums. It was impossible not to like him; at the same time, he represented everything I was dying to leave behind.

Most afternoons I spent on my own, in a back booth at La Maison du Café. I had replaced my tartan kilt with a pair of navy corduroy trousers and a cream button-down crepe shirt, thereby spending all of my eight pounds monthly allowance. I smoked Gauloises until my lungs ached, pretending to read the local paper, *L'Isere,* and drank endless cups of café au lait. Occasionally, I ordered a croque monsieur from my friend Leon, the waiter, who kindly ran up a tab. I knew nothing. I had a great feeling of importance about myself—though I had no idea where it came from. I was exhilarated, free, happy to be on my own. I started to bring a notebook with me to write down my "thoughts," plus a copy of Jacques Prévert's poems, which at sixteen I considered astonishingly insightful.

Romance was constantly on my mind.

Cet amour si vrai
Cet amour si beau . . .

seven
Château de la Vinouse 2005.

It's February and a lot colder than I could have imagined. The fields of unplanted earth around the château are a foreboding dark brown, and sheets of icy water lie in the furrows. I am here to start the restoration of the house. I feel a mixture of excitement and terror. And because I know nothing about French contractors, I've asked an Englishwoman, Nicola, to help. She has been living in the village for several years and is familiar with the local workmen. Divorced, an attractive mother of two, she has large chestnut eyes and a commanding, no-nonsense voice.

"You know what they say about contractors," she announces cheerily on our first meeting. "If they're available, they're no good."

And I laugh because I presume she must be joking.

She arranges for two of them to come to the house. The first is a M. Hinard, a small, man with flushed cheeks and a crushing handshake. His partner— taller, more sophisticated-looking, and with an important French nose—is introduced as M. Corbusier, a name that immediately inspires confidence.

It's cold in the house. Flakes of snow are whirling outside and a treacherous wind whistles under the front door. Both men seem cheerfully oblivious, however—*"Belle maison, Madame,"* they say, adding appreciative murmurings about the classic high ceilings, then start by going upstairs. Nothing more is said. But as we walk from room to damaged room, M. Hinard's face assumes the connoisseur's air of impending tragedy. "Every beam will have to be reinforced," he announces gravely. "And most likely the ceilings will have to come down." We are standing now in what I hope will be the master bedroom. M. Hinard has picked up an old plank of wood and is poking at a dark hole at the top of the chimney piece. Something else I hadn't noticed. "Rotten," he says— *pourri*. And to demonstrate his keen eye, he jabs again, more violently this time, with a pole-vaulter's thrust, so that two sizeable chunks of plaster come crashing at our feet. *"Voila!"* he says, looking remarkably pleased.

After that, he goes over to the windows. He tries to open one, then another. He yanks at the old iron handles; they rattle but won't move. "They'll all have to be replaced," he says. *"All* of them?" I ask (there are more than forty in the house). *"Mais oui!"* he says, barely hiding his disdain. I tell him I'm very attached to the warped frames and that I am particularly fond of the ripples in the original glass. I will regret it, he says, because of the winter drafts. "And what about the floors?" M. Corbusier says, his eyes fixed critically on the 200-year-old tiles under our feet. As was the custom in the early nineteenth century, large sections have been painted red. A dark, bloody hue. "Impossible to get off," says M. Hinard dismissively. I try not to panic. But this seems more of a tragedy than the ceiling. In a corner, behind a door, I see a beautiful stretch of pale rose where the tiles have been untouched. "Surely with some strong paint remover, some *decapitant,"* I suggest. *"Non,"* says M. Corbusier, speaking as the expert. He has been quietly sketching each room, listing the various disasters on his yellow pad. "Many people have tried in old houses like this," he says. *"Mais c'est impossible!"*

Not the last time I will hear those words.

In the kitchen, there is little to inspire—an old boiler, its thick funnel disappearing into a charred ceiling, and beyond that, modified in the 1950s, a makeshift bathroom: home of the three-legged tin tub and two prison-cell windows. *"Ça, alors!"* M. Hinard murmurs, old lightbulbs crunching under his feet. Further words are unnecessary. The whole room will have to be gutted.

Despite the grim assessment, they seem perfectly qualified to do the job. I'm even congratulating myself, relieved to have found a contractor so soon. But then there's the question of availability. According to Nicola, M. Hinard is in the middle of remodeling a school nearby. Could he really be done there, then finish at La Vinouse in time for the summer? *"Pas de problem,"* M. Hinard says, regaining some of his vigor. No problem. He will go home and write up a detailed estimate, the *"devis."*

In France, an estimate is serious business. A signed devis is a binding contract: each item of work to be undertaken—every detail, however trivial—must be listed, and the final price is the final price. Or so I am led to believe.

The following day, a second contractor arrives. Eric is strong and wiry, his face lined like a ploughed field. He's eager to take on the job, and his handshake is also impressive. He is, however, a man of few words. As we tour the house, his eyes scanning the holes, the water-stained walls, he just nods or simply murmurs, *"Oui, je comprends."* He never writes anything down. No need, he says, tapping his head, *"C'est ici."* Apparently it's all stored up there. But I'm worried about the amount of work to be done, and I'm probably not asking the right questions; at the same time, I don't want to seem like the desperate foreigner (being the desperate foreigner). I mention deadlines. "My husband is coming in August," I say. He smiles, unconcerned. Fine. Not that he's *available.* Not right now, that is. "But August is a long way off," he insists. On his way out he gives me a crushing but affirmative handshake and promises to write up the devis.

"How soon?" I ask.

"Soon," he says. *"Bientôt."*

I hear from no one for a week. Nicola leaves messages with M. Hinard and Eric, but the calls are not returned. I have nothing to do but wait. At Kathryn's I lead a monk's life. Though brisk and sunny in the daytime, it's bitterly cold at night. I eat simple dinners of scrambled eggs, *mâche,* and goat's cheese. I turn off the radiators to save on the heating, then like a fugitive scurry up to bed with my meager meal, a bottle of wine under my arm. Sometimes it's barely seven o'clock. Wearing flannel pajamas, socks, and a bathrobe, I immerse myself in the practical details. I read books on French gardening and indigenous trees; I study brochures of bathroom supplies, taps, and sinks. Downing half the bottle of wine, I spend a useful hour on construction words: *enduit de lissage, massette, lambris.* But by ten o' clock I've nothing more to do and, though exhausted, I can't sleep, so I kill off the other half. The wind whistles outside. The floors creak incessantly and cold air leaks around the window frames—frames, I notice, that are similar to mine at the château. By two in the morning I am still wide-eyed, staring at the wood-slatted ceiling.

In L.A., I'd be in a state of panic by now, my mind racing, wondering if I should take an Ativan. Or another Ativan. I'd be thinking of every tricky relationship I ever had, my capacity for error, my dwindling career, wallowing in self-pity. But not here. I am calm, floating. How good it feels to be on my own. What luxury, knowing I only have myself to please. I am almost embarrassed to feel this happy. Wrapped in a blanket, I wander downstairs to the kitchen: thick beams, an Aga stove, two country sofas, and a tall pine cabinet, the shelves stacked with Kathryn's old VCR collection. I inspect the spines and see, with detached amusement, one of my own films, with Vincent Price. Then another, directed by Roman Polanski. A former life, ancient history. Although I still get letters—*Dear Miss Lewis, I am a great admirer . . . Ich bin ein grosser fan.* For some reason, most are from Germany, a nation devoted to horror movies, it seems. *Please to autograph these photos, madam*—written in loopy adolescent scrawl, a plastic folder enclosed containing fuzzy pictures of the naked or semi-naked me, acquired from God knows where—probably late-night TV. Who was that girl? The creamy skin, the milkmaid eyes, the hint of boredom. I make a cup of *verveine* tea, then go back to bed, to my builder's dictionary, my thumbed copies of *House & Garden* or *Maisons Côté Ouest.* Days go by, and I've barely spoken to anyone, except my husband.

"So how's it going?"

"Great. I'm lining up workmen. Just waiting for the estimates."

"Do you miss me?"

"Of course." It's true. Left on my own, I become calm, loving, the person I always hoped to be.

"But what do you *do* all day there?"

"Well, not much. I drive around."

And that's exactly what I do. I drive around the countryside. With my iPod balanced on the dash, I play the old favorites: The Stones, Billie Holiday, Simply Red's "Holding Back the Years," I tear along the deserted lanes, the morning sun blinking through the poplars, the mist rising from the fields like a mirage, drowning in nature.

"It's winter but so beautiful. Don't you miss the seasons?"

"No," he says, in case I'd forgotten. "I can *visit* them."

On my way back from these excursions, sometimes going as far as Puycelsi or Bruniquel—a hilltop town where in the sixth century Princess Brunehaut, daughter of the king of the Visigoths, once ruled (and who was subsequently tied to a horse and torn limb from limb)—I stop at Raymond's to pick up a baguette. Better acquainted with the clientele now, I get a few sly nods and a wave from the rosy-faced man in the zigzag sweater. There is even a forceful *"Bonjour, Madame!"* from the farmer with the wandering eye.

Then I drive over to the château. I wander through the rooms, trying to imagine them finished—yes, even furnished. I go down to the freezing basement, to poke around in the dirt floors, to look for the tunnel. The one Guy Moulin assures me exists. An old escape route once used by the aristocracy, or by fleeing Protestants, depending on which century we're talking about. I find nothing, just empty wine bottles and old bits of farm machinery. So I go back up the rotting stairs to the hallway to stare at the luminous green linoleum. It plagues me. The next morning, I bring a builder's knife with me, the kind with a retractable blade. I put on thick gardening gloves—awkward for cutting but good for tearing out big pieces with abandon. And after a few hours' work, the green strips are scattered across the kitchen and salon like so many dead snakes. What's obvious now (alarmingly so) is that *every room* on the ground floor is covered with an inch or more of gray cement. I go outside. In the barn I find an old crowbar and a heavy piece of brick. I then start to chip away at the floors. It's laborious, backbreaking, and hardly efficient. After an entire morning, I've only managed to remove a foot or so. But what's underneath is encouraging: a section of the original floorboards, wide planks, 200 years old. All I have to do now is remove another 3,000 *square feet of cement.*

Nicola is puzzlingly optimistic; she is also blessed with a vitality I can only presume to be the result of years living an idyllic life in the countryside. It's two weeks since M. Hinard and Eric came to look at the house. We've both left messages, but for some reason the estimates are never ready. Soon, they assure us. *Bientôt!*

"I'm not worried," I say to Nicola, obviously worried. And even she agrees it might be a good idea to start on the plumbing and the electrical.

The old pigeon house at Château de la Vinouse with Mme. Moulin's gas tank.

"I'll arrange for M. Boudet to come round," she says. "He's an expert in both fields, the best in the area. Of course, he's booked up for two years." She thinks, however, she can convince him to take on the job, as he will "do anything for her." Tactfully, I don't ask why.

M. Boudet is a short, cherubic man, charming and compellingly polite. He's also fit and tanned, despite the cold, which suggests that he takes his winter vacations elsewhere, and is therefore expensive. Nicola hasn't mentioned money, and M. Boudet is unwilling to divulge even an approximate cost because of the binding nature of the written devis. What I've found out, however, is that building prices vary enormously. There is the *prix Anglais,* for example, rumored to be marginally elevated; the *prix Americain,* considerably more costly; and then, the most exorbitant of all, the *prix Parisien.* Naturally there is a *prix local,* but that takes years of trust and familiarity, and at this stage I can hardly expect to qualify.

Right away, I know I'll be hiring M. Boudet. *"Bonjour—belle maison,"* he says, sweeping past me with an air of efficiency, his black Sharpie already uncapped. The old plumbing and electrical will have to go, he announces—the dangling wires, the ancient sockets, the fizzing plugs. "How many bathrooms do you require, madame? Three? And central heating?" "Well, I . . ." He moves energetically through the rooms, asking me to point out where I want the sinks, the toilets, where exactly each new plug, switch, fax, and TV cable outlet should go, and where I'd like the main junction box, which naturally throws me into a panic of indecision. Still, I'm swept on by his enthusiasm, plus a nagging fear that if I don't make some headway, nothing will get done. One arm outstretched, he deftly scores *x*'s and arrows along the crumbling walls. He talks about low kilowattage and the need for a *parafoudre* (lightning conductor), this being a high-risk area for blackouts.

He strides ahead, moving at an amazing pace—perhaps, I think, trying to catch up with that two-year backlog of work—and I follow. In the second bedroom upstairs, soon to be my bathroom, I tell him I'd like to put a bath in the center of the room. He tries to talk me out of it. Though

French plumbing has come a long way in the last decade, the notion of converting an oversize bedroom with a marble fireplace into an area used solely to wash oneself obviously smacks of Hollywood madness. When I mention I'm thinking of hanging an old chandelier over the tub, he looks astounded. He mimes a large object hitting my head. "When it falls, you will be electrocuted," he says—*electrocuté, madame!* Although this somehow produces a satisfied smile.

He has all the information he needs to do the job, he says. Encouraged, I ask when he might be able to start. He gives me a look of genuine surprise. *"Aucune idée!"* He couldn't possibly say. And so, illogically, I ask when he thinks he might be able to *finish*. By August? Well, he couldn't say that either. But he will definitely send me a written devis.

"Soon?" I ask, trying not to sound too desperate.

"Yes," he says. *"Bientôt."*

Arguably one of the most misleading words in the French language.

My husband suddenly decides to come. He is stopping by for a few days on his way to Bulgaria, where he is producing a movie. So I get the train to Paris to collect him. I greet him in the hotel lobby wide-eyed, aware that I look oddly astounded, almost feral, as if emerging from a lengthy hibernation. Two weeks alone, and I've retreated into my covert self. I see his tanned face, the cynical scowl, saved by the forgiving green eyes, and tell myself to *get a grip*. After all, this is Paris. The eternally romantic city. Particularly as we're staying at the Ritz. We walk together through the hotel's arcade, past the glittering jewel-box windows, to get to the old Hemingway bar, now refurbished and called something else. Two stools are available; the tables are already taken by tourists like ourselves— Americans, happily chatting in corners. "Look," my husband says as we order drinks, "everyone pretending they don't mind paying forty dollars for a martini!"

"I forget how funny you are," I say, laughing. It's true. As if I always have another man in mind.

"That's convenient. Did you miss me?"

"Yes," I say, busy knocking back the first vodka, relieved to feel the warm glow. I squeeze his arm. "I'm happy you're here."

"You should be."

"Well, I *am!*"

"After all, I bought you a house in France!"

We laugh again. We have another martini, then eat a late lunch at Chez Georges, an old favorite, just off the Places des Victoires. We go to dinner at Benoit to meet some investors, French film financiers who may or may not fund a future movie with Sean Penn. As the producer's wife, I ooze fake charm over the gravlax, while my husband talks realistically about getting a good script first. He refuses to pander to get the money. It could happen, he likes to say, but probably not. For once, I see his struggles instead of my own, his quiet anxiety.

Finally, after the *turbot à la vapeur*, plus a second bottle of Sancerre, we fall out into the street. It's raining slightly. Arm in arm, sliding on the wet cobblestones, we head down the Rue de Rivoli, joking about one of the men's dyed blue-black hair, his slick comb-over, his saucer-sized Rolex. Back at the hotel, quite drunk, we undress quickly, then fuck on the peach-colored silk bedspread. We sink into each other, the familiar grooves; I feel his strong arms, his oddly dainty feet, the legs I've always envied for their smooth shapeliness. It took years to get to this, I think, to feel safe. It doesn't work without trust, or love. And I have to hold on to that, to preserve it. At this stage, I can barely remember fucking anyone else. We are tender together; we don't go in for anything acrobatic sexually. Occasionally, he'll ask me to parade across the room naked, wearing a pair of $800 shoes. I never say—So what are you going to do to turn *me* on? Once, perhaps, to punish him. But now I want to be seduced and be seductive, to dive into the peachy depths, to reaffirm my desire for him. I climb on top of him. I lean back, the chandelier orbiting my head. A blur. Then he pulls me down, shoving me over the side of the bed until my head hits the carpet and, choking with laughter, we manage to knock the phone off the Louis XVI night table.

After this, silence. A limbo-like calm. Holding his hand, I gaze up at the ceiling, the ornate plaster with pink and gold swirls, suddenly remembering that I was here with my first husband. When was it, 1982? Decades ago. Not in this room, but something equally elaborate down the hall. I was miserable back then, almost suicidal. In fact, I wanted to kill us both. Instead, I spent half the night crying in the bathroom. I don't mention this now. After all these years, I'm still trying to hide my vulnerabilities. Still putting on a good front. But back in Los Angeles, when I have nightmares, shooting upright in bed, gasping, my husband gently talks me back to sleep.

In the morning, we inspect our hangovers in the bathroom mirror. I kiss his unshaven cheek, his cultivated three-day growth, his *jolie laide* look. "What does that mean?" he used to say. Pretty ugly? "No. Like Belmondo," I'd say. Cute, a little gnarly but sexy. "Am I jolly laid today?" he asks now. "Yes," I reply, "Jolly *well laid.*" I'm feeling cocky.

After breakfast, we go for a walk. We do a tour of the Place Vendôme, then cross the Rue de Rivoli and walk through the Tuileries. The soft dampness of the gravel, the smell of compost and leaves. Heaven. Arm in arm, we head for the Rodins where, despite my husband's so-called misgivings about Paris, he whispers, "Magnificent."

A good sign. Yes, I think, *this is going to work.*

But Paris isn't France. And by the time we arrive at Gare Montparnasse to get the train south, I start obsessing about the house. So far, all he's seen is a few bad photographs, and I'm nervous. I'm nervous about him liking the countryside, and I'm nervous about the train, which like most of my old travel fantasies did not include packed carriages with screaming children and a third-rate sandwich bar.

We arrive just before dusk. We are staying at Kathryn's farm, her rambling collection of stone houses and barns, her idyllic storybook version of life *à la campagne,* complete with horses, chickens, and cats. Five to be exact. Out here there are wild cats everywhere; at night they leap from hedgerows across the car's headlights like young panthers. I don't mention this to my husband because of his allergies. Before leaving, I locked Kathryn's in the pigeon house with some cans of food, then vacuumed the rooms. But somehow the essence of cat remains, particularly in the bed where we're sleeping. In the middle of the night, he can't breathe and has to spend several hours outside, sitting in the front seat of the rental car with the doors open, trying to recuperate. He downs an Allegra, without complaining, though every throaty wheeze makes me feel unreasonably resentful.

The next morning, he says he's fine. "Why wouldn't I be fine after only two hours sleep and with chronic jet lag?" he murmurs, giving me one of his glacial looks. At the bar in Monclar, we get coffee, plus a *galopin* for him (a breakfast beer), then drive over to the château. It has rained heavily during the night and the landscape looks forbiddingly bleak: one continuous brown smudge. There are deep, watery potholes in the driveway, and as we get closer to the house I notice a few more chunks of crépi have fallen off the north wall. If I was nervous before, now I'm panicked. We go inside. My husband walks around silently. Naturally the photos couldn't show the extent of the damage: the brown patches of damp, the broken fireplaces, the collapsed ceiling upstairs—plaster chips still floating down after M. Hinard's rigorous prodding—not to mention the cement floors littered with strips of green linoleum. Obviously there are no ruined houses in Los Angeles, so I start to see everything through his eyes. I watch him pacing, hands buried in his pockets, trying to hide his concern. Finally, he turns to me. "It's a *disaster*," he says. "Far worse than I imagined."

"Would you like to go down to the basement to see the original bread oven?" I say, sounding more English than I've done in years.

"No."

Instead, he walks out the back door, down the stone staircase, and into the garden, where a few flakes of snow are now blowing in from the west. This, unfortunately, is the bad side of the house, the virtually windowless side that, admittedly, in winter, exudes about as much charm as a women's correctional institution. He goes to a point beyond the big cedar and looks out. More bleakness. But just then the clouds part, the sun appears and, miraculously, the hills rise up bathed in waves of shimmering light. "A disaster," he says, "but with a great view. So where are you going to put the pool?"

I hadn't thought about a pool. In my romantic vision of life in rural France, a swimming pool seemed too conventional, too L.A.

"Because that's the only way I could possibly come here," he says.

A word here about the money. The truth is I've always had a problem in this area, especially when it's not mine. "But you're married now!" say the seasoned California wives. "It's yours too!" Legally, perhaps. But as a late bloomer, a woman who's still trying to escape the grasp of mothers and lovers and husbands, asking for what I need financially is difficult. I feel beholden. Of course I *am* beholden. Particularly now. Having spent the initial $300,000 on the house, I need more to restore it. With no working electricity or plumbing, no bathroom, kitchen, or even a sound ceiling, there are moments when I wonder what the hell I'm doing. How far does a girl have to go for *freedom*? A few days ago, waiting for the estimates, Nicola drew up a rough building budget. She predicted a cost of about $100,000. In Paris, I asked my husband if he would loan me the money. "Think of it as an investment," I said, unconvincingly. "I'll pay you back when my ship comes in." "I *am* your ship!" he replied coolly. But he agreed. So once again, I feel guilty and grateful—annoyed that I feel so grateful because I'd sworn to myself (since when—the '80s?) I wasn't going to feel that way again with a man. Therefore, illogically, I am blaming him as well as myself for being the woman who has to rely on a man for her happiness. In order to reinvent herself, to build the house that *will save her.* . . .

Nicola knows someone reputed to be a pool expert. And the next day, at the appointed hour, we are standing with this man in one of his client's back gardens, to check out an example of his work. A medium-sized pool, it looks perfectly acceptable, except for its odd blue color. In fact, considering the weather—the blanket of impenetrable gray above—it looks almost turquoise. I put my hand in the water. The sides feel strangely soft and spongy. My husband puts his hand in too. "Plastic?" he says, his eyes widening. Apparently the pool walls are entirely covered with a "liner," as if someone has literally laid down a giant blue garbage bag. "What is it the French have about *plastic*?" he asks. On the drive over, we'd passed a new housing development, rows of depressing pink boxes, swing sets, and plastic molded chairs parked on their front porches. When I tried to make a point about ordinary people having to live somewhere too, he said, aggravated, "You don't have to defend the *whole* of France, you know." But now, on our knees, our hands plunged into the icy water, poking at the spongy lining, we can't help laughing. "Are they *kidding*," he says. No. In fact, the pool man is adamant. There is simply no other way to build one, he says.

When I call other companies and ask about an alternative to the plastic, they are confused. "What would it be made of?" they ask. If I suggest plaster, they are dumbfounded. "Plaster? What *kind* of plaster?" "Like an American pool," I say. After a brief hesitation comes the inevitable response: "You won't get anyone to build that here. *C'est impossible!*"

My husband is discouraged, the pool at this point representing an important link to the civilized world, to be accompanied, he hopes, by a plasma TV (just coming on the market) and a decent Internet connection. That is, if he decides to come.

"Why do you keep saying that? If you don't want to come, *don't*," I say, on edge.

And the next day things get worse.

M. Brocco arrives. According to Nicola, a man who knows how to build a *piscine Americaine*, or something close to it. The three of us stand in the garden, on a strip of land below the chestnuts. A grassy plateau where Mme. Moulin used to dry her washing. A perfect spot, we agree—a little on the tilt, perhaps, but directly in line with the view. However, if it's to be done by the summer, we'll need to start right away.

My husband is pacing off the land, trying to imagine a not-too-laborious walk from the house in the morning, carrying an *International Herald Tribune* and his cup of espresso. M. Brocco, armed with a can of spray paint, follows him, sinking plastic stakes into the ground, then spraying orange lines to mark the boundaries. Kathryn once suggested that having just bought eight acres of land, a pool might be better farther away, perhaps hidden behind a wall—a delightful discovery at the end of a stone pathway, flanked by Provençal urns. I'm wondering now if she's right, but M. Brocco is shaking his head, saying something about expensive retaining walls. Nevertheless, I walk to the very edge of the plateau, a spot farthest from the house, and mark the site there. M. Brocco crosses out the first neon lines, comes over, and sprays new ones.

"Too far!" My husband shouts.

"No. We don't want it so close to the house. Do we?"

"I think we do."

"But this is the countryside. We're not in Los Angeles. This isn't a *suburban backyard* in the San Fernando Valley, for God's sake," I say, realizing immediately that I've gone too far—the Valley representing the boundary beyond which he thinks there is little, if any, taste. "That's insulting," he replies. Then, shouting to M. Brocco, he walks to a spot even closer to the kitchen than before. "Over here, *s'il vous plaît!*" he says, and M. Brocco obliges. He pulls out the stakes, crosses out my lines, and sprays a third set. "Too *near,*" I shout defensively, suddenly tearful about this bleak strip of land. *My* land. "I want it here," he says. "But I don't!" "Fine. Then forget it!" he yells, and leaves, marching up the back stairs and into the house. M. Brocco seems unfazed by the argument, even amused. After all, we're married. This is France. Casually, he crosses out the last orange lines and then, reminding me it's a quarter to twelve, tells me he's going home to lunch. He knows exactly what we want, however, so he'll send over a devis.

The next day my husband is leaving for Bulgaria. We shuffle silently past each other, busy showering, taking vitamins; in the kitchen, we toast stale slices of yesterday's baguette like martyrs. By nine o'clock his suitcase is packed, even though his plane isn't until three. Feeling bad about the quarrel, I book a table for lunch in Toulouse, at the Brasserie les Beaux-Arts, Chez Flo, as it's locally called, a traditional fin de siècle establishment, its walls romantically appointed with opaline sconces and walnut paneling. On the drive down, we barely speak. But when the maître d' shows us a front booth, my husband's mood brightens. The place is packed: there's a tantalizing sound of laughter, of tinkling glasses, and the waiters are suitably hostile. "Ah, civilization," he says, sinking back. He's in heaven. We order foie gras, langoustines with homemade mayonnaise, and a bottle of the palest rosé.

"I'm sorry we argued," he says.

"Me too," I say. I slide my hand over his under the table, like I used to do in restaurants years ago, when we were married to other people.

"It's just that the house is *your* thing. Your love affair with France."

"I know."

"Don't get defensive."

"I'm not," I say defensively.

"It's your passion. It's just not *mine*."

"Yes. I understand."

"Listen, I'm only trying to explain to you why—"

"You don't have to. And you don't have to tell me *everything* you feel all the time."

"You know I do!" he says. He's laughing, at the same time giving me his slant-eyed look, showing me how patient he's being.

"It really is an investment."

"Good. When can we sell?"

"Sell?"

"My guess is you'll get tired of it in a year or so, anyway." Silent, obviously wounded, I withdraw my hand. "Well—it's a *possibility*, isn't it?"

What can I say, honestly? That I don't know how to live with him anymore in L.A.? Or for that matter, live with myself. I certainly can't say that leaving him might actually solve our marriage, because I'm not even sure the marriage needs solving.

"I'm thinking out loud, that's all," he says apologetically. And then, because he can't help himself, he adds, "I'm just trying to figure out what the fuck we're supposed *to do* there all day."

"Nothing," I say, looking away. "That's the whole point."

It's now March 10, a month since I arrived. No one has delivered an estimate. I leave more messages with M. Hinard's wife, with both Eric and
M. Boudet's wives, and with someone possibly related to M. Brocco, the
pool man. No one calls me back. Finally I manage to reach M. Brocco
during his lunch hour, forgetting, of course, that the only time to reach a
Frenchman is between the sacred hours of twelve and two. A young girl
answers. I hear the clink and scrape of crockery in the background, then
she hands him the phone. "*Where,*" I ask, barely able to restrain myself,
"is the promised estimate? And why didn't you call me back?" (I am unaware at this point that French workmen never call back.) I hear a sigh.
He tells me he can't do it. He doesn't want the job. The slant of the land,
the probability of shifting cement. "*Non. C'est impossible!*" Impossible, he
says again, and hangs up.

eight
Grenoble.

Most of my wanting to become French was about French men. I can't remember how Michel came into my life. I think he just sat down one day and started talking. I'd seen him before in the Maison du Café. About twenty, unshaven, slightly rumpled in a gray serge suit and white open-necked shirt, he would stroll around, hands in his pockets, wearing the self-satisfied look of a man who has yet to be disappointed in life. Not that I had such insights at sixteen. But I could see that women liked him, and he knew it.

In the beginning, he just flirted with me. He called me his *petit lapin*, his adorable *chou*. Of course, I'd never known a man in this way, or been the object of such adoring familiarity. All that dark masculinity and rushing words. In the daytime, we wandered around with Guy, his best friend, who was always trying to pick up girls. Or we sat in one of the smaller cafés, like Le Zinc, a dusty hole where we played table hockey and the *patron* arm wrestled with the clients. After dark, we necked passionately in the front seat of his decrepit Alfa. In those early days, I didn't know what I felt about him; I was still too astonished that he liked me. And I was sure he was seeing other girls, most likely sleeping with them. When we strolled past other cafés on Place Grenette, I would see him shoot looks at women he knew, ivory-legged beauties who in return gave him a knowing smile, or a raised eyebrow—probably because I looked so young. In my jeans and frosted pink lipstick, I resembled a healthy twelve-year-old. Still, we went everywhere together, and on the weekends he drove me to Alpe d'Huez to teach me to ski. I begged my parents to send me money so I could buy the latest stretch trousers with elastic loops on the bottoms, and a pair of ski boots.

I was busy creating my new French life, something I knew only from memories of my summer vacations, or from movies. To go with my Jean Seberg haircut, I'd bought a striped matelot T-shirt like the one Jeanne Moreau wore in *Jules and Jim,* and a tight black gabardine skirt. I found a portable record player in a second-hand shop and spent afternoons lying on my sagging mahogany bed transfixed, my heart thumping, listening to 45s of Edith Piaf singing "Non, Je Ne Regrette Rien" or Françoise Hardy's "Oh Oh Chéri."

Love had taken the place of education. Occasionally, I had to make an appearance at the faculty to qualify for my end-of-year *certificat d'études,* but I was learning more French with Michel. And he was happy to be the dilettante tutor. He didn't have much to do, either; he was taking a year off before starting work for his father, who was in the office equipment business. Walking down the Rue Alsace Lorraine, he would point out his parents' apartment, two second-floor balconies in a belle époque building. There was never any question of taking me up to meet them, and I wouldn't have expected it. I'm not sure what I expected. I didn't have an opinion about anything. Our romance filled me up—although so far there'd been no real sex. But he had told me he loved me. It was a December evening, foggy and freezing, and we were standing on the corner of Rue de Tilsitt. He opened his coat to wrap it around me. "I love you, *petite Anglaise!*" I told him I loved him, too. *"Je t'aime,"* I said, gazing rapturously at his face—words that up until then I'd never uttered to anyone in English, let alone in French, and no one (including my parents) had said to me in any language. The thrill was immediate and terrifying. But I was aching to be in the throes of love, and to *be* loved. On those nights, I didn't get back to the pension until late. Not that anyone would notice. There were no rules or supervision, something that would have shocked them at home. But when Michel had to make an appearance at home for dinner, I would join the others at Madame's.

By this time, Madame's son, Maurice, had moved in. Recently separated, he'd come home with his son, a hollow-eyed nine-year-old who spent most of the day moping around outside the kitchen. Maurice was a *voyou*, a thick-lipped brute with a meaty, unshaven face. Full of himself, his moods ranged from outright hostility to playful contempt and were mainly directed at the female lodgers. Sweeping into the dining room, a napkin already tucked into the neck of his shirt, he'd shout, *"Salut les gonzesses!"*—Hi, girlies—then treat us to one of his salacious laughs. At table he held court. He started with politics: De Gaulle, the economy, the atom bomb, the Common Market—which the papers were full of. "The olive branch has failed," he was only too happy to report, because the British had been refused entry into the European Economic Community. "And who needs them, anyway!" There were cracks about the Americans—"All money, no finesse." Then, warmed up, he'd have a go at the Algerians: *"Salles etrangers,"* he barked, with another throaty laugh, cabbage juice trickling down his chin, "all here to steal French jobs!"

A lot of North Africans were pouring into France then after the war of independence. School authorities had warned us to stay away from certain streets and seedy bars. Dens of iniquity, we were told, where young unsuspecting girls could be whisked away on the back of a Vespa to become slaves, or worse. In fact, they were rather tame Kasbah-type joints. Michel and I would often go there in the afternoons. One or two had juke boxes, and we'd dance around to tinny mountain love songs, kissing, showing off, while the dark-eyed waiters in their rubber sandals and nylon shirts stood watching, shocked by such blasphemy.

Maurice was a photographer by trade, and Madame had converted an old linen closet on the third floor for him to develop his portraits and wedding pictures. But he fancied himself for better things, and at dinner he would make suggestive remarks about one of us posing for "modeling shots." "Come on, girlies, come on. Why not?" he would say, taunting us, pursing his big lips, until Madame, thinking he'd finally gone too far, had to crack her stick across the back of his chair and shout, "*Ça suffit!*" Still, when he got the chance, he propositioned each of us privately. I had my turn. I was on the stairs one night, on my way to bed. Suddenly, he stepped out of the shadows and barred my way with his foot. It was dark, the push button contraption on the wall allowing twenty seconds of light had just clicked off. "*Très mignonne*"—very cute—he said, sliding a hand around my waist. He was grinning, whispering in my ear with his meaty breath. "*Et très photogénique!*" I pulled away, but he yanked me back, my Anglo-Saxon timidity obviously an amusing challenge. "You have undiscovered talents," he went on suggestively. "Wouldn't you like to earn a little pin money? I know people at some important magazines in Paris, where a little nudity in good taste. . . ."

Unable to think of anything clever to say, I smiled stupidly, kicked his leg, then fled to my room.

But sex was imminent. One night Michel parked his car in a dark side street and we did it. I can see myself now, lying across the front seat of his Alfa, legs sticking out the open passenger door, my head rammed under the steering wheel. My knickers were off, my skirt bunched around my waist. It was a dark gray angora skirt with a matching sweater, something I'd bought at the local Galeries Lafayette with the money my parents had sent me for the ski trousers. Michel was panting with exertion. I could hardly breathe, or rather I was holding my breath because of his dead weight, suffocating, my head banging against the dash with every shove. I was drowning in him, the smell of his body, his oily hair. "*Ça va, chéri, ça va?*" he kept asking, as he yanked at one of my legs and pushed it up the front seat so he could ram a little harder. I felt like I was splitting in two. "*Oui, yes, oui,*" I gasped, but I was sick with worry—not about doing it but that someone would walk by and see us. And I was sure I was going to get pregnant. Or at least a few weeks later, when my period was late, I told myself I'd known it all along. It happened because I was too willing. There was some misplaced Catholic guilt here, but not enough, I thought, to feel so unfairly punished.

By this time, I was living in another pension—an apartment owned by an elderly woman Michel knew, a Mme. Perrin. Michel had insisted I move from Mme. des Francs after he heard about Maurice's advances. I made an excuse to my parents about my room being too noisy at Rue de Tilsitt and they transferred the funds. My memories of the place are vague: a dark landing with the usual forty-watt bulb, a pair of brown armchairs, and a smell of damp carpets. Mme. Perrin herself seemed invisible. The only evidence she existed was the plate of stuffed dates she left for us every night on the hall table.

I was sharing a room with an English girl called Marjorie, someone I'd run into on Rue du Vieux Temple, on one of my rare school visits. She epitomized the Marjories of this world: pale and mouse-like, she was struggling up the faculty steps, a pleated wool skirt trailing around her ankles, clinging to a pile of books like a life raft. But she was clever, a real brain box, and unlike me, she could read Montaigne and Voltaire in French. I was arrogant enough, however, to think I was just as smart: despite her intelligence she couldn't *speak* French, and by then I was able to order a few groceries from the local charcuterie. Her family photographs were already lined up on the mantelpiece. I pushed them aside and put up my own, including a picture of Michel. *"Mon petit ami,"* I said—"My boyfriend." "Oh, he's so handsome," she said, blinking shyly. "Yes, isn't he? He looks like Jean Marais. You know the actor in *Beauty and the Beast, La Belle et La Bête.* Cocteau's classic. Have you seen it?" No, she hadn't. I went on about my other favorite films: the genius of Godard and Truffaut, quoting lines I'd read in magazine reviews. I talked about myself, about clothes, giving her a few not-so-subtle hints about her own disastrous wardrobe. But what I couldn't tell her, the day it finally dawned on me, was about being pregnant. I couldn't tell anyone. I lay in bed terrified, overcome with shame. It was already the end of the school year, and I was meant to be going back to England. My father kept sending telegrams asking, "What is going on?" because he hadn't heard from me for so long.

I didn't blame Michel. I wasn't that naive. And there was never any question about having the baby. He got the name of a doctor from an old girlfriend and one miserable rainy Saturday morning dropped me off in front of an anonymous brown door on Quai Mounier. I climbed a staircase, clutching the envelope of cash he'd given me, to a dingy waiting room. In those days, it was a criminal offense in France to have an abortion, and the room bore all the marks of professional subterfuge—dirty furniture, a threadbare rug, a pile of well-thumbed magazines. Eventually, the doctor came in—or, rather, he stood glaring at me from the doorway. A compact man, he had short hair, cropped military-style, and a bright red face, his cheeks still blazing from that morning's shave. Apart from the white coat, he might have been a serial killer. "How old are you?" he barked. "Twenty-one," I said, obviously lying. The question was merely a formality. He wanted to know if I had the money. I held up the envelope. He came over and counted the notes, then waved me into the examining room. "Take off your skirt and underpants and lie down on the table," he said. The table was an old-fashioned leather box, like a piece of gym equipment, and had thick straps and sliding metal stirrups on poles. It was also icy cold. Half-naked, I sat shivering on the edge. He threw me a blanket, ordering me to lie back, then he pushed my knees apart. I heard a *ching* as he lifted the steel syringe from the basin, then felt the pain, a piercing knifelike jab as he injected some liquid into my cervix. "Be quiet!" he said—I was obviously groaning. Then he added, matter-of-factly, "We have to pay for our pleasure, don't we, my dear?"—"*Eh bien, il faut payer pour le plaisir, n'est ce pas, ma petite?*"

Afterward, he wrote down a number on a piece of paper. "Call me if anything goes wrong," he said coolly, then told me to go home and lie down. After a while I'd start bleeding and it would be over. But I was in terrible pain right away and rolled around for hours on someone's bed, clutching a pillow. I wasn't even sure where I was. A flat perhaps loaned by one of Guy's girlfriends. Michel held my hand, but he was sheepish and impatient with me, as men are when they realize they are the cause of great unhappiness. "Is it that painful?" he kept saying. "What do you *think?*" I groaned, furious that he looked so scared.

Later that night, I was still bleeding and the contractions were worse. Michel called the doctor. The number turned out to be out of order, or nonexistent, so there was nothing to do but take me to the hospital. It was two in the morning. The nurse demanded I tell her the name of the person who had performed the illegal abortion. I feigned innocence. I explained that I was pregnant and had just fallen off a horse, as Michel had instructed me to say. But she was obviously used to this kind of lame story. And there was blood on my clothes. "Do you realize you could be arrested?" she barked. "Yes, even though you're a *foreigner.*" I was too terrified to reply, so she went to get the night doctor. He came over. I obviously looked quite pitiful, doubled over, pale and sweating under the greenish hospital light, because he agreed to perform a curettage. On the operating table, I felt another painful stab, but must have been given an anesthetic, because when I came to, I had vomited all over my night-gown. It was seven in the morning; I was lying in a ward full of pregnant women, all smiling and chatting about babies. I didn't envy them. I was relieved it was over.

I had to go home. Somehow I convinced my parents not to come pick me up, and Michel and Guy drove me back to England in Guy's car. It was a long way to the coast, and I'd lost a considerable amount of blood. So for most of the journey, I lay across the back seat, near cata-tonic, wrapped in a quilt. I couldn't speak, nor did I want to, and for hours just stared out the window, watching the tops of the trees whip past. Then as we approached the Channel, and the radio switched from play-ing Charles Aznavour to Adam Faith, I was suddenly terrified. I was sure my parents would guess what had happened. Certainly my mother would.

She didn't at first, although she looked at me suspiciously. I was thin, and as pale as white bread. But my father was happy to be in the company of young men. Arriving from the office in his pinstripe suit, his shirt collar starched to throat-cutting perfection, he hugged me, then opened a celebratory bottle of champagne. In his semi-polished French, he trotted out his war adventures for Guy and Michel, sweeping through the Strait of Gibraltar, being shot at on the bridge. "Do you know why the Germans lost the war?" he asked, albeit rhetorically. "Because they didn't know how to *improvise!*" As usual, his charm was effective. But I could see the awkwardness on Michel's face. He looked ashamed to be sitting with such nice people; he was impressed by my parents, by the car in the driveway, even by our house—which to me seemed more drearily suburban than before. That night, he and Guy stayed overnight in a bed-and-breakfast joint on Westcliff Esplanade, then came back the next morning. I have no memory of that morning, but later my brother told me he'd watched me standing in the street saying good-bye. Apparently I was sobbing as the car pulled away.

I'd never explained to my parents what the relationship was, except to say that Michel was my boyfriend—that vague and all-encompassing term. Besides, what *could* I say? In our family, feelings were never discussed. But one morning, a few days later, I walked into my bedroom to find my mother going through my drawers. She was holding up the flannel nightdress covered with vomit. "What's this?" she asked pointedly. I was speechless. Why, I wondered, hadn't I thrown it away? Did I want to be found out? "Oh, that," I said, trying to sound normal. "Well, the thing is, I was in a car accident, in Spain, a few months ago." This part at least was true. One weekend, early on at Madame's, a few of us had driven across the border for the weekend. We went with an English student from another pension, the only person we knew who owned a car. John was a skier, a champion downhill racer, and a big drinker. On the first day, speeding through a village, he swerved at a corner and ran into a stone wall. Thrown from the back seat, my head hit the dashboard and I was knocked unconscious for a few minutes. I was driven back to France then delivered to a clinic in Perpignan, where I got six stitches in the corner of my right eye. John was mortified. "Oh my God, I almost *blinded* you," he said. Which the doctor confirmed.

None of this I'd told my mother. "I didn't mention the accident at the time because I thought you'd worry too much," I said, which hardly explained the nightdress. Sitting on the bed, I was staring at her home-made curtains, the swirls of pale mauve roses. The nausea I'd managed to suppress for the last forty-eight hours flooded my throat. "I went to a hospital because I had a slight concussion, nothing serious really. They gave me some medicine that made me throw up."

Obviously she didn't believe me. "Well, you know, dear," she said, giving me one of her penetrating looks, "I never like to pry." And that was it. She obviously couldn't bear to ask more. I was relieved, of course. One good thing about my mother: at least the bad was ignored along with the good. After that, I moped around the house, or went in the garden to smoke my Gauloises, waiting for a letter from Michel. I never told my mother or anyone else about the abortion. Westcliff seemed an alien place. I didn't belong with my sister at the Saturday night yacht club dances, twisting to "I Want to Hold Your Hand," or with the girls at the bar giggling over their Dubonnets, talking about fancying boys and wanting to get engaged. All I could think about was escaping to London to find a job.

Michel did write to me. Romantic letters. I was his ideal woman, he said. *La femme ideal.* He missed me terribly. As his military service wasn't coming up until February (mandatory in those days), he suggested we meet that Christmas. He also said his father had told him if he wanted to get married, he would give his permission. When I read these letters now, the talk about marriage shocks me, because I have no memory of it. What I do remember is standing in the kitchen in Seymour Road one afternoon, bent over the sink, sobbing my eyes out. I'd just spoken to Michel on the phone and he'd told me he wanted to end it. My parents were completely taken aback; they'd never witnessed such an outpouring.

"What shall we do?" my father said, hovering awkwardly in the doorway. But my mother saw the desperation. She said nothing, but she knew. She'd already put the kettle on for a cup of tea. "Why don't you go over to France to see him, then, dear?" she suggested calmly, before my father could protest.

The trip to Paris is vague, though the weather was memorable; it rained continually, the streets bathed in that misty gray that evokes such romantic sadness. Two moments stand out: The first, I am in a cinema somewhere near Rue Corneille. It's about four o'clock, and I'm killing time, waiting for Michel to finish his afternoon appointments. He is working for his father now, in Paris temporarily, representing the family's office equipment company. Nothing is resolved between us, and I'm sitting in an empty theater, watching *Les Parapluies de Cherbourg,* or barely watching it, listening to the music echo off the walls. The film is a classic, all-singing Technicolor-drenched weepy. And by the time it gets to the romantic climax, the bittersweet reunion when the newly married Catherine Deneuve drives her Mercedes into a petrol station and sees her first love, now a lowly pump attendant, I can hardly breathe. Sunk in my seat, watching the ill-fated couple perform their final duet, I'm overwhelmed by a sense of dread and impending loss that feels strong enough to kill me.

Then it's the next morning. I'm in the hotel—the traveling sales rep room with flat cream walls and transparent curtains. We have just made love and I'm lying naked on the bed, facedown on the cheap counterpane. Rain is cascading down the windows and Michel is telling me we have to end it. "You're too young," he says, "and I have no money"—reasons that to me seem completely illogical. He is already dressed, standing at the foot of the bed, agitated that he has had to repeat this several times, and because he's late for work. Also because I keep crying. "I'm heartbroken too," he says. *"Mais c'est fini."*

But the affair wouldn't end itself. Neither of us knew what to do. We were tortured by too much emotion. In the letters that followed, marriage is mentioned again. Our life together. By this time, he's twenty, in the army, in officers' school, and we're talking about meeting for the summer in the South of France. A few months later, he writes:

> *When I was with you I was the happiest of men. I had become "habitué*
> *à la bonheur"—accustomed to happiness. I have loved you more than*
> *I have loved anyone. And to keep you I would have done anything.*
> *But it is impossible to stay together any longer without being mar-*
> *ried. And you are too young to share your life with someone . . .*

The eloquence of his letter still moves me. But did he mean the situation was untenable? Sleeping together without being married, or that he was exhausted by it? Or that he really didn't have enough money? Because I also have an urgent note from Nanou, a friend of his. She begs me to write to him, as he's so desperately lonely: *Il ne va pas bien, tu lui manque beaucoup*—"He misses you so much."

But that was four months later, and I didn't answer.

Looking back, it's painful to think how careless I was with someone who loved me so much. How abruptly I let it go, particularly in light of how difficult it was to find love later, when sex replaced everything. But I *was* careless. I convinced myself I was powerless to orchestrate my life, that things just happened to me. It was a way of not dealing with emotions, avoiding pain. I was seventeen, a naive mixture of bravado and fear. I didn't believe I could change anything, not in a profound way, except perhaps by earning some money.

Though Michel hadn't left my life altogether, by this time I was living in London. I felt suddenly independent, desperate to move on. I was sharing a bed-sitter in South Kensington with a model named Jacqueline Bisset. The real '60s (it was now 1964) had begun.

nine
France.

M. Bruni is standing in the hallway, smoking a cheroot and staring at the floor. It's unusually hot for mid-March, a minor heat wave, and he's stripped to his shorts, a pair of plaster-stained baggy trunks, minus fly buttons. Fortunately, he is wearing underwear. He is going to try to sand off the cement covering the ground floor—not with a commercial sander, which would seem preferable considering the square footage, but with an ancient hand machine, which is attached to a scary-looking extension cord, the webbing noticeably frayed at one end. When I express my doubts, he says, a note of triumph in his voice, "In France there is no such word as '*impossible*'!"—which I have to admit makes a change.

He arrived a week ago, having been recommended by M. Da Cruz, the local taxi man, who'd somehow heard I was having difficulty finding workmen. M. Bruni, he said, though officially retired, might be available. He was the consummate worker, a veritable artisan, according to Da Cruz—credentials that were immediately confirmed by M. Bruni himself. "I've been in the business fifty years. I should be rich by now, but I'm not. Why? Because I *care* too much," he announced by way of introduction, in rapid-fire French. "And because I'm too *honest*!"

At sixty-three, trim and muscular, with angular features and his hair slicked back, he could still pass as a ladies' man. Obviously, he thought so. In fact, he reminded me a little of my old Uncle Mike, also the owner of a lascivious but not unattractive leer.

He'd been working since he was fifteen, he said, and made a small fortune. "But do you know why I've got nothing left for my retirement? Because I spent it all—*everything*. I blew the lot!" Grinning now, he pulled out a packet of cigarillos, lit one, and clamped it between his teeth. "I stayed in three-star hotels—Cannes, Nice, Saint-Tropez, you name it. I bought smart clothes, went to nightclubs and fancy restaurants— you know, those high-class joints where they debone the fish *before* they serve it. I didn't mess around. I lived!"

Warmed by the thought, he paused to see how this was going over. Was I impressed? Yes, I *was* impressed, and relieved and many other things. Above all that he was willing to take on the job. Also that he was *available*. He shook my hand—he had big worker's hands, like lumps of clay. "I'll start next week," he said, then he ducked down the hall to cast his professional eye. After he'd taken in the damage in the salon—the water stains, the crumbling plaster—he reappeared to give me a look of exaggerated horror. "This is going to cost a fortune to fix up," he said. "For the money you could have bought a nice new place instead!"

M. Bruni shows up every day at 8.30, except when he doesn't. He's been having trouble with his teeth and sometimes has to spend the day at the dentist. Being officially retired, he's also often missing after lunch, particularly on Fridays when he plays petanque in Montauban with his pals. But most days he arrives in good spirits. Whistling, he strips down to his underpants, pulls on his ruined shorts, secured with a grubby piece of string, then gets down on all fours and starts sanding. The dust is terrible. It's backbreaking work, and he refuses to wear kneepads. When I arrive one morning with face masks to protect him (and myself) against the poisonous fumes, I'm rewarded with a disdainful *"Ha! Je suis Bruni!"* one fist pummeling his chest. Then, defiantly, he lights up another cheroot.

He seems tireless. He grinds away, following the original dips and grooves in the wood, and after three days he's managed to sand about a third of the long hallway. The difference is startling. I gaze at the beautiful pale planks. And even he's impressed. *"Pas mal, eh!"* he says.

But nothing else is being done. There's been no word from the elusive M. Hinard, or from Eric. No devis, even though Nicola or I call every few days.

Not surprisingly, I have headaches. No worse than at home, but somehow I'd expected them to miraculously disappear in the countryside—acres of unpolluted air, a rush of well-being. But the daily stress of trying to get things moving is taking its toll. They are still there, along with various other ailments. "You're a hypochondriac!" my husband likes to say. "No, I'm just sick a lot," I reply coolly, refusing to rise to the challenge. In Los Angeles I have cupboards full of supplements. And these are now lined up in Kathryn's kitchen: bags of vitamins, alkalizing powders, homeopathic drops, probiotics, and boxes of herbal teas. The battle to stay young, to ward off the inevitable, to maintain a competitive sexual allure—at least on the surface—what is translated in California as *health*. I admit,

M. Bruni sanding the salon floor.

however, that swallowing these huge quantities of pills and potions doesn't necessarily make me feel any younger, or better; it merely reminds me that I'm getting old and therefore must be more vigilant in taking them.

Nicola calls to tell me she has found a local mason. What's more, she says, he's available. Something of a coup. Apparently, M. Escalet has a three-day window in his current schedule. That is, if he can start immediately.

The robust M. Escalet comes round. Broad-shouldered, clear-eyed, and smiling, he is the storybook version of a country workman. And his arms are huge. I take him upstairs. In the bedroom I tell him I want to knock a hole in the wall, into what will eventually become our bathroom—the one my husband now refers to as Versailles, due to its extravagant size and pink marble fireplace. "Where exactly?" M. Escalet asks.

"Ici," I say, roughly outlining a door with my hands.

Of course, I'm so used to long discussions and promised estimates that when M. Escalet says he can start immediately, it doesn't occur to me that he means *right now.* He goes downstairs. A moment later, he appears holding a sledgehammer. Then, without warning, shoulders braced, he starts swinging at the plaster. Bricks and mortar fly. I stand back, thrilled by such wanton destruction. So mesmerized, in fact, that I don't hear the footsteps behind me. "Madame Lewis!" a voice shouts.

It is M. Hinard, pink-faced from climbing the stairs and accompanied by the elegant, though noticeably aggravated, M. Corbusier. M. Hinard has several pages of typed notes in his hand, what looks suspiciously like the prepared devis. However, seeing M. Escalet at work, he promptly shoves them back into his coat pocket. "You've already *started* with someone else!" he says, incredulous, his face turning almost purple. And before I can reply, or even complain about the five weeks it's taken for him to *get back to me,* or explain about M. Escalet's temporary three-day schedule, he and M. Corbusier are gone, clattering down the stairs, muttering outrage on their way to the front door.

Needless to say, it would have been preferable to have hired a professional contractor rather than a lone mason with a three-day window. But it's too late now. I will have to find carpenters, plasterers, and painters myself. Even Nicola seems concerned. "French workmen aren't always happy to deal with a woman on her own," she says, "particularly a foreigner." M. Bruni, however, is more optimistic. He tells me there are plenty of local artisans around, such as himself—although, he warns me, it might be a "little late in the season now."

Naively, I had no idea there were seasons for workmen.

Another week slips by and no artisans are found. To calm my nerves at the end of the day, or sometimes in the middle of the day, I go outside to sit on the limestone steps, my back against the wall. There's an old rose bush climbing over the balustrade, and I have an intense longing to stay here and watch it grow. With my little iPod balanced on a window ledge, I listen to Django Reinhardt's "Cette Chanson Est Pour Vous," Jean Sablon singing, feeling giddy as I always do when he gets to the *chère madame* part.

The magical (and often imaginary) past still thrills me more than it should, I know. Though I'm now trying to fix it in the present. But it looms again. There is too much of it, too much nostalgia and longing, and the doubts resurface. *What am I doing? Can I do this? Yes, I must.* . . . On this warm April afternoon, lulled by Sablon's swooning voice, I surrender. Peace and beauty and an old chanson. M. Bruni is also a little carried away. It reminds him of his youth, he says, when he used to glide across the dance floor in some club in the Midi. He takes another cigarillo break, then, like an old vaudevillian, looping his thumbs inside the top of his shorts, he performs a deft two-step down the hall. I fetch a bottle of rosé, kept in a bucket of water near the stairs. A drink *pour chaser la honte du jour.* I can't find a corkscrew, but M. Bruni obliges. He hammers a nail in the cork, then pulls it out with a pair of pliers. This trick is performed with impressive speed. Bravo! "Unfortunately," he says, "my doctor has forbidden me to drink wine, except on Saturdays." So I don't offer him a glass. "What! You think I care what my *toubib* tells me?" he says, grinning, showing me a healthy slice of pink gum. *"Je suis Bruni!"*

. . .

I'm more patient now. I'm also learning a few things. When I call local workmen—*ouvriers*—at random, listed in the local yellow pages, each one tells me, without question, that he's busy. But as I've discovered, "busy" does not always mean "unavailable." Gentle persistence is required. And what has become almost as thrilling as someone starting work is someone arriving to *discuss* the work, even when they assure me they're booked up and have absolutely no time to *take the job*. Because if I manage to get them on the phone (during meal times), with a little flattery and some polite begging, after complaining about how *inondé*— overbooked—they are, invariably they admit they might be able to drop by the house next Tuesday as they'll be working in a village nearby. Of course, they can promise nothing.

Over the next week, I manage to secure a carpenter and a plasterer and a man to unplug the well. At the somewhat terrifyingly vast emporium Lapeyre, in Montauban, I order French doors for M. Escalet's new hole in the windowless kitchen wall. What I now need is a balcony to go on the other side. Some small, elegant piece of wrought iron that will match the original balustrade at the back of the house, running down the stone steps.

There is only one artisan in the area, but M. Sebastien Gastaldi is never at home. I have spoken to his wife several times, but she tells me he's definitely not available until September.

But one day, unexpectedly, Sebastien does arrive. He is young and startlingly thin, and has the trademark look of the consummate artiste— in his case possibly borrowed from a film noir: large sleep-deprived eyes, a wispy goatee, and dressed entirely in black. "I'm completely booked up," he says right away. Nevertheless, he's brought a clipboard and a yellow pad. Over the next two hours, he draws a scale diagram of the existing balustrade. He takes photographs, measures the distance between the cross struts and the rosettes and the diameter of the ball-shaped finials. Lighting one cigarette after another, he stands contemplatively in the garden, in the middle of what will be, if my luck changes, the swimming pool, to determine the exact height and width. Finally, his voice whispery, acquiescent, he says he might be able to build a balcony by the beginning of August. Does he, I enquire casually, have any idea about the price? Impossible to say, he says, but he'll send me a devis. I smile. I tell him to go ahead. *Go ahead anyway. Without a devis. PLEASE!*

That night I call my husband at the Grand Hotel in Sofia—the location for the movie he's producing, soon to start shooting. The operator asks me to hold on. I hear a few seconds of static, then into the void comes a blast of Russian marching music: an army of baritones accompanied by a deafening brass band. Eventually, he's put through.

He wants to know how everything is coming along. I explain about the new doorways, about M. Bruni and the floors, and for once he is indulgently patient. Calmly we discuss the balcony and the possibility of taking down a wall in the guest bedroom to make a bathroom. He also wants to know when I'm coming to Sofia. "The restaurants are surprisingly good. And the service is excellent," he says. "What's more, there are modern shops *everywhere.*" The subtext is obvious. Lying contentedly in his hotel room, how could he even imagine living in the French countryside, *in the middle of nowhere,* for an entire summer. Ignoring this, I carry on about the workmen. I elaborate on Sebastien, the *ferronier,* his artistry, his attention to detail, aware that I'm overdoing it a bit. "How old is he?" he asks. "I don't know. Maybe thirty," I say. "I'm just relieved I've found someone to do the job."

"Well, you like French men. You've always fallen for the artistic type."

I laugh. I know where this is going. "True," I say. "But if I'm thinking of running away with anyone, it's not going to be a workman. The next guy will have to have a plane. Ha ha!"

This is the part of our marriage that always works. By fooling around with the idea of leaving each other, it can never happen.

"Of course, I wouldn't blame him for coming on to you," he continues. "You still look beautiful."

"Thank you."

"That is, for an older woman."

"You could have left off the last bit."

"Well, you don't look thirty-five."

"I realize *that*."

"I'm just being honest."

"And I'm saying that you don't have to be. It's not always required. *Hold back.*" I feel myself getting annoyed. Unreasonably so. I hear a knock on his hotel door, then the click of wheels in the background, the room service trolley arriving. His civilized life. He says a few words to the waiter, then comes back on the line. "What I mean is . . ." I start. But he knows what I mean. And he won't be goaded. I hear the rattle of crockery, a cork being pulled. "The wine here is also excellent. I'm having a very good Bulgarian Merlot." He wants to talk. And he wants me to listen while he eats his grilled salmon. And I do, because I'm in the habit of listening, even if my mind is elsewhere. "I feel very relaxed here. After all, I grew up in a hotel. As a kid, I used to play with the bellhop. The doorman was my best friend." "Yes, I know," I say, a touch wearily. He senses it, but he wants to go on, to explain his position, to *state his case*. "Look, I'm going to *try* to like it in France, okay? Isn't that good enough? The trouble is you want me to be someone I'm not. I'm a city person. I like living in cities."

"Yes . . ."

"I *like* streets full of people. You know, Woody Allen once said he never wanted to leave New York because it had everything. He could go out and get wonton soup at three in the morning. Not that he *wanted* wonton soup, of course, but he knew it was there, just around the corner."

He likes to talk about Woody. He's a big fan, and not only because of his talent. They once shared a girlfriend. "I'm thankful," he goes on now, "because Woody made it okay for cute girls to like nerdy Jewish guys. It helped a lot of us get laid." I tell him he underestimates himself, but he thinks they look similar. He's taller, better looking, but his vulnerability is endearing.

"Come on, you're far more handsome than Woody."

"No. Not really. I'm afraid you'll have to be beautiful for both of us."

"Quite a responsibility," I say. But I manage a laugh.

ten

London. October 1964.

I imagined myself in one of the smart burgundy-and-yellow uniforms, the ones I'd seen the ground staff wearing in the British Eagle Airways main office on Conduit Street. In my proposal letter offering my services to this small airline, I also mentioned my talent for languages.

As it turned out, I ended up in a back room upstairs, working with about a dozen other girls. We wore our own clothes and sat two to a table, facing a set of antiquated metal boxes with rows of blinking orange lights. Our job was to log the phone bookings, and as fast as possible.

I was excited to be in London. Every morning, I took the bus from South Kensington to Green Park. Sitting on the top deck as it careened around Hyde Park Corner, my sense of being part of such a sophisticated world was thrilling. But I was comically bad at my job. It required the kind of concentration I simply didn't possess, even for the exalted sum of eight pounds a week. My shift began at nine a.m. About a minute later the calls started. And the drill went something like this: Bookings had to be entered in pencil on an index card ("Legible, please") with the traveler's name, address, the date, and method of payment. There was a separate column for flight numbers and destinations, which had to be written in code. These codes—columns of figures as indecipherable to me as hieroglyphs—were located in the airline directory. As there were only three of these directories for twelve girls—massive ring binders, so heavy they had to stay on the floor—we shoved them back and forth between us with our feet. And it was impossible to memorize anything because the flight timetables kept changing, not only with the seasons but on certain weekends, bank holidays, Christmas, Whitsun, Shrove Tuesdays, and the Queen's birthday. Also, according to British Eagle rules, while taking a booking, the next caller (a new blinking light) could not be left waiting for more than five rings. As the day wore on, the calls backed up. An impending visit to the bathroom induced a feeling of sheer panic. With the receiver wedged under my ear, the directory balanced on my knees, I might accidentally misdirect passengers, send a party of four to Glasgow instead of Bologne, for example, or I inadvertently cut them off. Sometimes not so inadvertently.

From a glass booth, we were watched by the floor manager, Mr. Stanley—a heavyset man with damp, thinning hair, who sweated through his shirt, even in winter. He would listen in on our calls, then interrupt us if we weren't working fast enough. And he singled me out in the first few days. "Pay attention, Miss Lewis—*hurry it up!*" Fortunately, I was helped by a girl named Bunty, an old hand. Inexplicably cheerful, Bunty exuded a kind of head-girl vigor for what seemed to me painfully complex work. She was engaged to a guards officer and was perfectly capable of leafing through a bridal magazine *while* she dealt with a barrage of calls. Luckily, a week later, when I was put on night duty (for which there was the fabulous salary increase of ten shillings), Bunty was on my shift. She brought in blankets and sandwiches, and most of the night we camped on the floor by the radiators to keep warm. It was impossible to sleep. Every time a truck came down Conduit Street, the plate-glass windows banged in their frames. If a call came in after midnight, she told me to ignore it: "Who cares? They'll ring back in the morning." I lay there bored, watching her sketch bridesmaid's dresses, amazed that the eight hours of drudgery never bothered her. Of course, she was about to be married. Her life was determined, her role as a woman complete.

I didn't feel like the other girls at British Eagle who'd apparently accepted their lot, and were just waiting to find Mr. Right. During the lunch hour, a few of them used to stand with their noses pressed to the office windows, gazing down on Bond Street. The game was to pick out a prospective husband, some flush-faced office junior or insurance broker striding along in a new bowler and a velvet-collared topcoat. "Oh, look at him. Gorgeous!" they would shout, then fall back in a swoon across the radiators. Of course, since Michel I felt different. Nothing was that simple. And despite my lack of sophistication, France had left me feeling I was destined for better things than British Eagle, though I had no idea what. So in a way, it was a relief when I was fired. One afternoon Mr. Stanley caught me on the phone having a personal conversation, which was strictly forbidden. "Come to the office," he said, cutting in. "Just a minute!" I replied airily, despite the fact that my box was lit up like the *Queen Mary*. He was waiting in the booth, sweaty and steely-eyed. A strand of damp hair normally welded to his scalp hung loose.

"You were talking to someone for ten minutes," he said. "And in *French!*"

"Yes, my boyfriend."

"It's against the rules."

"I know."

I might not have been so cavalier, but I'd been talking to Michel. And I was so elated to hear his voice that I couldn't hang up. I also didn't want him to think I had the kind of job where I could be so easily intimidated. He was still in the army. We hadn't spoken for several months, though he had sent me another letter explaining why we couldn't get married. He loved me, but I was too young. Perhaps he was waiting for me to contradict him. I didn't. I couldn't explain how I felt, or even *what* I felt. After the abortion, it was more than I could handle. Which is why I'd escaped to London. And now here we were, on the phone at British Eagle, chatting about his military service, about Guy, about his car, for God's sake, like old pals. I was crying a little by then. Because it was still there, that big emotional wave that was going to kill me.

"I'm giving you the sack," said Mr. Stanley.

"Well, you can't," I said indignantly, "because I'm leaving anyway!"

I had no idea what I was going to do—about a job or Michel. As usual, it was easier to bury my feelings. Somewhat numb, I walked up Bond Street to Fenwick, the department store. For weeks I'd been covetously staring at a black crochet evening sweater. I bought it, writing out a check for nine guineas, thereby emptying my checking account.

After British Eagle, I somehow drifted into modeling. I say that because I'm not exactly sure how it happened, but things did just happen in those days. I was just eighteen, living in a flat with Jacqueline Bisset. We'd moved from a bed-sitter in South Kensington, one woefully small room with a rusty sink and a gas ring. "Oh. You're quite attractive, aren't you?" she'd said on that first day, watching me climb the three flights with my blue Samsonite. "Thanks. You too," I replied. We'd never met, but via a friend I'd heard that a girl he knew was looking for someone to share a bed-sitter. "We're not allowed to smoke in the house," she warned me. But I did, still manically puffing on my Gauloise, and soon after the landlady threw us out.

We found a larger flat in Belgravia, in Chesham Street, for seven pounds a week. Though it was a fashionable address, it was hopelessly run down. Places like this don't exist anymore—Georgian houses in grand squares, loosely partitioned into flats that hadn't been touched since WWII, with pipes running up the walls and a makeshift bathroom on the half-landing. The place reeked of genteel shabbiness: old carpets, dried flowers in the hall, and decades of dust. Our rooms were on the top floor, one on either side of the staircase. Once red, the walls were now faded to a misleadingly dreamy pink, and matched the bed covers and the sagging pink armchairs. There was no kitchen, just a hot plate and a sink hidden behind a curtain suspended across our "living room." We rarely ate there. The idea was not to eat much at all. As models, we were on permanent diets, and we had no money to speak of. When we ran out of shillings, we fed the gas meter with foreign coins. We survived on tinned sardines and Ryvita, or we toasted slices of Wonderloaf in front of the fire, waiting for someone to take us out for a meal. Sometimes we put on furry false eyelashes and high heels and went downstairs to the pub next door, the Lowndes Arms, for a Scotch egg and a bottle of Mateus rosé. The Lowndes Arms was frequented then mainly by the chauffeurs and nannies from the larger houses in Belgrave Square. But there was one woman, I remember, always perched on a stool at the bar. Heavily made up, her cheeks on fire, she had what my mother called a ginny voice. "Hello, dearies," she would rasp as we came in, her eyes swiveling seductively at half-mast. "Ooh, lovely frocks!"

It was 1965. The transition from postwar timidness to full-blown hedonistic revolution was taking place. Skirts had risen to the shocking height of four inches above the knee, the Beatles were established, and the Rolling Stones were terrifying parents across the country.

Though we were still teenagers, Jackie was years ahead of me: she had gone to the Lycee, her mother was French, and she had a certain enviable poise. We had similar '50s bodies, with large breasts—hardly suitable for modeling, which by then demanded greyhound-thin girls. We also had unfashionably curly hair, which had to be straightened daily with hot irons. But unlike me, Jackie had perfect skin and slender thighs and a kind of misty classroom stare that in photographs looked both beguiling and intelligent. By this time, I'd spent a few weeks at the Lucie Clayton Charm Academy, learning how to walk down a runway (wearing a pill box hat, girdle, stockings, and white gloves), but I was still self-conscious about my looks, in particular my legs.

So far, I'd only had a few modeling bookings, although earning fifteen pounds posing for a Cadbury ad seemed fantastic after British Eagle Airways. And most days, I went out to look for work. You had to do the rounds, which meant making endless journeys on the tube or bus to present yourself to photographers. I didn't have much confidence I'd succeed, but I knew getting a job required a certain brazenness, and sex had become the accepted currency. I was a young eighteen, a country girl with a moon face, so that even with thick makeup—black eyeliner and caked-on mascara—I exuded an air of virginal saintliness. Something that men seemed anxious to remove.

Early on, I remember going to see a man whose studio was in a garage behind a house in St John's Wood. He was the traditional upper-class type and wore a Norfolk jacket with a hunting cravat dotted with little fox heads. Someone who'd taken up fashion photography to meet girls. After flicking through my Kodak box of photographs, he looked up and said, rather dubiously, "Well, I might be able to use you. Of course, you understand, Fiona, there will have to be a bit of pokery-poo." Five years earlier, a well-mannered Englishman wouldn't have dared bring up the subject of sex unless he was blind drunk. Now, things were wide open—though, in his case, there'd been no time (or necessity) to master the art of seduction. I stood looking at him stupidly, unable to speak—which, naturally, he took as a yes. And so catapulting me backward over the bed, he tried to shove it in quickly without the bother of removing my underpants. I managed to push him off. "I have to meet my mother for lunch," I said tartly. Fortunately the word *mother* seemed to resonate.

Jackie had boyfriends, some of them well-known photographers. Photographers were gods. Particularly the cocky working-class boys who'd made enough money to buy houses in Holland Park and who were now congratulating themselves for being able to take nice middle-class girls to dinner. Terry Donovan was one of them. When he arrived to pick her up, he usually waited in the street, giving a few blasts on the car horn. You didn't encourage men to see how you lived. But one night when Jackie was late, he came in. I was cooking my usual dinner of fried eggs and bacon on the hot plate. I remember the sound of his Chelsea boots on the stairs, then his confident, mocking voice calling to Jackie, who was still in the bathroom, ironing her hair. "Blimey, darlin', smells like a bloody chip shop in here. Mind you don't stink up the Rolls."

I was intimidated. I didn't know men like this, although I wanted to.

Jacqueline Bisset.

At the same time, I was also ill-at-ease with the kind of well-brought-up men who wore monogrammed shirts and asked what school you'd gone to. Everything in London was different. I felt ridiculously suburban. I was embarrassed by my lack of education, and what little sense I'd had of myself in Grenoble with Michel had disappeared. I hadn't a clue what being a woman was supposed to feel like. I knew men found me attractive, and was utterly seduced by the idea. At the same time, the fact that a man could make you feel better about yourself simply by noticing you was shocking. In a way, this was the real loss of innocence. Suddenly I was only concerned with how men saw me. Was I pretty enough? Thin enough? Groovy enough? I took diet pills. I ate nothing and drank instead. At least once a week our Chesham Street bathroom echoed with the sounds of induced vomiting as Jackie or I stuck the handle of a Mason Pearson brush down our throats. A last resort if the Ex-Lax hadn't worked.

I went to see a slimming doctor, famous for injecting sheeps' placentas into girls' thighs, reputed to reduce cellulite. It cost five guineas. His practice was on the ground floor of a house on Harley Street. In the waiting room, an old wood-paneled dining room atmospherically lit like a funeral parlor, the models were lined up. It was a lucrative trade; the doctor had a full schedule, and you weren't encouraged to linger. When I walked in his office he was already standing, holding up a syringe. He was also dressed formally, as doctors were in those days, in a stiff collar and a morning coat. As he advanced, his breath reeking of scotch, he said casually, "Just lift your skirt, my dear. No need to remove anything else," then he swiftly plunged the needle through my tights.

Sex was everywhere. On a Saturday afternoon on the King's Road, the pavement was packed with girls in short skirts spilling out of pubs, or standing around admiring their reflections in shop windows. Men would drive past with their radios blaring, shouting provocative remarks: "Ooo, nice knickers, love. Give us a kiss." There was no coyness, no offense. Girls were expected to be seductive and playful. And clothes were essential, particularly if you had no idea who you were. It was a way to define yourself. I bought a yellow shepherdess smock from Mary Quant, successfully camouflaging my breasts, a pair of fake white Courrèges boots, and a trailing Guinevere skirt. I hoped the rest would follow.

But I wasn't comfortable about sex. I told myself it was because of what had happened with Michel; the truth was, in London I didn't know how to relax with men. I liked the flirting and everything that led up to sex—the passion of kissing, the hot thrill—but when it came to doing it, I simply froze. Sex made me feel too vulnerable. Yet I didn't know how to refuse. If a man took me to dinner, and then over dessert the inevitable question of going back to his place came up, I was at a loss as to what to say. I didn't know how to tell him I wasn't sure, that I didn't fancy him, or I just didn't *feel* like it. It seemed easier to get it over with, to sleep with him then escape afterwards. And I had to anesthetize myself to get through those evenings, knocking back enough wine or brandy to slay a horse. It was a terrible way to learn about men, or about myself. But I was afraid of looking unsophisticated, and I was still plagued by good manners. Manners were the great impediment to good sex.

One night I went home with a Lloyd's broker—a tall, well-groomed man in a pinstripe suit. Back in his drafty bachelor flat in Knightsbridge, he looked about as uncomfortable as I was. We barely spoke. When he fucked me he did it silently, teeth clenched, temples pulsating, as if this was his first attempt since the school whack-off. There was no intimacy, no emotional reciprocity. And I didn't expect it. I lay there until dawn, then ran out to catch a bus to Chesham Street. Only later that morning did I realize I'd left my father's watch behind. Gold, inset with rubies and diamonds, it was something he'd picked up in Gibraltar during the war, he said, in exchange for a bag of onions, very scarce at the time. Too garish for him, he never wore it. But I treasured it. Yet I couldn't even bring myself to phone the man the next day to ask him to look under the bed where I'd put it for safety.

I made excuses to myself for this sort of behavior. And I envied Jackie, who seemed to know instinctively how to deal with men. Later, I found out there were plenty of girls who were just as confused as I was about sex in the early '60s. Escaping the confines of a respectable home, suddenly being free to do what you wanted, was one thing; few of us were emotionally equipped for the rest. There was a lot of talk about love, but in my first year in London, my only relationships with men were sexual. Women's liberation didn't go beyond that. And most of us had to get blind drunk to get through a one-night stand. Then waking up the next morning in a strange flat, your hairpiece lying on the pillow like a dead rat, mascara streaming, you would walk home, knickerless, last night's dress trailing along the pavement, trying to convince yourself how bold you were. When you didn't get a phone call the next day—or the next—you pretended not to be disappointed. After all, things were different. Sex was supposed to be mutually enjoyable; past niceties no longer applied. At least girls were at pains to make it seem that way, so as not to be considered uncool. But it didn't sit well. We didn't own our sexuality. We were literally trying to hurl ourselves into the modern world.

And no one really talked about the fucking. It was too new. Those slippery fantasies about giant penises and threesomes, about gladiator girls on acid transcending their bodies to embrace freedom—that came later. When Jackie and I arrived home after an all-nighter, we never probed for details. "Have a good time?" she'd ask. "Oh, yes, fantastic." "Cup of tea?" "Lovely—maybe a couple Aspirin . . ." Then one of us would turn on Radio Caroline and we'd skip across the bedroom in our underwear, singing along to Roy Orbison, or to the Stones' latest: "(I Can't Get No) Satisfaction."

I wandered around in an emotional fog, longing for romance. I didn't know how to find love, so I went on having sex, in the hope that it would get better. It didn't. I think it was terror, really. Sex changed the odds, whether you liked it or not. And in my case there was a genuine fear that if I did relax, if I abandoned the know-it-all child and gave in to a man completely, I would lose my identity altogether.

Young people having celebrity status was new. And rock stars, actors, people you were seen with gave you importance. It was a way for a girl to be publicly admired. You didn't expect to be asked about yourself, or asked what you did. I remember being taken to Alan Price's flat one night, the keyboard player with the Animals. He was jamming with the boys, and there were several girls there, like myself. We hardly spoke; we sat on the sofa, swaying in unison, our feet rhythmically tapping to "The House of the Rising Sun," our miniskirts riding up our thighs. "Yeah, great, fab"—what else could you say? And these kinds of nights went on for hours. The other girls looked like they were in heaven, but all I could think was, *What am I doing here? Who am I?* Though, naturally, I was incapable of asking the man I was with to take me home.

If I was insecure, I was also full of myself. By 1965, being a part of the great youth-oriented phenomenon meant you were primed to succeed. People still in their twenties were writing plays, movies, designing furniture, making shoes and dresses. Ossie Clarke had opened Quorum; I bought a turquoise snakeskin bomber jacket, some crushed velvet

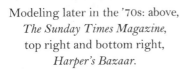

Modeling later in the '70s: above,
The Sunday Times Magazine,
top right and bottom right,
Harper's Bazaar.

trousers, and a hat from James Wedge's boutique Top Gear. I'd been on
the cover of *Honey* magazine. Jackie had just landed a walk-on in the
film *The Knack . . . and How to Get It,* along with Charlotte Rampling
and Jane Birkin, whom I would often run in to breezing along the King's
Road, fairylike in a Liberty print smock. There was no reason, I thought,
why I couldn't become something too.

eleven
France 2005.

It's raining today. Just a slight drizzle, with a blanket of mist hanging over the woods, turning them a mysterious pale purple. I am walking around the back of the house with Fabrice, the gardener. He's come to see about pruning the *buis,* the old boxwood hedges behind the cedar that are hopelessly overgrown: a solid wall, reaching almost thirty feet high. There are also dead lilacs, a dozen diseased elms, and thickets of knee-high weeds.

"One of the big fig trees should come down too," he says. "It blocks the view." The tree is beautiful, so the suggestion is made tentatively—as if he hardly dare mention such sacrilege, and not only for my sake. Fabrice is a gentle young man, shy, though not timid, and he is deeply connected to the earth. He lives in the village and looks after several of the neighboring gardens, including Kathryn's; he knows when to plant irises (August), how long the rain will continue (until the next full moon), and exactly the right time to pick my *tilleul* (lime) blossoms to make tea. Although so far, he's been reluctant to divulge this last piece of information.

We walk up the driveway toward the old château entrance—what's left of it, that is. Two marooned wrought-iron gates, barely attached to their enormous brick pillars, and crowned with a pair of elegant bronze urns. To the left is an expanse of weedy ground running down to the woods, the hectares that used to be M. Moulin's melon fields and that are now mine. "Look at the light. Look at the way it turns the tops of the trees golden," I say, a touch dramatically. He must think I'm deranged. But no, he's smiling, also moved. "So what do you want to do there?" he asks.

When I lay awake at night, I think about these fields. I fantasize about rows of pruned hedges, espaliered fruit trees, herb labyrinths, perhaps a romantic tunnel of limes. I have, I admit, a weakness for topiary. For some time I've been carrying around an old book called *The Formal Garden in England*, by Sir Reginald Blomfield, RA. Among its inky plates is an illustration of a house in Canons Ashby, Northamptonshire. In the front garden, behind a pair of iron gates not unlike mine, are rows of gigantic boxwood balls flanked by turrets of clipped yew. I'm picturing something similar here, a combination of Petit Trianon geometrics and a Rousseau-inspired *jardin paysager,* an "escape to nature" with winding pathways overlooking rolling fields of green. Of course, this isn't England, or eighteenth-century France, and to most people (my husband, for one), even attempting something like this seems excessive— particularly because the first toilet has yet to be installed. But when I mention this to Fabrice, he's surprisingly enthusiastic. *"Oui, j'adore ça!"* he says. Then, blushing, he turns his big frame away. Tomorrow, he murmurs, he will show me photos of the Château de Villandry, famous for its parterre and topiary balls. I feel exhilarated, standing in the waist-high weeds with this gentle young man, talking about irrigation ditches and planting. "When can we start?" I ask. He smiles patiently. "It's too late. Already too hot." (It's only April.) "We'll have to wait until the autumn." He has all the time in the world, of course, whereas I feel as if mine is running out. I have to do everything *now.*

I'm trying to make myself slow down. After all, I can do anything I like—or do nothing. Eat, or not eat. There is no male meal, no dinner arrangements to be determined a minute after breakfast: *What's the plan, sweetheart?* No wifely obligations, no dread of permanence. I pamper myself instead. I take long baths. I sleep, or I don't. I read all night. I get up early (unlike in L.A.). And on the weekend I look for flea markets, local *brocantes*.

On Sunday, I drive to Caussade, a small town twenty minutes north of Montauban. At eight o'clock, the sun is just breaking through the clouds, the trucks are lined up, and the dealers are unloading their wares: the big mirrors and gilt candelabras, the art deco armchairs, the bunches of silver forks tied with pink string, and stacks of old patterned plates. The cafés are already full, the bakery is open. I buy myself a warm slice of bacon quiche, wrapped in wax paper, then walk around. The thrill of the bargain.

Right away, I see an old armoire. It is magnificent, more than two and a half meters high—large even by French standards, the front panels cut from great polished planks of walnut—*noyer massif*—and deep enough to hide a few dauphins. There is a piece missing from one of the legs, but it's barely noticeable. A fact that is immediately confirmed by the dealer. "*Mais on ne le voit presque pas!*" he says, hands waving. A typical southerner, with wild black hair. I nod, feigning disinterest, trying to pass as the seasoned bargainer. But from his expression I can tell he sees the excited novice, the tourist who has fallen in love. "How much?" "Well, it's Louis Philippe," he says. "But the real one." "*Le Vrai!*" he adds, raising a finger for emphasis. I have no idea what he means. Was there a fake one? And if so, what period for furniture was that? I remind myself to look up the kings of France. The wardrobe, he assures me, comes apart easily, and for a little more money he will deliver it to my house. "Okay," I say quickly. "*Merci!*"

I am elated, and not only because of the wardrobe's beauty. This is the first piece of furniture I've bought for the house. After that, I spend twenty minutes bent over a table of linen sheets. More than a hundred years old, they are piled up, freshly washed and pressed, part of a bride's trousseau, the initials in big swirling letters embroidered across the top. Who could have parted with such beautiful things? But I've already spent too much. At another stall, I buy silver spoons and forks, ten of each for forty euros, then two chairs with rush seats for thirty-five. There is some termite damage to the back legs, but then they're Louis Philippe, I am told. The real one or not, I have no idea.

It takes Fabrice three days to do the work. He arrives in a green zippered jumpsuit, gloves, heavy work boots, and carrying a chain saw. He's very particular about his clothes, just as he is about his tools, which are oiled, sharpened, and arranged neatly on hooks in the back of his old Deux Chevaux. It's a perfect spring morning, a few puffy clouds on the horizon, and when he slices through the thick box branches, the effect is startling. The sky opens up and the view extends east, revealing M. Moulin's irrigation lake, a strip of shimmering water flanked by poplars.

The next day, Fabrice hacks down the fig tree, then something called a Christ tree that's growing too close to the house. It comes crashing down in a blaze of leaves, its black pods flying. By the time he starts on the diseased elms, *les ormes*, I'm watching from a corner of the house, sickened by so much destruction. But Fabrice is calm. "The bad must go in order for the good to live," he says prophetically. I help him pile up the branches. Some he chops for wood, the rest we drag down the hill to make a bonfire. It's exhausting going back and forth. I've lost my gloves; my hands are raw and my feet ache. But there's something satisfying about the physical exertion. When I lie down for a minute, I can't get up again. An hour later, I'm still drifting horizontally. Grass, clouds, the smell of the lit fire. Guilty pleasures. In L.A. I can never laze around like this, because I'm always worried I should be doing something more worthwhile.

By now, M. Bruni has finished sanding the hallway and is halfway through the kitchen. There is an occasional screech as he hits a corner then silence, punctuated by an exasperated *Putain! Merde!* The cement dust is terrible. Great clouds of it billow from the windows, coating the walls and poisoning the air. At the end of the day, he emerges like a ghost, wheezing, his face a deathly gray. When I tell him I'm concerned—looking concerned—he thinks I'm talking about the state of his clothes. "Don't worry," he says, mocking me with his little grin, "my wife owns a washing machine." But on the advice of his doctor—or perhaps his wife—he's now agreed to wear a mask because he can't stop coughing. I witnessed a bout a few days ago: he was choking, doubled over by the stairs. I ran to get him a bottle of water; he took a quick swig, then handed it back. "I'll feel better when I've had a cigarette," he said, laughing. Nevertheless, this morning he arrives with a serious-looking contraption: a rubber breathing apparatus with double ventilators, plus a pair of goggles.

The next day M. Gomes, the plasterer arrives. He is Portuguese, sturdily built, and appropriately white-faced. He has a low center of gravity, like an opera singer, and walks shoulders back, leading with his stomach. I give him the usual tour to inspect the damage. Like everybody, he is halted by the gaping hole upstairs in the bedroom ceiling, now big enough to see the rafters above and, alarmingly, I notice, several slits of daylight. *"Madame Lewis,"* he says—his voice is also operatic, a deep baritone, and he pronounces it *Low-eees*—*"tout est pourri!"* Yes, I say, I know. Rotten. The only thing to do, he says, is to cover the damage with

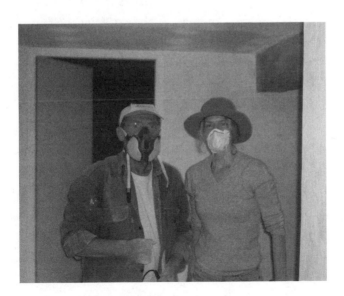

M. Bruni and me.

boards, suspend *placoplatre* (fiberboard) in every room upstairs, then plaster over that.

"Will it look *authentic?*" I ask. I am suddenly imagining the sleek overhead runway of an insurance office in downtown Los Angeles. Will it look brand-new? Given the age and beauty of the house, I assume preserving its original integrity—the *esthétique*—is understood by everyone. But for the owner, the aesthetic choice is often overloaded with emotion. Having fallen in love with the ruin, tampering with so much as a rusty doorknob is like a stab in the heart. And though I know how important it is to explain exactly what I want, I often forget to say what I *don't want*. My French is good, but when it comes to the precise words for steel runners or even *placoplatre*, I miss a few things. When M. Gomes assures me it will look *propre* (clean), as opposed to impossibly *ruiné* (ruined), that there is simply no other solution short of replacing all the ceilings at enormous expense, I accept his judgment. When he tells me the steel runners needed to attach the new boards will have to be "hung" lower due to the existing bulges from the water damage, though I'm tempted to ask if this will interfere with the tops of the windows (extremely high, the frames ending only a few centimeters below the ceiling), I don't. I presume he cares enough not to spoil the *esthétique*. Admittedly, there are times when instead of voicing my concern, I'm mumbling an unctuous *"Merci,"* only too grateful that a workman has shown up in the first place.

A few days later, I arrive at the house and M. Gomes's army has started. Four men are on ladders, busy drilling the steel runners into the walls. Already finished in my bedroom, the fiberboards are in place. Not only have they covered the tops of the windows, making it impossible to hang a curtain pole, but they have also "leveled" the charming 1810 slant to the ceiling so that the cross beams now look crooked—comically deep at one end, shallow at the other. My heart sinks. And the ugliness of the stark white boards is somehow personally wounding. "The runners will have to come down," I tell them. "You will just have to reattach the boards *flat* against the ceiling, *without* runners." There is an awkward silence. The workmen stare at me from the tops of their ladders like angry circus performers, their faces fixed with utter disbelief. "Come down? *Impossible!*"

"No, *pas impossible*," I reply firmly. *"Imperative!"* A minor victory. Even so, I walk outside, up the driveway, and duck into the magic circle to calm down. I suddenly feel overwhelmed by the details, and we've barely started. M. Escalet has not returned to finish the hole in the kitchen wall for the French doors. M. Boudet is still unavailable. And earlier that morning, I noticed something odd about Bruni's floors. I was staring at what I'd presumed were the natural brown knots in the wood. Except that they seemed to be getting bigger. I mentioned this phenomenon to M. Bruni. He was silent for a moment, then sheepishly he raised his hand. "Guilty as charged." After checking with the experts (whoever they might be), he admitted he should have wetted down the wood first. The so-called knots were in fact scorch marks from his sander. "Perhaps a *new* sander," I suggested, trying to stay calm. *"Non, non,"* he insisted; his old one was still perfectly serviceable. He would just do the floors again. His fault, he admitted. "So to be fair, this time I'll only charge you *half price!*

I am tempted to call my husband. Not to complain. That would be a mistake. To reassure him—and myself—that all is well. But I don't call. I open a bottle of Kathryn's Clement Termes blanc instead. The sun sinks: a spectacle of mauve and orange streaks behind the wintery black trees. For an hour I sit at the kitchen table composing arguments in my head, promising myself to take a stronger stand against the workmen. Then I call my husband.

It's Saturday night in Sofia, and he's having dinner in the hotel restaurant. I hear a low rumble of voices, piped music, china clinking. But he's not in a good mood. There are certain problems concerning the movie, about which he doesn't care to elaborate.

"You wouldn't understand. It's too complicated."

I'm tempted to hang up. Instead, I say as pleasantly as three glasses of wine will allow, "I hate it when you use that tone of voice."

"It's the same tone I've had for twenty years."

"Exactly."

"You're always so goddamned sensitive."

"Well, knowing that, couldn't you try and . . . ?"

"What?"

"It's just about manners."

"Oh, you have to stop with the English thing."

"You're right. It must be *me*."

What am I trying to prove? After all, people change, but they don't change much. It's your perception of yourself that fucks you up. *Try to be objective.* I ask about the weather, my other English preoccupation. Well, it's cold and he is alone. He's not happy being on location. He misses L.A. He *always* misses L.A. Normally on a Saturday he'd be on Riviera golf course. He loves to play, he says. He loves the concentration it requires, a sport that keeps him firmly in the present.

"Remember you once promised to take lessons but never did," he now remarks accusingly. "Imagine. If you played golf you'd be the *perfect* woman."

"Well, if I was the perfect woman, what would I be doing with you?" It comes out. Just like that. Perhaps I'm still preoccupied with M. Bruni and the scorched floors.

"I presume you're kidding," he says.

"You know I am."

"Good," he says. "Then why don't you get on a plane?"

twelve
England 1965.

I was often lonely and went home on the weekend, catching the train from Liverpool Street station. Standing under its cavernous roof that smelled of coldness and soot, I would see other girls like myself: young, wan-faced things in fashionable London clothes, wearing too much makeup, waiting to go down to Dagenham or Ipswich and carrying a bag of laundry for their mothers to wash.

By 1965, my family had moved from Westcliff-on-Sea to South Hall, a brick Georgian house in the country, near the village of Paglesham, a few miles down the Thames Estuary. My father used to cycle past it as a boy, he said, when it was a cattle farm with 100 acres. Now reduced to two and a half, it still had an orchard, a small cottage, a barn, and stables, and when he bought it for 12,000 pounds (then about $30,000), no one had touched it in years. Nailed to the tack room wall was a note listing how many bushels of walnuts had been collected in 1948. Under the carpet in the drawing room, painted across the bare boards in giant red, swooping script, someone had written "God save the Queen" to commemorate Victoria's 1900 jubilee. My sister said that leaving our box in Westcliff for South Hall was like moving to Buckingham Palace. We had entered a world of cricket, village fetes, plowing matches, shooting sticks, and Wellington boots. And to complement our new status, my father had moved up in the legal world. He was now a deputy crown court judge, owner of an impressive nineteenth-century shoulder-length wig. "Second hand," he said proudly, "acquired from a clerk I know in the robing room at the Royal Courts of Justice."

Living in a large country house was seductive. Being part of the safe, undynamic middle class (what level I could never determine—middle-middle or upper-middle) meant social mobility, particularly in the 1960s, when you could claim your ascendancy by acquiring the right things. More silver appeared on the sideboard; there was a baby grand, elaborate gilt mirrors, damask napkins, and table mats stamped with hunting scenes. My mother, thrift-conscious as ever, did a lot of the decorating herself. Curtains and bedspreads were run up on the Singer; she made wastebaskets from jumbo-sized tomato tins and covered them in chintz. At night, she lay awake figuring out plumbing problems because Mr. Ramos, the builder, insisted that in a house this old (some parts dated

South Hall, Paglesham.

from the sixteenth century), they were unsolvable. She argued with him, and he bowed to her expertise. Unlike her middle child, she knew how to deal with workmen.

My fondest memory is Sunday lunch in the garden. A hot day, the hum of bees in the herbaceous border, the trestle table set up by the old green-house. My mother wheels out a trolley loaded with giant domed silver salvers, as if we are on a cruise ship. Dishes of roast beef and Yorkshire pudding or pheasant pie. She gets the pheasants locally, then plucks and guts them herself. There is a vegetable garden—homegrown beans, let-tuces, and asparagus. By sheer willpower it seems she has turned herself into a gourmet cook. My father is effusive, full of wonder: "Look at that. *Marvelous!*" And she's pleased to be singled out for a star turn. My sister is often there with her new husband, a charming local man who builds boats. "The porthole king," my father calls him, oblivious to his feelings. After all lunch has to be *entertaining*. And in case no one is up for the task, he's going to supply it.

But first, there is talk about food, recipes for apple pie. "Do you par-boil the apples or leave them raw?" "Parboil. And use the *white* of the egg, not the yolk, on the crusts." My sister, having thrown herself headlong into marriage—and also drowning under an avalanche of china and sil-verware—is now very close with my mother. They carry on about fashion, the terrible short skirts: "girls walking around practically showing their knickers." "And with those dreadful *white* high heels," adds my mother (the ultimate fashion faux pas, of which I am guilty). All of this bores my father, and so, fired up after a couple glasses of Beaujolais, he starts in on the war. His war: the freezing cold, the terrible food. "We were liter-ally *starving*! All we had were ship's biscuits or tinned monkey—cheap corned beef. Or what we called a 'train wreck'—one sausage and a smear of ketchup!" He articulates the words for full effect, eyes sparkling, his wine glass on the tilt. "To make a piece of bread last, we had to slice it in two, although most of the time you could only eat the middle; the rest was *green* with mold!" I am laughing, naturally, still his faithful cohort.

My mother, meanwhile, stares wistfully across the mossy lawn—a hint of girlishness here, one hand (plus cigarette) waving coquettishly above her head. The sylph-like blond who, during those grim bombing nights in London, had fallen for the upstairs lodger, my dashing law student father. "Do you remember when the back end of the house was blown off? The fire literally *jumped* five feet out of the grate!" he says now, laughing. "And what about our honeymoon at the Waldorf? I was called back to sea and you had to spend the night with your bridesmaids!"

When my brother is there, home from boarding school, my mother is in heaven. Her darling boy. And at fifteen, he'd become something of a comedian. He suffered (as did I) from the English fear of being a bore, and entertained us with impersonations—John Lennon, Harold Macmillan, Peter Sellers—or with the latest Tommy Cooper joke: "Last week, I went on a whiskey diet . . . so far I've lost *three days!*" And he was duly rewarded for the effort, my mother clapping adoringly, my father leaning back in his garden chair and laughing, "Ha ha ha!"

Only later did his relationship with our father sour. What I did with my life wasn't important, but my brother had to succeed. When he started to fail his exams, when he announced he had no intention of becoming a lawyer, my father's affection slipped into his famous courtroom froideur: "You have to buck up, boy. You're a *bloody disaster!*" When he announced he'd started a rock band, it was tantamount to admitting he'd taken heroin.

I loved Paglesham. It was Essex flat, with an enormous sky and open fields running down to the sea wall. The land was marshy, with little inlets leading from the River Roach that at low tide turned into banks of oozing mud. It was the end of the line, a Thames backwater. The pub at Church End had a dirt floor, and the regulars played shove ha'penny. In the winter, the winds roared straight across from Russia. My love for the countryside began there. It gave me the same sense of relief I found later in France, and on a lazy summer afternoon, I would escape to the sea wall. There, stretched out on the grassy slope with my notebook, I'd try to write.

My idea of writing was as passionate as it was vague. I had no idea how you became a writer. I'd never even met one. I also thought I was unqualified because of my pitiful lack of education. At St. Teresa's, Mrs. Hugget had been my brief champion. She was stocky, with large breasts under her old jumper, which we tried not to look at, and her gown was always smeared with cigarette ash. But I had a crush on her, and not just because she gave me A's on my essays; she also introduced me to T. S. Eliot's "The Waste Land," the only poem I remember reading at school. It made a great impression on me, mainly because she took the time to explain it. Sadly, after a few terms, she had to leave. I collected a few shillings from the girls in my class, who were decidedly less enthusiastic than myself, and bought her a black cigarette holder studded with fake diamonds. As a parting gift it was an odd choice. I was heartbroken to see her go, though apparently not brave enough to say so or to let down my cover of being "amusing." Unfortunately, she was replaced by a Mrs. Gledhill, a smart, no-nonsense redhead who wrote "too flowery" in my margins and gave me a C. She was probably right. It often took hours and many overworked adjectives to squeeze out a paragraph. But wanting to write stayed with me.

I'd never had the courage to mention this to anyone. Then one weekend, I decided to tell my father. We were taking a walk together, strolling up the local farmer's lane. "I'm thinking of becoming a writer," I said, blurting it out. He was a few paces ahead, wearing his old green hunting jacket and a tweed cap. "You, a *writer?*" he said, starting to laugh. There was an amusing follow-up line, something about whether I could, in fact, "write my name in the dirt with a stick!" But by then, I was laughing too because the idea did seem a bit far-fetched. I was hurt, but I don't think he meant to be unkind. He just didn't see me that way.

I wrote in secret. I composed little poems, jotting them down on the backs of envelopes, leaving them in coat pockets or inside some book to be discovered decades later. Not that I owned any books then, apart from T. S. Eliot and a copy of William Blake's *Songs of Innocence*, which I still have. According to the inscription, it was given to me by someone named Kevin—"Despite everything," it says, although I have no memory of Kevin or what I did or didn't do. Besides a few chapters of *The Mayor of Casterbridge*, half of *Peyton Place* (swiftly confiscated by Mother Clare), and *The Colditz Story* (my father's), I'd read almost nothing, though there were plenty of books around the house. It sounds incredible now, but it took me a long time to realize that to write I also had to *read*.

Those weekends in the summer were heavenly. Living the life. Going down to the Plough and Sail for pints of shandy and meat pies, watching the handsome farm boys play darts and the old men propped up on benches. I loved the locals. I loved the smell of the wheat fields when it rained. I loved the quiet. I remember one autumn evening hearing someone practicing the trumpet a mile away. To listen to Hoagy Carmichael's "Skylark" wafting across the night air was a wondrous thing. But I never lasted very long. I couldn't keep it up, pretending to be some other girl—the one happily traipsing around in Wellingtons and an old Dacron mac, the one who wasn't having sex and drinking. When my mother asked, "So what are you up to these days in London, dear, apart from the modeling?" I didn't know what to say. What we said to each other was rarely what we meant, anyway, and it was impossible to tell if she knew. So I kept the two versions of myself separate: the virgin waiting to find a nice upper-class man to marry, preferably an old Etonian, for her sake, and the anxious London girl who'd recently gained ten pounds because of the pill.

Soon, however, a new status was conferred upon me that impressed both my parents. I became an actress.

Like many models, I slid into acting. Not out of any vocational desire but because the kind of films they made in those days often required "birds" to stand around dressed provocatively in bikinis or miniskirts. This wouldn't happen now, but several careers, including Jackie's, started this way. Wearing a pound or two of Max Factor, our job was to swoon or scream when something momentous happened to the male lead. Occasionally, you were given a few lines.

There were a lot of girls required for the James Bond movie *Casino*

Royale, and every model in London was auditioned. As Jackie had already been cast in the part of Giovanna Goodthighs, a sizeable role, she managed to get me a small part—a walk-on, really, and it was hardly glamorous. To get to Pinewood Studios at six a.m., I caught the five fifteen train. It was freezing at that hour, and no warmer inside the studio, where I had to stand in a drafty corridor with a dozen or so other Bond girls. With nothing on but flimsy robes over our bra and underpants, we were lucky if we could get an assistant director to fetch us a cup of tea or a fried egg sandwich while we waited to go into wardrobe and makeup. And these institutions, particularly the hair and makeup teams, were holdovers from the old black-and-white days. Turning yourself over to a man who had done Bette Davis in her heyday was a terrifying experience. You went in a girl of twenty and came out a woman in her forties, with a bouffant of ringlets, a mask of Pan Stik on your face, orange lipstick, false eyelashes and, in my case (cleverly matching my eyes), two half-moons of electric-blue eye shadow. Not that any of us were brave enough to complain.

Casino Royale's celebrity cast included Peter Sellers, David Niven, Woody Allen, and Orson Welles. I remember little about the shooting—a string of interminable days standing around the baccarat table with the other handmaidens, plunging necklines to the fore, while we waited for someone to shout, "Laugh, girls!" or "Look surprised!"

The only thing truly memorable was a vivid encounter I had with Orson Welles. Above the soundstages was a floor of dressing rooms. One lunchtime, I was looking for Jackie and mistakenly walked into another girl's room. She was someone I knew slightly. A dark-haired Mata Hari type who at that moment was on her knees, naked, facing a long mirror. And Orson, bent over, trousers around his ankles, was taking her from behind. It was a rigorous performance, and due to his size there was a lot of panting and enthusiastic shouting—a vision I might say is almost impossible to forget. I stood there for only a few seconds. The girl saw me in the mirror, but Orson didn't, although he'd obviously heard the door open. I can only presume that when he shouted cheerily, "Come in.

Won't be a minute!" he thought I was an assistant director calling him back to the set.

I wasn't shocked, but I remember feeling slightly depressed. Not about the sex itself but the sheer casualness of it: the girl's willful look in the mirror, the semblance of fun—something passed off as an innocent lunchtime romp with an actor who most likely would never speak to her again.

My first real job was with the director Roman Polanski. I was twenty, *Repulsion* had just been released, and he was suddenly London's celebrated genius. I knew little about him. But Jackie had landed a part in his next film, *Cul-de-Sac,* so he invited us one night to the Ad Lib nightclub. The club was the hot spot to be. A dark room on the top floor of a building in Leicester Place, with smoke-mirrored walls and a glittering view of London. The noise was incredible, the music thumping—"Rescue Me," "Stop! In the Name of Love," "Get Off My Cloud"—the dance floor packed with bodies, heads rocketing back and forth, arms snapping. That night, Paul McCartney was at one table, Julie Christie at another. And I remember my outfit because with the extra pounds it was too tight. I was wearing a beige tube skirt from Biba, the waist unfashionably secured with a safety pin; a tight pink sweater; and brick-high platforms.

Roman sat in a corner with his producing partner, Gene Gutowski. We pushed through the crowd, and Jackie slid in next to Gene. I stood there awkwardly until Roman said, "Hey, c'mon. Sit here." So I did. He wasn't fluent in English then, so we spoke French. "What are you doing here? In London?" he asked: *"Qu'est ce que tu fais ici? À Londres?"* He had a gravelly voice and spoke in short bursts, as if he permanently lacked oxygen, the strain all the more apparent over the crashing music. "Well, I'm a model," I said, shouting back. *Mannequin.* And to acknowledge this lack of professional originality, I added provocatively, "Or maybe an actress, like every other girl in this room!" The last line was said in English, but he laughed anyway. The following week he screened *Knife in the Water* for me and *Two Men and a Wardrobe,* and by that time we were having an affair. I thought his films were extraordinary, and I'd never met anyone like him. He was a volcano, bursting with energy and curiosity, and unlike British men with their veiled references, he said exactly what he thought. He told me I wore too much makeup and he didn't like my clothes. "*Ça ne va pas du tout!*" he announced when I turned up at his house in a pair of black wool culottes, fashionable at the time. Roman was right. I had no idea how to dress, although apparently no other man had noticed. And I was never comfortable with my looks. What I saw was a kind of sloppy prettiness instead of sophistication. I was jealous of the sleek, athletic beauties such as Charlotte Rampling, who I'd once witnessed at a tea party casually eat her way through an entire jar of strawberry jam. How did she do it? Starving, I swallowed diet pills and picked at my food. At dinner, Roman watched me impatiently. "What are you doing? You're not eating enough," he protested. "You look great! *Eat!*" Then, sliding half his steak onto my plate, he'd add, with a parched-throat laugh, "You want me to *chew* it for you too?"

Gérard Brach, his old friend and screenwriting partner—a paradigm of creative angst—barely left the house. Roman was the opposite: an excited schoolboy. He was wickedly interested in everything: art, music, cars, politics, and particularly girls—all girls—an enthusiasm I attributed to a lack of success when he was younger. Now a celebrity, he was trying to catch up. (I didn't know then about his childhood in Poland, his mother dying in Auschwitz, his ghetto life, or about him hiding in the streets to escape Nazis.) Small and muscular, he was flagrantly open about sex, the great adventure, and would jump up and down on the bed with glee. In his mews house, around the corner from my flat on Chesham Street, there was a life-sized sculpture in his living room, a nude by the artist Allen Jones. Gamefully submissive, this anonymous woman was positioned on her hands and knees, a sheet of glass balanced on her back. Roman's coffee table.

We were lovers, most of all friends. And we went on seeing each other on and off until *The Fearless Vampire Killers* when Roman fell in love with Sharon Tate.

Roman thought I had promise as an actress. He must have seen something, but the truth was I couldn't even begin to understand the creative process. For all my hamming around as a child, it didn't translate to anything believable on the screen. Even so, by then I'd already been in two foreign movies: one French, in which I joined a group of wayward teenagers trying to foil a murder; then a low-budget Italian film, shot in London, where as a rock singer I wiggled around for two weeks miming into a microphone. *The Fearless Vampire Killers* was a comic take on the old Dracula story, and Roman cast me as the serving wench at the inn. I only had a few scenes, but he patiently acted them out for me, talking softly in his flat, accented voice, showing me how to throw away a line. I copied him. I mimicked every inflection, every pause, and managed to give a passable performance. However, one of the stars, Jack MacGowran, noticing my difficulty, suggested I should take acting lessons. He helped me enroll in an American school run by Patrick O'Neal, to study the Stanislavski method. But I couldn't grasp it. Even if I understood the theory of drawing on past experiences to portray emotions, I was still incapable of tapping into the real stuff. It was buried too deep. When I was asked by one of the teachers to go onstage and *become* a tree—already an alarming, if not incomprehensible, idea for a down-to-earth English girl—all I could do to camouflage my fear was to clown around, grimacing and shaking my arms until I made the students laugh.

Still, I was drawn to the concept of fame, the idea of being admired—that old childhood fantasy. And working in movies was the perfect escape. Looking back, I think that on the few occasions I was able to relax, I had a certain allure on-screen, which is why any director even bothered to work with me. I see young actresses now, passionate about their work, and feel embarrassed that I didn't appreciate my luck. At the same time, there were too many distractions. Not only the clubs and the music and parading along the King's Road, but the idea that you could do anything and make money, which produced its own mixture of self-glorification and fear. *Oh, yeah, I'll be something someday.* I was offered what was then the huge sum of $2,000 pounds to shave my head on camera for a

Jack McGowran, Roman Polanski, and me as the
serving maid in *The Fearless Vampire Killers.*

shampoo commercial (I declined; my thin hair would have taken years
to grow back). The only criteria then was to be young, and better yet to
be working class. The English disdain for ambition, what Cyril Connolly
called "the English distrust of the intellect and prejudice in favour of the
amateur," had suddenly disappeared. There were no limits. Even so, when
people ask now what "swinging London" was like, I say, "Compared to
what?" I didn't know anything else.

In 1967, I met someone called John Velasco, a young entrepreneur
who decided I had the right wide-eyed look to become a pop star. I was
already taking singing lessons to improve my acting voice, to open up
those clenched British vowels. My teacher, Mr. Csaszar, a Hungarian
war refugee, had a studio on Charing Cross Road. Soft-spoken, painfully

polite, he would tap my diaphragm with his baton and say pleadingly, "Here, vrom *here, please.*" We were working on an unrecorded piece written by the then-celebrated Jimmy Webb. I got as far as the studio to make the demo, but after two days, John gave up: "You're not breathing correctly!" And I couldn't really sing. As with acting, I still wasn't brave enough to let go.

But at some point I must have shown John my poems, the ones I'd been laboring over for years, and he encouraged me to write lyrics. He introduced me to a folk singer, Colin, who was about to perform at the Royal Albert Hall, opening for the Four Seasons. I wrote a song called "Always," a somewhat saccharine ballad, which they bought for five pounds, and Colin decided to play it on the first night. It was a big thing for me. So I asked my parents to come up for the show.

Things hadn't been going well between us. By then, there had been words about my sex life and, uncharacteristically, I'd argued with my mother. A photograph of me had appeared in the *Daily Mail,* a provocative, partially naked still that was lifted from one of my movies. It was the headline, however, that confirmed my disgrace: FIONA'S AFFAIR WITH ROGER VADIM!—the French director who at the time was more famous for his sexual liaisons than his talent.

He was forty. His real name was Roger Vadim Plemiannikov, and his father—a Russian aristocrat from Kiev—had once been vice consul to Egypt. I had met him in London at the Hilton Hotel when he was auditioning actresses for a film. I didn't get the part, but soon after, he invited me to stay with him in Paris. It was an unsatisfactory relationship, a bond lasting longer than it should have and based initially on the not-so-spectacular coincidence of my birthday falling on the same day as Brigitte Bardot's, one of his ex-wives. Still, I was very taken with Vadim. He had a dark, exotic air, and a rather feminine way of crossing and uncrossing his legs.

He was also very seductive, a soft talker. One of those deceptively attentive French men who have a way of making a girl feel unique, if only for a short while. "Fiona, you should come to Paris. You should be with me. I want to *show you things*," he said, as though tempting an eleven-year-old with a pony.

Part of me knew I was drifting again, capitulating to a man, living his life, acting out some parody of myself, aiming to please. But I was flattered, and so I went. I didn't know anyone in Paris. I had hardly any money, so I hung around waiting for Vadim to fill my days. He usually got up late and took his bath around eleven. It was a small bathroom, a turn-of-the-century addition to his apartment in the Marais. The tub was shallow, and he filled it entirely. I was standing in the doorway one morning, dressed and waiting. He'd gone out the night before without me, and I was looking forward to our lunch. He was lying back, relaxed, his hands sculling the water, his famously large penis wafting back and forth. *"Ah, chéri,"* he said smoothly, "I didn't realize you wanted to have lunch with me today. *Quelle dommage.* What a pity. I have an engagement with an old friend. Could you pass me a towel?"

It was clear that the friend was female—*une amie*. I didn't make a fuss. I wasn't uncool. "Oh, okay," I said, wondering at the same time if I had enough cash to get back to London.

He left town for a few days and his friend, the actor Serge Marquand, suggested I sleep with him. When I reminded him I was Vadim's girlfriend, he assured me Vadim wouldn't mind, which I realized was probably true. Despite this, our relationship continued on and off for more than a year. He came to London, I went to Paris. Jane Fonda and he had split up some time ago, but her things were still in their country house. The art deco furniture, the Jax pants hanging in the wardrobe. In awe of Jane, I felt spookily de trop in their bedroom, with her face creams still on the nightstand. I decided I had to leave. Vadim didn't protest. There were no tears. And I can't honestly say I loved him. But I was still very susceptible to people who said they *loved me*.

There were more reports about the affair in the *Daily Mail*, more revealing photographs. A line up of his ex-wives: Bardot, Annette

Stroyberg, Catherine Deneuve—all clothed—then me, the lesser siren, braless, in a shirt slashed to the waist.

For my mother, the scandal was unforgivable. Normally any break with tradition was met either with complete silence or a change in the conversation, but this was too public. She rang me in London. "Your father can barely show his face, Fiona!" she said, her voice an octave higher than normal. "He can't even go to the office, he's so *humiliated*. Have you forgotten he's a *professional* man!"

I'm not sure why I was so shocked. My cheeks burned. All the old childish frustrations rushed in and made me feel weak with shame. At the same time I tried to come up with something clever to defend myself. "It could have been worse, you know," I offered lamely. "At least he's not *black*." Her deepest fear.

Much worse, for God's sake. What my mother had apparently missed, or chosen to ignore, were the daily reports in the papers and on TV about orgies and overdoses, the drug-induced flights from top-story windows, about politicians' sons killing themselves on LSD. Even so, when I hung up, I was miserable. I threw myself on the sofa in tears. The real heartbreak, of course, was the fact that I'd disgraced myself in my father's eyes.

We didn't speak for a while. They did, however, come to the Royal Albert Hall for the debut of my song a few months later. I couldn't get us seats together and arranged to meet them during the intermission, after Colin had finished his set. I can see myself now, running into that glamorous gilt and mirrored bar feeling important. They were waiting with their gin and tonics. When I asked what they thought of my song, my mother gave me one of her impenetrable smiles. "Well, dear," she said, "not exactly our cup of tea."

As hard as it was for a girl to pull herself out of the 1950s, it was impossible for her parents; the differences between the two decades were so profound. And in those days, I wasn't the only girl who had a combative relationship with her mother.

Victoria was a girl who saved me. I'd never had a real confidante, and so I was relieved to find someone to talk to. She was a much better version of myself. She had the kind of pale, luminous English skin that people write about, a short bowl haircut, and wide-set eyes. Her parents had both been spies during the war, and it was rumored that MI5 had tried to recruit her too. At the time, I had no idea why she was interested in me; she seemed so exotic. We would swan around all day, arm in arm, doing nothing. Or we'd get drunk at San Lorenzo then—laughing hysterically, smoking our foul Gitanes—walk to Harrods and spend as much money as possible (usually hers) on clothes. I never knew where the cash came from. In the evening, sailing forth in a cloud of Fracas, she'd take me to a smart dinner party where we'd get even drunker—the difference being that we didn't have to go home with a man. She was fearless. Her first husband had pushed her down the stairs when she was pregnant, and so she'd willed herself to be strong with men. She had a fuck-you attitude that I worshipped, plus a touch of madness that made her a superior being. What's more, her self-esteem was never dependent on anyone's approval—at least it looked that way to me. It was years before I realized the toll it had taken on her. But she was patient with me. When I'd start moaning about feeling lonely or lost, she'd say, "Get a grip, baby! *Ne perde pas ta valise!*"—her unique translation ("Don't lose your suitcase")—and run me a hot bath. Pouring in half a bottle of Floris *Malmaison*, she'd then kneel behind me to rub Tiger Balm on my forehead. I felt loved, and for the first time, I valued myself. We were twenty and twenty-one, two girls from the countryside, similar in many ways, not the least being her difficult relationship with her mother. Many years later, we'd talk about those years in the '60s. When we had to move in with a man because we didn't have enough money to exist independently, and the fact that neither of our mothers saw fit to comment. "How did they think we were *living?*" she would say in her beautiful, old-fashioned voice. "How did they think we were surviving on no money? Didn't they *care?*"

Like me, Victoria had never had much encouragement about her abilities or her looks. And this didn't change as she grew up, even though she was considered a great beauty in London, and clever. Finally, when her mother was dying of pneumonia, lying in Victoria's arms and barely able to breathe, she managed to whisper to her daughter, "You know, dear, you're very pretty"—a remark that so astounded Victoria she burst into tears. She was telling me about it thirty years later. And by this time, she was living with a famously rich man in a grand country house in Oxfordshire. We were lying on her four-poster bed, the butler had brought in tea, and outside the winter sun was casting shadows across the lush 900-acre park. She hadn't lost her wit. "Very pretty!" she repeated, exploding with one of her big laughs. "Thanks, Mummy—bit fucking late, don't ya think?"

In London, there were plenty of women, beautiful women with brains, who didn't marry for conventional reasons but who couldn't get beyond wanting desperately to be admired, who needed money and got used to men giving it to them, and who instead of promoting themselves were stuck in a '50s world of silent obligation, resenting men, and hating themselves for it. The unfulfilled. The casualties. The non–career women. On drugs or lost. I could easily have been one of them.

thirteen
Bulgaria 2005.

The approach from the airport is less than inspiring, the landscape bleak, the sun a distant streak of low-voltage yellow. We drive past fields of blackish earth, past abandoned plots dotted with swampy-looking strips of water that shimmer like oil slicks. There are burnt-out cars, rubbish heaps, then rows of tenement buildings. Tall, graffiti-covered slabs, some missing chunks where the facade has fallen away, some with balconies, a few of these still intact and strung with depressingly hopeful lines of laundry. I feel as if I've just landed in some postapocalyptic outpost of old Russia.

In fact, Todor Zhivkov, loyal to the Soviets for thirty-three years, was deposed in 1989, and soon after, the People's Republic of Bulgaria held its first free elections. Yet something remains; the shadows are still here.

But as we approach the city, everything changes: the traffic thickens and we're entering wide boulevards and tree-lined streets. Driving down Knyaz Alexander Dondukov Boulevard, I realize we've arrived in a perfectly normal-looking European city. Not only are there attractive turn-of-the-century buildings and open parks, but rising dramatically like a Disney mirage is the Alexander Nevsky Cathedral, all brilliant green and gold onion domes.

. . .

The business of making movies is stressful. There are the usual location problems, more so in this case because Sofia is supposed to be passing for 1940s Los Angeles. But in the world of independent financing, Bulgaria has become a viable location. Deals are made with the government; tax breaks will be given. There are also foreign investors involved, some with dubious reputations. My husband has been reassured, however, that everything is ready to go. Except that it's not. The furniture for the first day's shooting has been lost somewhere on the Black Sea. The dummy for the dead body looks like something out of a Saks window, and a man is flying in from Los Angeles with the right kind of rubber. The old Chevys have not arrived. My husband, of course, is prepared for this kind of thing. After more than thirty years as a producer, there are no surprises. He's written books about the business: the perils of moviemaking—cautionary tales from the front line. And he's famously tough. If the money people quibble too much about the script or the budget, he tells them, "Don't make it then!" And he means it. He has no illusions. The movie business is not for the faint-hearted. When we first met, he said to me, "In this town your character is measured by how you handle *defeat* not success." That was sobering. No self-pity there. I was still starry-eyed, the actress-turned–budding screenwriter. But as usual he wanted to give me the truth. One day we were driving in the hills near Griffith Park and he stopped near the old HOLLYWOOD sign. "There should be another one underneath," he announced drily, "saying NEXT!"

While it's still light, we take a walk on Vitosha Boulevard, the main drag. It's packed with shoppers. He's right, of course—the shops are modern, rows of gleaming plate-glass windows that might have been lifted from an American mall: Nike, Puma, Adidas, with flashy lingerie stores in between. The essentials for up-to-date living. What's more surprising is that the young women working in these shops are beautiful, amazingly so. Naively, I was expecting girls with mustaches, but these Slavic-eyed creatures are slim-hipped and have creamy white skin. The men, however, are cement blocks. Big Russian no-necks with pockmarked faces and bloated waistlines, a difference that genetically seems almost impossible.

Wider, more menacing versions of these men are stationed outside the restaurant that night. They are the local mafia boys, the tough-looking *mutri*, leaning against their big Mercedes and SUVs. Dressed in wide-shouldered black suits and wraparound shades, they have all the comic swagger of goons from an old Stallone movie.

We are having dinner with the director and some of the actors. Scarlett Johansson has just flown in from Los Angeles. She arrives for dinner, accompanied by two of the players, and is precocious and funny. My husband has been in Sofia for close to a month. A news junkie by habit, he is suffering from media withdrawal. He has CNN in his room, but the clips are on a loop and repeated every hour. When he asks Scarlett what's going on in the world, she replies, "Oh, the usual. The War in Iraq. The economy. And in case you didn't know, there's a two-for-one sale on cardigans at the Gap." In the movie, she's playing the classic '40s femme fatale. Leaning back saucily in her chair now, her skirt riding up, her mouth a big red swirl, she runs a hand through her bleached hair. "Blond enough for you?" she asks the director.

I know the director, Brian De Palma. I've worked with him, albeit several decades before. A dedicated gastronome, plus a Hitchcock devotee, he's not famous for lavishing much attention on his actors. He asks Scarlett if he's going to hear her rehearse a few lines before they shoot. "Oh, well, I hate that," she pouts. "I'm really better when it's spontaneous." However, she's been watching old Marilyn Monroe films, she says, and swiveling sideways, tries out another sultry move. Her confidence is breathtaking. I'm in awe: her scrubbed beauty, her great Nordic glow. I'm trying to imagine having such poise at *twenty*. I can't. Even now, when I adopt the mannerisms of the older, wiser woman, the groundwork is shaky. But when you're the person who takes too long to get ready for dinner, that's what you rely on. Sounding smart. At some point, there's a conversation about female intelligence. The great lament: that we are still not taken seriously. "Well," I say, quoting from Virginia

Woolf, "no one minds a woman thinking, as long as she's *thinking about a man*." That gets their attention. High-minded while they're cynical. After all, I'm the producer's wife, although it occurs to me I should be wearing a lot more jewelry.

My husband is up late, on the phone to Los Angeles. The next morning, he leaves to deal with the ongoing problems. There are new locations to be found, the old ones having apparently been "lost" after the wrong (insufficient) amount of levs were slipped under some official's desk. I was planning to visit the sixth-century Banya Basli mosque and the Russian Church, but it's raining hard. So I happily lie in bed. And our room in the Grand Hotel Sofia is oddly relaxing despite the garish post-Glasnost decor. Everything is green and glossy and over the top—as if the designer was asked to recreate the Frank Sinatra suite at Caesar's. The drapes are electric green, dotted with soup bowl–sized gold medallions, and match the bed cover and the wall-to-wall Kelly-green carpet. The furniture, oversized and stained a dark Eastern bloc brown, is, as far as I can tell, unmovable. But the room is quiet. Just the soothing hum of a vacuum cleaner out in the corridor. I love hotel rooms. I feel like I'm floating in limbo. As usual, I start thinking about the old days with my husband. Going back, always going back. Trying to relive those magical firsts.

"Do you remember that time at the Beverly Wilshire?" I said to him last night, reminding him of one of our after-lunch trysts. Our first *cinq à sept*—in a hotel, that is. Embarrassed, he had hidden behind a pillar in the lobby, pretending to read a newspaper, and I had to get the room. "This is all new for me," he'd whispered, which at the time I thought unlikely (he looked like a fighter; in fact he was all poetry at the core). "Do you remember? You were so nervous."

"I had every reason to be," he said. "I knew my life was over."

"Oh. Have I been *that* difficult?"

"Yes."

"Always?" I was laughing, but he was giving me one of his cunning looks.

"Yes! You have!"

No. Not always. In those early days, I was pretty accommodating. And I certainly didn't want to break up his marriage. Having spent seven years as an unhappy housewife, I felt bad for his wife. At least that's what I said to him, congratulating myself for taking the moral high ground. The truth was I was too scared. I didn't have much faith in my ability to commit to anyone so soon, not on a permanent basis. I loved him. I was often obsessed, but once the clandestine meetings were over, who knew if it would last? "There's also the possibility," I pointed out, "that this affair might make your marriage *better*."

These conversations took place daily. Like all doomed lovers, we talked for hours, hidden in a back booth of Le Dome, or sitting in his car outside my apartment, necking, laughing, unable to say good-bye. Honesty was still a big topic. He had to tell the truth, to *confess*, because, as he reminded me, he was incapable of not doing so. Though apparently, his wife had so far been spared.

"I can't just leave her."

"I don't want you to."

"What happens later? There's no guarantee."

"No. There's no guarantee. We should end it."

"How many men have you slept with? I mean before you were married. Five?"

I presumed he must be joking. "I'm *thirty-eight*!"

"I can't trust you."

"You shouldn't."

"How many?"

"Well, you know what they say. A woman with a past. A man with a future."

"Clever."

"Oscar Wilde."

Then, his head sinking in despair, "I've been married for *twenty-two* years. What am I going to tell her?"

"Nothing. Just stay."

And I meant it. He couldn't trust me any more than he could trust his own emotions. And despite his years in the movie business, when it came to my being an actress, he was a bit of a prude.

I hadn't talked about my film career because at that time I was concentrating on writing. At the beginning, in the months when we were pretending we weren't going to have sex, we'd still meet as producer and writer, ostensibly to discuss some future project together. He was encouraging about my screenplays. My ideas were good, he said, although he thought the women had far too much clever dialogue. "Oh, you think they should be *stupid*," I remarked indignantly. He wasn't fazed. "No. But make it real. It's the small moments that count. What you leave out in a script can be just as important and still get the emotion across."

He hadn't seen any of my films, but a month later, I happened to be at MGM shooting a science fiction movie and he came to visit the set. I was playing a scientist, one of my more strident roles, the lab coat now having permanently replaced the push-up bra. I'd already done films in this genre in which, armed with the accouterments of sci-fi chic—a hypodermic needle and thigh-high boots—I would utter such statically menacing lines as: "Lie still. This will only hurt for a minute!"

Then one night he saw one of my movies on TV in which I appeared naked. After that, reviewing my credits, he was mildly shocked to find out I'd been nude in not one but several films, and that I'd also been photographed by Helmut Newton. Which made him trust me even less. In the middle of making love, he would stop to ask thoughtfully, "So—are you acting *now*?"

We ended it several times. But we couldn't stop talking on the phone. I was still daring him not to love me. Or perhaps I was trying to prove to myself that I wasn't lovable. Eventually, I got sick. A bad kidney infection. Doubled over one night, I was taken to the hospital. My doctor ordered me to stop drinking for at least a year. It was either that or face permanent damage. *No drinking?* No more hilarious lunches at Le Dome, sinking that fourth fatal martini. I was terrified. Not so much about being ill: I was more worried that, sober, I would lose my sense of humor and become a bore.

"Listen to you. Always so dramatic," he said. "And you don't have to be so funny all the time. I love you anyway."

I love you anyway. How could I not have fallen for this man?

That Christmas he moved out. I stayed in my apartment in West Hollywood, while he rented a small house for himself in Beverly Hills. It was all new for him. "Oh, this is easy," he said, running to the market for groceries, vacuuming the carpet, delighted by his bachelor domesticity. "I don't know why housewives make so much fuss!" Then, two days later, worn out, he would call me to ask timidly, "So how often are you *supposed* to change the sheets?"

I am still in the room. I have ordered a late breakfast, and now I'm thinking about France. As my husband would say, no matter where I am, I am thinking about France. Before he left this morning, having promised myself I would definitely *not* bring up the subject, I did just that. He was

My husband and me, Christmas 1989.

getting out of bed. "I have to go," he said, leaning over to kiss my shoulder. He sounded in a good mood, so I decided to mention the pool. *His* pool. I told him I'd found a company in Nice that could build what they called a Las Vegas *piscine*, one with a genuine plaster finish. "But it's expensive," I said. There was a slight intake of breath, a raised eyebrow. "Oh, is that why you came here, to get more money?" He was standing in the bathroom doorway, half smiling, half serious. But I recognized the tone. "That's not fair," I said. And I could have just left it at that. But I didn't. I brought up another big expense: painting the inside of the house. Mr. Martinez, the man recommended for the job, had given me a quote that seemed very high. "Although I should have suspected as much," I said, "when I saw him coming down the driveway in a new BMW." But he was supposed to be an *expert*, I pointed out, and painting, I'd discovered, was always expensive because of the cost of the paint. "Although why paint prices should be higher in France than anywhere in the known speaking *world* . . ." By this time, my husband was getting impatient. He had to take a shower. He had to have coffee, get going. Perversely, I kept on. Did he have any thoughts about color? Because I'd been trying to decide between white or off-white walls, or a pale gray . . .

"It doesn't matter," he said, poised in the bathroom doorway. "You're obsessing on the details. It's a summer house. I'll only be going there two or three weeks a year. *At most.*"

Two or three weeks. Well, I probably deserved that.

Later that afternoon, we go to Alexander Nevsky Square to see the great cathedral. My husband is of Russian descent, from Kiev, and so visiting churches devoted to Christ are not out of the question here. It is one of the largest Eastern Orthodox cathedrals in the world. Built in the Neo-Byzantine style to honor the Russian tsar and the 200,000 soldiers who died during the 1877–78 Russo-Turkish War (resulting in Bulgaria's liberation from Ottoman rule), it can hold 5,000 people. Inside there are throngs of whispering foreigners, all dwarfed by the huge dome. We visit the Southern Altar (St. Boris), then the Northern Altar (St. Cyril and

Methodie—who, incidentally, created the Cyrillic alphabet); we pass the frescoes, then walk back outside. It's raining now, an icy wind whipping across Battenberg Square. At one end is a small flea market, with half a dozen rickety tables selling souvenirs and antiques. We stop at the first stall. I buy an old nickel-plated pocket watch from a man with a creased, ruddy face. He turns the watch over for me with his chapped hands. On the back, in relief, is a Soviet-style train roaring across a wasteland. I can't help thinking about the driver or stationmaster who was rewarded with this after thirty years of drudgery, and now it's being sold in the square for just a few levs. I don't have the heart to bargain. "*Da. Blagodarya,*" I say. All the words I know: "Yes. Thank you."

On our way back, we somehow make a wrong turn and it's as if we've stepped into the dark ages. Only one block away, the streets are cobbled, pot-holed, the buildings broken down, and in between the banged-up Soviet cars, the gutters are swimming with garbage. All the old suffering is here. There are women in doorways wearing frayed shawls and finger-less gloves, one selling pencils from a tin cup. It's still a city on the brink. Disheartened, we turn back to the world of conspicuous consumption, past the glittering Nike and La Perla shops, to the men in black, the *mutri,* and the puzzlingly beautiful young girls.

We stop for tea in a modern café. Steaming espresso machines sit behind the counter, and at the back is a small restaurant with orange plywood walls and an enormous fish tank. The waitresses are young and, naturally, good-looking. My husband is already a regular customer, and as we come in they shout their welcoming hellos in perfect English. He grins at them, pleased. Then, as if to remind me how lucky I am—in case I'm thinking of spending more than *two weeks* a year in France—he says, "Ask any of them. They're all dying to come to America."

Perhaps it's true. In their pointy shoes, or with Levi's tucked into their boots, the girls greet him like a savior, someone who might facili-tate the next step, away from their suety leather-jacketed boyfriends and on to Vegas.

"Look, not all foreigners want to come to America," I say, when we sit down. "Not everyone thinks life there is so *perfect*." And already I know the tone of my voice is all wrong.

"You, for example?"

"No. I just think *saying* that, it sounds rather naive. This sense of entitlement. Thinking life in the United States is always better than anywhere in the entire world."

"For them it would be better."

"You can't be sure."

"I'm sure. *You're* the one who doesn't want to live there."

"But I do live there."

"Yes. Though admit it, since you got the house, you've become anti-*everything* that's American."

"No. You always misunderstand this." And I'm still smiling, because I know what's coming. I can't stop myself. I know I'll start sounding off about having to live with people who think its okay to give their children McMuffins and buckets of corn syrup for breakfast. A country overflowing with methane-producing livestock, cows shot up with penicillin and steroids; the polluted drinking water, or the plastic bottles leaking cancer-causing phthalates; not to mention acres of genetically modified God-knows-what.

Ten years before, I would have steered clear of a woman like myself. Someone who couldn't order a meal in a restaurant without asking the waiter to list the ingredients in the salad dressing, who wanted everything on the side. Now it feels as if my entire life is *on the side*. "Don't make me start about the ruination of the planet," I say. "Monsanto and big pharma. Or about children on *psychostimulants*."

"I feel bad that we didn't have children. Or adopt children," he says.

"That's not what I meant—"

"I know it upsets you . . ."

"It doesn't anymore. It's too long ago."

And it's definitely too long ago to bring it up. But he's being serious. He wants me to be real, or he wants me to be the woman he married years ago.

"I'm talking about doctors prescribing drugs to children," I go on relentlessly, "sometimes to babies under *five*. They say it affects their brain chemistry—"

"Who are *they*? The experts?" And to show the waitresses how indulgent he is being with his whacky wife, he starts laughing. One of the girls, the tall redhead with mahogany-colored knee boots and the matinee smile, arrives with the cappuccinos. Normally I don't drink coffee because of my digestive problems. Now I take a healthy swig.

"It's well-documented."

"*Where?* Show me."

"You know what I'm saying. You agree. You're just being argumentative."

"Well, if you think all this horror isn't arriving in France in the next minute, you're wrong."

"Exactly," I say, feeling a wave of acid crawl up my throat and lodge itself behind my frontal lobe. "That's why I'd like to have a few summers there first!"

Later that evening, we are having a drink in the Cigar Bar, a low-lit corridor off the hotel lobby full of gliding waiters and more shit-brown immovable furniture. One of the actors stops to say hello. He asks me how the work is coming along at the house in Provence. "Fine. Thank you," I say. "But it's the Southwest." He grins. Then he turns to my husband and, with a look that suggests France might have been the subject of many a riotous evening, asks, "So you're actually going to *live there* now?"

"No. That's my wife's idea," says my husband, with his signature smile.

And so, to further ingratiate himself with the producer, the actor adds: "Well, maybe you never really have to go there. Maybe you can just *say* you own a house in France and keep passing round the photos!"

Hilarious. We laugh heartily and order more drinks.

fourteen
London.

When Ian La Frenais came into my life, it was a great relief. I didn't know if I was in love, but I wanted to live with a man even if it turned out to be the wrong one. I moved into his Chelsea flat on Old Church Street, off the King's Road, a Victorian brick building populated by graphic artists and designers, including the young debutante shirtmakers Deborah & Clare.

In a way, Ian saved me. He allowed me to survive. He was kind and affectionate and that most alluring thing: a writer. He'd come down from Newcastle at the time when it was fashionable to be working class or lower middle class, when northerners were flocking to London. "There was no game plan," he said, "you just had to get there." His first job was cleaning flats for a company called New Pin Domestic, but the clients were continuously disappointed. "Are you on the stage or in the films?" the women would ask. They only wanted to hire out-of-work actors.

When I met him, he and his partner, Dick Clement, had just begun writing the TV series *The Likely Lads,* which later became very successful. He looked the opposite of the traditional BBC man, who still wore patched tweeds and threadbare corduroys, and instead dressed like everyone else whose territory was the King's Road: rakish in a crushed velvet jacket and drainpipe jeans. He was also the first man I slept with who made me feel comfortable about sex. "Look, sorry, I'm just not that relaxed about it." I could tell him anything. It was as if we were best friends. "Hello, pet," he would say in the morning and bring me a cup of tea in bed. "Why don't you stay there and I'll make you a nice breakfast?"

As a couple, we did the kind of things girls used to do together. We got our hair done at a new place in Beauchamp Place, some trendy scissor wizard who straightened mine and blow-dried Ian's Beatle bob. He even looked like Paul McCartney, or at least an elder brother. We shopped for clothes; we had facials. We were like children, luxuriating in ourselves. He bought a vintage Rolls. We spent our nights at Alvaro's, pressed against the plastered walls next to Terence Stamp and Michael Caine; we danced at Club del Aretusa to "Sgt. Pepper's Lonely Heart's Club Band." The sound effects alone were a psychedelic experience: harps and harmoniums, bells and cellos and dogs barking. I downed a Mandrax, smoked my Sobranie Turkish cigarettes, and pranced around, one night dressed in a *churidar*—a serene Eastern being—the next, eyes black with kohl, playing the disenchanted heathen. You might say I was in a state of permanent delusion. But at least Ian gave me the confidence to let go. And if I felt a bit short on love, or what I understood to be love—some mournful, poetically inspired longing—I walked down to the Physic Garden, on Royal Hospital Road, where I would scribble a few feverish lines in my notebook.

I considered myself a romantic, but I thrived on drama; it was a way to feel consequential. I would create arguments with Ian then be unfaithful, despite the fact that we were supposed to be engaged. I'd run off with someone for a few weeks, then reappear at his flat, mortified, full of apologies, and in the beginning, he was nice enough to take me back. While I was in Ireland doing *Where's Jack?*, a costume drama about the exploits of a famous eighteenth-century criminal, he came to visit me. By then, I had happily embraced my make-believe movie-star life. I lived in a rented manor house near Bray Studios. I'd adopted a Dalmatian puppy that systematically destroyed the furniture—I didn't care. On

Friday nights, I went to the pub with my driver, Paddy, who naturally became my best friend. For these special outings, he wore his "drinking suit," a snappy PVC two-piece that allowed the overflowing booze, or any gastric mishaps, to run off onto the saloon floor. What a riot! I had a cook named Bridic who made terrible lamb stew but who took care of me—not, of course, that I thought I needed taking care of. And when Ian arrived, having driven the length of England and then crossed the Irish Sea by boat, I was brazenly screwing one of the actors. "What are you *doing?*" he demanded, as if I'd lost my mind.

I had lost my mind. I was ungrateful. I couldn't connect. I didn't know how to be loved. Ian had started coming with me when I went to Paglesham for the weekends. My father liked him immediately—two comedians sitting around after dinner with the claret, telling each other stories. My mother was more skeptical: about his accent, his obvious working-class origins. But fame is the great seducer. And by then he was becoming well-known as a television writer and screenwriter, earning a considerable amount of money. At South Hall, Ian and I slept in different bedrooms. We didn't even admit that we lived together in London, and, naturally, my mother couldn't bring herself to ask. It was comical, really. If she called the flat looking for me, she'd say cheerily to Ian, "I wanted to talk to Fiona and I was wondering if she might have *dropped round* this morning."

We told them we planned to get married. Yes. Why not? How positively normal! My mother was delighted; I was reprieved. Except that I could already see the china and silver piling up, the dinner parties, the cut flowers on the mantelpiece. It was in my DNA.

I tried to make it work. We went away on trips. We drove up to Whitley Bay where Ian had lived as a boy. It was cold. We walked along the beach, the big black clouds rolling in, the waves crashing under the lighthouse. The North Sea was dark green. "You'd have to man up to go in there," said Ian. We laughed. We visited the beautiful priory at Tynemouth, then drove around the little backstreets lined with bungalows where he'd been brought up. "Them were the days, pet," he said, full of Geordie humor. At a different time, I thought, I could see myself happy here, living in a cottage on the bay, cooking, and having children. But later in Sardinia with him for a two-week holiday, I sat on a rock staring out at the Mediterranean, weeping from frustration. He was the nicest man I'd ever met, but I had to go. Obligingly, he drove me to the airport. As it happened, there was a strike on; no planes could leave the island for a week. The lounge was mobbed, and we saw one irate English businessman screaming at a ground stewardess, "For God's sake, I have to get back to *Lincolnshire!*" We started laughing. I couldn't even make *that* drama work. So he calmly drove me back to our rented villa and the break-up was postponed.

Ian wrote several screenplays, and I appeared in two of his films. *Otley*, with Tom Courtenay, and *Villain*, with Richard Burton. Burton's role was as a sadistic, mother-obsessed killer, modeled on the real-life London gangster Ronnie Kray, and I was the girlfriend of one of his henchman, played by Ian McShane. Sometimes I would spend the lunch hour with Burton, sitting in a pub near Shepperton Studios, knocking back greyhounds (vodka and ginger beer), while he waited for Liz. She would finally arrive, looking extraordinary in furs, and stay well into the afternoon to keep an eye on him. They were the biggest stars in the world then, but Richard was a generous actor. One day I remember feeling particularly jittery on the set. It was a difficult scene: I arrive suddenly at our flat and surprise McShane, who is having a secret homosexual affair with Burton (risky cinema in those days). Burton, who has been hiding in the bedroom, suddenly bursts through the door and shouts, "Get outta here, slag! *Get out!*" He said it so ferociously, and so convincingly, I was thrown. After several bad takes, Burton took me aside. He squeezed my arm and whispered, slipping back to his gentle Welsh lilt, "C'mon, Fiona, you're good. You can *do it!*"

But I didn't feel I was that good. I loved the independence working on a movie. I loved having money (although compared to today's salaries, we were paid nominal sums). I loved the camaraderie, cracking jokes with the gaffers between takes. But I still wasn't comfortable acting. I didn't think there was anything natural or profound about my performance. I was so practiced at being a pleasant person that most of the time my face refused to give much away. Still, after a few films, I did get better, even if it meant I had to drop another Mandrax just to stop shaking on the set. And it worked. Mandrax (the equivalent of Quaaludes in America) had become my drug of choice. The first time I took one, I remember thinking to myself, *Oh my God, this is how I'm supposed to feel.* A little swimmy-eyed, I managed to relax. I became oddly focused—that is if I didn't overdo it and start tripping across the furniture. And eventually I got a few good reviews. This immediately went to my head. I started to have an opinion about the script, and if I didn't like something the director suggested, I would object.

Later on, in Ken Russell's *Lisztomania,* I walked off the set in the middle of a scene because Russell shouted at me. *Fuck this!* I was playing Countess Marie D'Agoult, Liszt's mistress—a French aristocrat in love with the handsome young Franz, played by Roger Daltrey of the Who. Perfect casting. Russell's take on the story was to portray the composer as the original eighteenth-century rock star, complete with phallic imagery, hair-raising sexual orgies, and pantomime clothes. Ringo Starr played the pope.

Ken, a thick-chested man with an air of buffoonery and malice, was considered something of a demented genius, particularly after his musical fantasy film *Tommy.* He was also notoriously rude to actresses. He liked to push them until they broke down and cried. I was determined not to. But I came close. On this particular afternoon, Ken was in his canvas chair, his customary bottle of wine at his side, directing with a bullhorn—one of his many affectations, even if the action was taking place only a few feet away. "You are stupid, Fiona, utterly *stupid,*" he boomed, one hand whirring above his head. Apparently, I wasn't talking fast enough, or with enough conviction. It was an odd scene (no odder, however, than the rest of the movie that featured Rockettes-like dancers and a giant inflated penis) in which, performing a kind of Chaplinesque fantasy, Daltrey and I had to "act" with jerky movements to simulate the projection of a silent movie. After fifteen minutes of Ken's gleeful insults, I told him to royally fuck off, then left the set and locked myself in my dressing room. I informed the producer, David Puttnam, that I would stay there until Ken apologized. I'm sure he never did, so I must have eventually come out. But by that time I didn't care if I was fired or not.

For *One More Time*, a sequel to the dismal *Salt and Pepper*, directed by Jerry Lewis, I was arrogant enough to demand my name be taken off the picture. Shot in London, it was a dated Rat Pack story in which the euphoric duo, Sammy Davis Jr. and Peter Lawford, team up to solve a crime. I and another actress, Esther Anderson, had been promised substantial parts. But in the end we did little more than stand around in tight velvet shorts and stilettos, and were treated like Vegas hookers, both on and off the set. Even I knew that it was too late to have to put up with that. As it turned out, however, the movie literally saved my life.

Roger Daltry and me in *Lisztomania*.

On *The Fearless Vampire Killers* I'd become good friends with the actress Sharon Tate. Sharon was the classic Texan beauty. Women in London didn't look like her, nor did they have her sweet and confident nature. A beauty queen, with a body of Barbie Doll perfection, she'd been groomed by the old Hollywood system. She'd already been in several movies, including *Valley of the Dolls* (earning a nomination for a Golden Globe); nevertheless she was comically realistic about her career: "Let's face it, honey, I don't think I'll ever be doing Shakespeare!"

During the movie, she and Roman moved in together. We were all friends. They were getting married, and Roman had found a vintage white Rolls-Royce for her as a wedding present. A few days before the ceremony, I took her to lunch at Alvaro's, where Roman had instructed me to occupy her while he and Ian drove to Maidenhead to get the car. Later, when Sharon was eight and a half months pregnant and had gone back to Los Angeles, she invited me to stay with her at the Cielo Drive house. I had already booked my flight, but at the last minute I signed up for the Jerry Lewis movie. The Manson murders took place the week I was supposed to be there. I can remember the morning Ian called to tell me. The details were gruesome. For days I couldn't look at the papers, particularly the tabloids, with their banner headlines: RITUALISTIC KILL-INGS. They blamed Roman and Sharon's "degenerate lifestyle" for what were initially believed to be drug murders. It was brutal and horrifyingly sad. Not long after, Roman and I had lunch at Aretusa. He had aged. His face was ashen; he looked utterly defeated. He talked about his child-hood, hiding in the streets from the Nazis during the war, about his first wife leaving him, about his love for Sharon and his murdered unborn child. "There's nothing left now," he said. "They might as well send me back to Poland."

One of the great changes in the '60s was the breakdown of class barriers. Cockney boys and adenoidal northerners had become the new aristoc-racy, and young men from stately homes were investing in restaurants and dress shops. A prince handled the Rolling Stones' money; lawyers were suddenly in rock and roll—one year at Lincoln's Inn, the next, a road manager. It was a way for noncreative people to get in on the game.

Ian mixed easily with the upper classes in a manner that I, being from the stultified middle class, never could do. He was amused by his new celebrity and liked to tease the titled girls, the long-necked Sabrinas and Annabels, about their accents, their trust funds. Taken to meet their mothers, he'd say, "Smashing house, love," then ask if he could have a cup of tea or, better yet, something decent from the cellar. And they loved him. One weekend, Ian and I were invited to Alistair Londonderry's house, Wynyard Park in County Durham, a mammoth place where, due to lack of funds, only one wing was heated. We were shown around the echoing halls, and when we got to the ballroom, Ian remarked breezily, "Bloody hell—glad I don't have to clean these floors." But I was in awe. To begin with, the houses were so beautiful: the lush parklands with obelisks and follies, the silk-curtained bedrooms, the libraries with coffered ceilings. Seeing so many priceless things in one place was utterly daunting. Rooms full of history and gravitas. Unlike Ian, I was on my best behavior. I didn't know how to react, and so I pretended I was in the habit of seeing Turners and Canalettos in the drawing room, or a marble-pillared hallway. Wynyard did have a marble-pillared hallway. It was immense, its Doric columns topped with ancient Greek heads—stolen a few decades earlier, I presumed, by some enterprising ancestor.

Alistair was tall, playfully handsome, and eccentric. And recklessness was encouraged. One night, after dinner, he suggested we go roller-skating. Each of us was handed a pair of roller skates by the butler, and then—as if this were the most normal thing in the world—we were escorted to the marble hallway for a rousing game of football. The idea was to wind our way in and out of the pillars at full speed, kicking the ball, or throwing it as high as possible while we tried to—or tried *not* to, the rules were never clear—knock the heads from their pedestals.

There was an unmistakable glamour to these upper-class boys: their blatant irreverence, their disregard for public opinion. They were often good-looking too, in that Rupert Brooke way: lanky and impeccably mannered and deceptively shy, which meant I read a lot more into their characters than possibly existed.

A few years later, in 1973, I started going out with Patrick Anson. An old Harrovian, ex–Grenadier Guard, and cousin of the queen, Patrick had inherited his father's title and was now the Fifth Earl of Litchfield. He had also inherited the family estate, Shugborough Hall in Staffordshire, a grand neoclassical house in an extensive park, dotted with follies and monuments. The National Trust had recently taken it over (in lieu of death duties), but he kept a thirty-four room apartment in one of the wings. During the week, he was a photographer in London—something his parents had apparently once referred to as "gone into trade." I'd met him once before in my early modeling days. Doing the rounds, I'd stopped by his studio in Knightsbridge. It was snowing. I was wearing an old tweed coat and my plastic fake Courrèges boots, which he was gracious enough not to comment on. Instead, he handed me a mug of tea, then walked me across to Hyde Park, where he took shots of me swinging on a lamppost.

Guests were invited up for the weekend (Up or *down*, I was never sure.) On Friday night, after a ritual tour of the house and gardens— the Chinese pagoda, the Triumphal arch based on Hadrian's, the Doric temple—a substantial amount of alcohol was consumed. On Saturday, fortified with beakers of Bloody Marys, we rode motorcycles back and forth across the front lawn. Then in the evening, we played charades and smoked joints in the nursery. The idea was to behave like privileged children left alone for the holidays. Patrick's father had been a notorious prankster. There was a story that one Christmas the tree had been decorated with a few hundred condoms to startle a visiting clergyman. That sort of thing. But it only went so far; basic traditions were upheld. The butler served potted shrimps for tea. Dinner was formal: black tie for the men, the women in long dresses. And there were rules. One Easter, Prince Michael of Kent was staying, and every time I passed him in the corridor, I was expected to stop and curtsey, despite the fact that he'd openly flirted with me the night before.

. . .

When I met someone, I assumed his life, his friends, and left everything of myself behind. Not that I expected to be transformed by a man, but lacking any identity, it was easy to be consumed, particularly if I convinced myself I'd fallen in love. And I was completely taken with Patrick. He was very handsome in a kind of dissolute way, with rosy farmer's cheeks and thick, wavy hair—a leonine mane, worn in an outdated pompadour, which exaggerated the size of his head. But he was debonair; he had a boyish humor and he oozed charm. It was also impossible not to be impressed by the house. So I was eager to play by the rules.

During weekend shooting parties I would stand gamely at his side for hours in one of his rain-sodden fields, freezing, clutching a hand warmer and a flask of sloe gin, to cheer him on. I was a good sport. I didn't complain. Nor did I say anything when he made me leave his room every morning, just after dawn. He kept two alarm clocks under his bed, set ten minutes apart, to make sure I'd be back in my own room before the butler arrived at eight with his breakfast tray. The butler knew, of course; that wasn't the point. It was about decorum. It was more important that he remain dignified for the staff's benefit. Occasionally, however, the old-fashioned manners had to be put aside to give vent to the aristocratic temper. One afternoon, I asked the housekeeper if she could iron a dress for me, soaked from the rain, and was severely reprimanded. "She doesn't do *that*," he shouted at me, his face scarlet. And instead of saying *okay*, or just laughing, I shrank like a stable boy because I presumed I should have *known*.

I knew nothing, but I was aware. For all his trendiness—the Mr. Fish silk shirts and flying antique scarves—like a lot of aristos, he didn't know how to value himself now that the rules had changed. He put a high premium on being taken seriously as a photographer, and he was very gifted. But in those early days, due to his royal connections, he was known mainly for the titled family portraits of the queen, or Duke and Duchess of Windsor. He envied the spivs, the artistic cockney boys, but there was lineage to think of, history and tradition. In quiet moments, I saw the

Patrick Lichfield.

confusion, the fear of not doing the right thing, whatever that was. But it would have been unthinkable to bring it up.

He said he ought to marry me. Late one night, about two in the morning, he had a sudden urge to pot rabbits, a sport that required parking his jeep on the front lawn and shooting at strays caught in the car's headlights. The top was down, and he was standing on the driver's seat, rifle in hand. I was next to him, freezing as usual, feigning enthusiasm. "I should marry you, Fiona," he said. "You're perfect." I thought it might have been his sister Lady Elizabeth's idea, someone I liked and who'd always been kind to me. But I couldn't speak. I was flattered into silence. It didn't occur to me to ask myself if I wanted to get married, or if I could be happy with this man. And naturally, I could not ask: *Do you love me, then?* It was mentioned only once and, scared of being unsophisticated, I could never bring it up again.

Other women I knew did better with the upper-class boys. The American actress Barbara Parkins, of *Peyton Place* fame, would sometimes come for the weekend. Better dressed than any English girl, outfitted for the part in a Burberry cape and a hat stuck with partridge feathers, she radiated confidence. There were no cloying remarks about the beauty of the house, no tiptoeing around the priceless furniture. Bossy and enthusiastic, she addressed Patrick and his titled friends in a nanny-knows-best voice. And when she suggested a game of Scrabble or a bracing walk to the bridge and back, not only was she admired but obeyed. She also gave the impression that she didn't rely on men, that they weren't important for her survival. You might say this was my first example of feminism—a woman who took charge of her life.

Patrick was always complaining about money, particularly because the National Trust had taken over the house. "They won't even let me buy a new bloody *Hoover*," he would say, which hardly seemed credible. If I took the train up for the weekend, he'd ask me if I could "pick up a few things" on my way: music tapes, books, or some smoked salmon from Harrods. "I'll pay you back, darling," he said. But he never did. And I was broke at the time. I'd done a film the year before, but the money was already spent on clothes and rent, or to pay off my perpetual bank overdraft. Still, I couldn't bring myself to ask for the money. I remember toward the end, when things weren't going well, I bought him a John Lennon drawing for his birthday (thirty-three guineas). I had to borrow the money and badly wanted to keep it for myself, but I was still putting on a show. I thought, how could a penniless girl who was not doing so well as an actress possibly be interesting to him otherwise?

There were also blunders. One evening, we were at a restaurant in London, having dinner with Princess Anne. Naturally, I was on my best behavior. We were at the end of the meal, having coffee. Relieved to have come through unscathed, I reached across the table for the bowl of sugar. As I did, my espresso went flying—with such force that it sailed by Patrick and spilled over Her Royal Highness's cream silk blouse. It was hard to get past a faux pas like that.

A few weeks later, Patrick ended it. In true English fashion it was never said in so many words; it was the slow burn of rejection. He was extremely busy, or going away on a shoot. And after that, I was no longer invited to Shugborough Hall.

For my mother, the affair with Patrick was a ray of hope in an otherwise bleak landscape. After all, Patrick was an earl. Marriage was a possibility, if I didn't screw it up. I was in her good books again. She was also beginning to be impressed by my career—not the acting particularly, more by my semi-fame. I took full advantage of this. When I came home to visit after months on location, I would spend the weekend lording around the house, smoking, flipping through magazines, or lying on the drawing room sofa, waiting for her to bring me another cup of tea. "You must be tired after all that work," she would say. "Exhausted," I whined petulantly. "Well, I'm making grilled sole for dinner." "Great, but please don't *overcook* the vegetables." Cockily I would show off my new Saint Laurent skirt or a pair of Chelsea Cobbler boots—"Cost a bloody fortune"—only too aware that she still saved to buy her good clothes. I played the star, pleased to finally get her attention. When pictures of Patrick and me had appeared in the papers, his royal connections featured in the headline, it was a big thing for her. Now I had to tell her the bad news. I was dreading it. Part of me was, that is. The cynical side couldn't wait. I drove to South Hall for the weekend. Saturday went by. I postponed saying anything until Sunday morning. She was in the kitchen, sitting at the pine table, slicing runner beans for lunch. "Beans from the garden, dear!" "Great," I said. "Oh, by the way, just so you know, it's over with Patrick. He's going to marry someone else. A titled girl. Someone who isn't a *commoner*"—meaning, of course, an ordinary girl like myself. A few seconds passed. She looked up, her face disheveled, unable to speak for fear it might all unravel. Then she said softly, "A pity, dear," and went back to slicing the beans. I ran out. I tore upstairs to my bedroom, to my old room at the end of the corridor, with the chintz curtains, threw myself across the bed, and sobbed. I was heartbroken. For her, for myself. More for her because I still so desperately wanted to be the girl she could be proud of. I had failed. The inimitable glamour of British nobility. After all, I could have been a countess.

But I couldn't, of course. Things hadn't changed that much. I wasn't aristocrat material. Besides, I didn't know the first thing about what it meant to be married, or about intimacy in a relationship. I had no sense of myself as a woman; there was something lacking. I remember after one weekend at Paglesham being on the train to London. It was late and the carriage was empty, except for a couple a few seats away. Young, perhaps in their early twenties, they sat huddled together, under a pool of amber light. She was wearing a flowered silk headscarf and the man was speaking softly to her, holding her face in his hands as if he was scared it might break. And I thought to myself, *How do you become that?* It was as though I lived in a different world.

fifteen
France. May 2005.

Like a *Mad Max* movie, they arrive. Two white trucks swerve across the lawn, a motorcycle follows. Cars pull in. A French Smart car, then a beat-up Renault that parks under the chestnut trees, the driver (M. Bruni) unaware that he's crushed a bed of white irises.

But I'm ready for them. I am standing at the front door like a valiant chatelaine, greeting the troops who've come to commandeer her château. I have croissants, a thermos of coffee, plus a bottle of Terre d'Ocre, a pale rosé, bought for three and a half euros at the local supermarket. This is to be opened at the first sign of things going well; though, possibly it will be opened no matter what. I'm trying to be optimistic.

The Boudet team troops in. It's a family business, and M. Boudet Sr. comes with his two sons: Christopher, the elder, the more serious of the two, and David, a skinny, long-haired twenty-year-old, owner of the Suzuki motorbike and an angelic grin. With them is their uncle, also an enthusiastic smiler. I hand out cups of coffee. Fifteen minutes later, their big metal toolboxes and orange extension cords line the hallway. Then the drills start. The speed is incredible. They attack the walls like a gang of professionals tunneling through to a bank vault next door. Chunks of plaster and red brick fly; by the afternoon there are electrical wires snaking across the ceiling and disappearing into holes in the floor.

Over the next three days, more workmen arrive. A heavyset man appears in the back garden rising dramatically over the top of the incline on a mechanical digger. "Here?" he shouts, "or down there?" At Nicola's request he's come to carve out a trench for the septic tank, the *fosse septique*. Where would I like it? I have no idea. Forgetting there are no sewage pipes in the country, I wasn't aware I needed one. Another man, a Mr. Smout, is waiting inside to install equipment for British Sky television. Illegal in France, so I've been told, it seems every English resident living south of Calais has it. It supplies full English programs, feeds from CNN, MSNBC and, most important for my husband, American sports. Mr. Smout, an expat who lives in nearby Puycelsi, needs to secure a dish to the roof then run connecting cables inside the walls to the attic. "Please coordinate with M. Boudet Sr.," I say.

Elated by the activity, I float around the house in a kind of misty-eyed reverie. Progress. Incredible! That is, until I hear shouting from the roof. It's Mr. Smout telling M. Boudet Sr.—and not for the first time—that he needs his wires connected *immediately*. M. Boudet, who works fast but at his own pace, isn't thrilled about an Englishman telling him what he needs, and certainly not in that tone of voice. And Mr. Smout, a man from the British school of get-a-move-on-mate, has little patience for the working foibles of the French. "*Dee-pechez voo!*" he screams, with his retaliatory Anglo accent. "Bloody hurry up!"

I hear my name called—"*Madame Lew-ees*"—echoing across the trees. But I'm already heading for the magic circle, a place that will become, as difficulties arise (and they do), my sanctuary. A refuge from these men who I'm not sure I can control. Of course, I should have stayed in the house to referee the argument. But I'm trying to avoid M. Boudet after our run-in a few days ago about the radiator pipes.

The house has no chimneys. At some point they must have been knocked off the roof, and the flues are blocked, so I've decided to install central heating. "Where will you run the pipes?" I asked M. Boudet innocently. Considering how many channels had been opened up, I presumed they'd be hidden somewhere *inside* the walls. But then there was the question of the *tiron*. This is a thick iron pipe that runs across the floor upstairs and is secured on the outside of the house by pairs of crossed iron bars. Something I'd imagined could be easily removed, except that it's literally—and rather alarmingly, I learned—holding the entire house together. It lies below the windows, snaking through all three bedrooms, and M. Boudet saw no reason why it couldn't stay there. "I'll just lay the radiator pipes behind it," he said smiling. He has the small boy's smile—winning, unchallengeable. "You can get somebody to build a long wooden box to hide them both. Once it's painted, you'll hardly notice it."

I would notice it, of course. But I wasn't up for arguing this early in the game. Instead, I tried to politely show M. Boudet (aware that French artisans are sensitive about their work) how inconvenient it would be. Positioning myself in front of the tiron—allowing enough room for the so-called "wooden box"—I leaned across to open the window. This I could manage. But when I tried to reach the latch holding the shutter in place on the outside wall, it was impossible. "Impossible," I said. That is, without jumping *over* the imaginary box and onto the window sill— which I pantomimed but didn't do. Smiling now—or, rather, grinning like a waiter—I explained that I would need to close the shutters to sleep. Particularly because M. Gomes's low fiberboard ceilings meant that hanging curtains were now more or less *out of the question.* There was a silence. M. Boudet didn't attempt to reach the shutter latch himself; I was obviously taller. And not wanting to risk spoiling our camaraderie, or interrupt the momentum—the noise of hammering and drilling going on in the rest of the house—I left it at that. But he wasn't happy. He walked off muttering, shaking his head. So I would obviously have to bring it up again.

She looks as if she's stepped out of an old film noir, a *Rififi* girl with voluptuous dark hair, olive skin, and slanted green eyes that close seductively when she tilts her head. She reminds me of Mme. Guerin from my childhood at Hôtel Les Palmiers, except that she's thirty years younger and showing a lot more cleavage. Celine is Fabrice the gardener's sister-in-law. She has come to help, to earn a little extra money. Miraculously, she speaks English.

As soon as she arrives, the workmen perk up. The Boudets, busy all over the house, emerge one by one to deliver their self-conscious *"Bonjours."* Only M. Bruni doesn't appear. He is busy in the salon, on his knees, sanding the last stubborn bits of cement by hand. For self-motivation, there is the usual swearing. But when I bring Celine to meet him, he stands up, dusts himself off, and extends a hand. *"Bonjour, mademoiselle!"* he says, with an exaggerated bow. *"Comment allez vous?"* And then, naturally, confronted by such an attractive woman, he can't resist launching into one of his self-congratulatory rants: "Let me tell you, I've had fifty years in the business. *Fifty!* I'm a professional. I can do anything," he blurts out, as if the subject is of national importance. "In fact, I've built *entire* houses by myself. From the ground up! *Oui, j'ai construit les maisons entières!"*

Celine stares at him blankly. She then turns to me and asks in English, "What do you want me to do?" "Well, why don't you ask Bruni?" I suggest, trying to reestablish his credibility, at the same time wanting to hurry things along. Twelve noon, the great exodus for lunch, is coming up fast. Bruni pretends to be unfazed by her lack of interest. But his tone changes. "You can pull up the old nail heads sticking up around the edges," he says, waving a crow bar, "and be careful around the marble fireplace."

In fact, the fireplace has already been taken care of. After the incident upstairs, I've boxed it in with cardboard and written ATTENTION MARBRE! across it in giant capitals, aware that M. Gomes's boys will be starting down here soon.

I can tell Bruni is unnerved by Celine. "You missed a nail there," he barks in his superior tone, or, "Use a chisel in the corners." In reply, she raises one dark eyebrow, or makes a little moue, as if to say, "Men!" And every fifteen minutes, she walks outside for a cigarette break. She drains a bottle of mineral water then, leaning back across the hood of her little Citroën, exposing about a foot of bronzed stomach, she lights up. Bruni ignores her. He stays in the salon, head down. But a few days later when Celine goes out for a smoke and David Boudet joins her, Bruni can't take it anymore. When he sees them laughing together, flirting, Celine tossing her head with voluptuous abandon, he's had enough. "I can't work like this!" he shouts, downing his tools. "She does nothing. And she's crazy"—"*Elle est completement folle!*" Then, embarrassed, aware that his outrage is utterly transparent, he packs up and goes home.

In France flirting is considered an art form, a way of life. There is no negative connotation, and it's considered separate from sex. Well, maybe. A separate talent, perhaps. But I can't help comparing my own behavior to Celine's. I am careful with the workmen. I address them with the formal "*vous*" and call most of them "*monsieur.*" I hover between geniality and anxious remove—one minute the stern benefactress, the next a chummy shop steward—in order to get the job done. Anything too overt, I'm afraid, will look like I'm trading on my femininity, as if I'm *flirting*. I'm flattering myself, perhaps; I'm a lot older than Celine. But the idea that a mature, relatively soignée woman in France is not necessarily invisible after fifty seems true. So I'm careful. On the other hand, as La Rochefoucauld once remarked, *Making a point of not flirting is in itself a kind of come on.*

Take M. Gomes, for example. He has a habit when he sees me of adjusting his genitals—an in-motion, leg-raised tweak of the crotch with his forefinger to accompany the morning greeting. Then, when we discuss various plaster finishes, his eyes drift to my breasts. "*À la campagne?*" he asks. "Rough or smooth, *Ma-dame Loo-ees?*" The tone is boisterous, suggestive. But when I ignore this completely, he reverts to his courteous self. Perhaps in France it's complicity that counts. Flirting has to be a two-way street, and manners count. Nothing so démodé here as a shrieking No! which really means Yes!

Then there's M. Danton, the septic tank man. Out of the blue one morning, he sidles up to me as I am trudging across the front lawn. "I can't believe one of the workmen hasn't asked you out," he says breezily, "or at least tried to *hit* on you!" Despite his anticipatory grin, I reply thoughtfully, "No, I don't think any of them would dare"—*Ils n'oseraient pas.* He nods. Nothing more is said, and we go on to talk soberly about sump pumps and gravel.

Joseph is different. A local carpenter, recommended by a friend of Kathryn's, I have hired him to make the new door frames and baseboards. Young, probably in his twenties, slim and well-built, with dark, unruly hair, he skulks around the house mysteriously, if not perpetually annoyed. Apparently, he doesn't like being told what to do by a woman.

Not that I noticed this at first. The awkwardness, the jerky shoulders, and the shifty *voyou* grin I mistakenly read as shy enthusiasm. Particularly as he was the only person willing to help with the tiron. When he first arrived, he was very impressed by the house, respectful of its beauty. Coming up the stairs, he marveled at the high ceilings, the old tile floors. Then seeing the big iron pole snaking across the bedroom floor, he looked shocked. "*Ah, non—pas acceptable.*" Unacceptable, he said, "Not in a magnificent old house like this!" I then explained the problem of M. Boudet's radiator pipes, and without hesitating, Joseph offered to fix it himself—albeit for a negotiable fee. He would drill a channel along the length of the south wall, slide in the tiron, and M. Boudet could place his radiator pipes beside it. Grateful, I asked M. Boudet to come and look. "I have no intention of putting *my* pipes in with the tiron," he said abruptly, as if he'd been asked to share a room. He was willing, however, to chisel out a row of floor tiles running under the windows and put them there: "Bruni can relay the tiles when he's finished downstairs." Fine. We all agreed, and for once M. Boudet relinquished a winning smile. I couldn't tell if it was for me, a conciliatory nod, or for Joseph, the newcomer, or perhaps a dry comment on M. Bruni's professionalism, who two days before had left for a dentist appointment and not reappeared. Still, it was hard for me not to look triumphant. A small miracle in the world of building *esthétique*.

Joseph and I discussed money. He wanted to be paid in cash—*en liquide*. Most of the workers ask for cash to avoid paying taxes. Taxes are very high in France, a fact that I'm reminded of almost daily, particularly by M. Bruni, who fancies himself an expert on the inflated euro. "Well," I tell him, attempting some logic, "maybe taxes *have* to be high. To compensate for the country's thirty-hour working week *and* the lack of declared revenue. Which means that by the law of diminishing returns, they must get higher every year." An opinion that is met with a blank stare.

It takes Joseph four days to drill out the channel, hide the tiron, and adjust the iron cross supports on the outside walls. During the process, he's pleasant and professional, and I am politely grateful. He nods, green eyes darting away, his big hands poised on his hips. He's attractive. And he knows it. A few decades ago, I would have tried to seduce a man like this—flirting while pretending to do the opposite. In fact, with Joseph I go to even greater lengths to assume the correct tone. "Thank you so much. *Merci infiniment!*" I say, on the run. I'm like the seasoned flight attendant, percolating with noncommittal cheer.

But when it comes to settling up at the end of the week, he starts to look shifty again. He's not happy with his envelope of cash. "The work was far more complicated than I realized," he says. He wants a lot more.

We are upstairs in the empty corridor. It's after five, still hot, and Joseph is standing in front of me, blocking the stairs, one sinewy arm propped against the wall. "Don't you think I deserve it?" he says sulkily. He has an unnerving way of standing too close when he talks, and there's an almost comic flare to his nostrils. "No one else would have done it!" he whines. He's playing me, I realize, trying it on. And when he repeats, "Come on, you know *personne ne l'aurait fait!* the sulkiness is replaced by a burst of anger.

Of course, I should have seen it coming. The day before, I'd suggested reversing a door in the bathroom because it opened the wrong way. "How much would you charge for that?" I asked, trying as usual to calculate the cost against my dwindling budget. "Oh, you think it's easy to turn a door around?" he snapped back, dark eyebrows shooting up. "Just like that?" No, I replied carefully, slipping back into my *patronne* reserve. I simply wanted to know if it would be worth it. "But you never consider the *work* involved," he went on. *"Le travail!"* I was insulting his craft by even mentioning money. Then, with another toss of his head, he said I was also insulting him *personally* by treating him like the other workmen. "Rich *Americaine!*" he shouted, then stormed off.

Now he's back. I'm still pinned against the wall, and he's smirking, full of self-confidence. The would-be Don Juan with the day-old shirt and the pungent arms. But I'm attracted to him, and he knows it. Or I might be attracted to him. A man who's as alluring as he is repellant. I look away, suddenly feeling as vulnerable as I did as a girl, but not nearly as amusing. "And who works for these kinds of prices, anyway?" he goes on. *"Pour ce prix la?"* I remind him that we had an agreement. A set amount. "And yesterday you said it *wasn't* about the money," I add weakly. His head shoots back, as if I've tricked him again. More dark looks, and I feel like I'm in a scene from *The Roman Spring of Mrs. Stone,* every word laced with salacious sarcasm. "But I did it as a favor," he says. *"Pour vous, Fee-onna.* Because you wanted it done *so badly."*

The implication being that if I were a man he wouldn't have done it at all? Or that it would have been even more expensive? Either way, as a *woman* I'm not grateful enough. Or not woman enough to understand him. He calls me Fiona, as he has from the beginning. And not wanting to appear standoffish, I call him Joseph.

Am I complicit? Have I been flirting, flattered in my old age by his crafty grins? Have I in some coercive way led him on, and now humiliated him? With a final glare, he snatches the envelope of money, then bolts downstairs.

The mature response would be to fire him. But I can't. And he knows it. I've already said (too often) how grateful I am, aware of how difficult it is to find a good carpenter "this late in the season."

But I'm unnerved. I walk up the drive to the magic circle. It's cooler now, a sharp wind blowing through the chestnuts. Stop being so emotional, I tell myself. Calm down. Despite the chill, it's soothingly quiet here, and patches of mysterious white flowers have sprung up in the long grass. I lie down for a minute, Ophelia-like in the weeds, and close my eyes. Then I come back to the house to call my husband.

"Hold on," he says. He's on the set. I can hear the rumble of machinery, an assistant director shouting "Quiet!" He walks outside with the phone. The clunk of a heavy door. Traffic noise. "I can easily call you back," I say. I'm not sure why I'm calling anyway. I'm in an odd mood.

"No, it's fine," he says. But he sounds frustrated. He tells me it's been a bad day. There have been arguments with the financiers. Yesterday, a certain sum that was supposed to have been put in escrow wasn't there. He threatened to shut down the movie. Brian De Palma was on his way to the airport. Today the money has miraculously reappeared. "I called their bluff."

"You're a genius."

"Hardly, but thanks."

"Well, you are." And saying it, I feel better. I want to remind myself how clever he is. "Besides, your mother said so. Do you remember? On your fiftieth birthday?"

His fiftieth. I'd made a video as a surprise, running around L.A. to interview his old friends, the agents and actors, and finally his parents. I sat them on the sofa in our living room, then asked his mother what she remembered most about her son. His mother—smiling, confident—looked directly at the camera and without a trace of irony sweetly said, "As soon as he was born, I knew he was a genius."

"Remember?"

"Yes, that was funny. I did get As at school, but if I'd got Bs she would have thought *that* was the best!"

"Must be nice. Better than being told you'll probably amount to nothing."

"Ah, the English curse! Are you still blaming your parents?" He's mocking me, as usual.

"No. I'm saying that the English revel in failure. They understand it. Don't get your hopes up, dear!"

"That's why you came to America."

True. That's why I came. That's why I eventually married a man who tells me what's what. Who sets me straight. But I don't want that from him now. I don't know what I want. I feel jumpy. I miss him. I also love being on my own in France. I'm full of contradictions.

"*Contra-diction.*"

"What?"

"It's French for 'contradiction.' It's the same word, just said with an accent. In fact, every word in English that ends in i-o-n is the same in French. Isn't that interesting?"

"I don't speak the language, in case you've forgotten."

"But you could learn."

To be fair, he had tried. He'd sat down with the Pimsleur tapes for a month but only picked up enough to order a glass of wine with confidence, or a meal, and when a waiter came back at him with a flurry of incomprehensible words, he'd given up: "I just can't do it!" It infuriated him.

This, of course, is a big part of the problem—not speaking French. Perhaps I'm only realizing it now. He's a raconteur, and his cleverness with words is the embodiment of who he is. He's also competitive. He likes to outtalk me with his stories, and not being able to express himself in France, he feels he loses his identity. Even so, I go on, trying to interest him.

"Another odd thing," I say. "Did you know that the French call condoms *capotes Anglaises,* and the English call them French letters. No wonder the countries never got along!"

Silence on his end. I hear a truck starting up and someone calling his name. "Look," he says, "I've got to go. I'll call you later."

sixteen
Paris 1970.

In the end, reading and writing saved me. That and going back to France. At a party in Paris, I met a man who changed my life. I was twenty-four, Philippe a few years younger. A writer, a self-confessed prodigy, at sixteen he had cowritten an erotic book called *Les Violons, Encore les Violons,* and for a while became a minor celebrity. However, he hadn't done much since and was tortured by the fact, albeit in his own superior way. A flamboyant dresser, he liked to stroll along Boulevard St. Germain in a long black jacket and a cream silk shirt, the sleeves flowing from the cuffs. His hair was groomed to a dark sheen and fell loosely to his shoulders (a work of art compared to mine), and he often walked with a silver-topped cane. He was delicately mannered, though not in an effeminate way. It was Byron without the club foot.

He was also aware of his narcissism, thoroughly amused by it. At the same time, he was fascinated by me. He couldn't believe I had these poetic leanings but had read absolutely nothing. So he introduced me to books. It was a revelation. Lying across his unmade bed in the Rue du Bac, he taught me to read Nietzsche, Faulkner, Camus, and Céline. We went to WHSmith on the Rue de Rivoli to buy the paperbacks in English. *Céline!* The thrill I felt when I saw the words, *Once one's in it, one's in it up to the neck.* . . . Who'd ever imagined writing like that? So I forgave the drugs and the mess in his flat: the awful reek of cigarettes, the empty wine bottles and dirty bedsheets. He had two claustrophobic rooms in the eaves of an old *hôtel particulier*, what had once been the maid's quarters. There was no kitchen and no real bathroom, just a sink and a toilet inside a cupboard with a portable bidet, a little tin thing you pulled out on wheels. But there were plenty of books. He had a full set, the parchment-pink Gallimard editions crammed to the ceiling. It was the genuine artist's lair, everything faded and worn from years of sitting around and thinking. But there wasn't much writing. Occasionally, I'd wake up in the middle of the night and find him at his desk, bent over a notebook, its pages covered with his minute, indecipherable scrawl. The next day they'd be torn out and thrown away. "I wanted to *read* them," I'd say. "I know," he'd reply, gazing at me with his huge brown eyes. "That's why."

I was very impressed by him, and by myself, living the bohemian life, learning about literature. I was amazed to discover that fictional characters had similar feelings to mine—more eloquently defined, of course, but there they were, put into words. When I read *The Wild Palms* for the first time, I was very moved, not only by the beauty of Faulkner's long sentences but also by the emotions he described. When he refers to the "mausoleum of love" and when, for instance, Charlotte says to Wilbourne: "Listen: it's got to be all honeymoon, always. Forever and ever, until one of us dies. It can't be anything else. Either heaven or hell."

Not that I could honestly equate those feelings to my relationship with Philippe, but I wanted to. I was still wrapped up in the idea of love, the agony and the drama, convinced that happiness could only come from being loved by a man. A writer—and, in Philippe's case, a supreme egotist. "The perfect woman is a higher type of human than the perfect man, and also something much more rare," he'd say, quoting from his tattered copy of *Thus Spake Zarathustra*.

"Am I the perfect woman?"

"We'll see." And with that he'd sling me across the mattress, a creaky

two inches of hard springs, quickly ripping off his clothes—all the better
to watch me take off mine while he lit a joint. His body was slender,
his skin shockingly white. Lying there with his hair spread romantically
across the pillow, he looked almost too delicate to be touched. More
like an exotic girl. And he always wanted me on top. He wanted me
to adore him as he adored me. He commanded me to go faster, slower.
And I did. In the pigeon-sized room, the air swirling with hash smoke,
our hair tangled together, it was almost like screwing myself. But I was
starting to loosen up. When he wanted to bury his face in my crotch,
or do *soixante-neuf,* I laughed. He was offended. *"Pourquoi tu ris?"* Well,
English men never did that, I said. At least no one had ever asked me to
do it. In my world, the blow job was still a novel idea.

Most mornings we got up late and walked to Café Flore. Philippe's favorite booth was at the back, the one Simone de Beauvoir had occupied,
he assured me, while penning her notes to Sartre. Breakfast consisted
of cafés serrés, buttered tartines, and often a cognac to deal with the
hangovers. We sat for hours, Philippe bent over *Le Monde,* one elbow
propped on the table, his pale nicotine-tipped fingers waving a cigarette, and me next to him holding a well-thumbed copy of *Journey to
the End of the Night,* many of its pages heavily underlined. It was all
very self-consciously artistic. Other writers and artists would come in:
screenwriter Paul Gégauff; Daniel Pommerol, the sculptor; Dennis
Berry, an American director who was then married to Jean Seberg; and
Maria Schneider (before her Brando debut). Stoned, she would traipse
in, overtly sexual in last night's dress, and throw herself exhausted across
the banquette. Then, raising her big panda eyes (complete with dark circles), she would make a big show of trying to seduce us both. Philippe
always encouraged her.

   We went out every night. To La Coupole, still authentic then, to
meet Danny and his American friends. Or we went to Lipp, where the
waiters knew him and, as a writer, he was treated with the reverence he
thought he deserved. He had no money. I think he got a small allowance

from his parents, and I never had much, either. I couldn't save a penny. But he didn't believe it. He thought I was holding out on him. I remember a particularly bad evening. We were sitting in one of Lipp's coveted booths to the right of the entrance. I'd ordered the *raie aux beurre noir* and a *baba au rhum*, and as usual and we were both quite drunk. When the bill came, Philippe wanted me to get out my wallet. "I've only got a 100-franc note left," I said. "My last," which was true *"Oh, merde, tu es radin,"* he said, looking pouty and adjusting his ascot. "What?" I didn't know what *radin* meant. "Cheap. You are being so *cheap!"* (In his bad English, he pronounced it *sheep*.) He kept nudging me to slide the money under the table, so as not to look radin himself in front of the waiters. "Give it to me," he demanded. "No," I shouted back. He made a big fuss. Eventually, the maître d' came over and we had to leave. Out in the street, arguments like this could go on forever. Walking ahead, he'd glare back at me. "Don't you know that it's customary in France to *support* the artist?"

"What artist?" I'd say. Why don't you *do something* instead of lying around your apartment all day staring at the ceiling."

"You don't understand how difficult it is."

"Well, how could I? You make doing nothing *look so easy!"*

"Salope!"

At this point, I would back down because he looked so hurt. Which merely encouraged him to berate me for my insensitivity and cheapness all the way to the Rue du Bac.

But his sense of entitlement was a bit of a game; by asserting himself, then going cold on me, he could find out if I really loved him. For all his brooding and airy ways, if I threatened to go back to London, he broke down and cried. He was sorry. I was an angel. Then he'd get hold of some money to buy me a present: a book, or a vintage scarf from the flea market. Even so, he was also cultivating a dark side.

At that time there was a group of men in Paris nicknamed *les méchants*—the villains, the wicked ones. They had money, they were educated. Some were successful writers, painters, and directors, such as Frédéric Pardo and Philippe le Roi. Preening *demi-mondaines* who dressed in the uniform black and hung out at Regine's or Castel, and who were notoriously sadistic with women. They admired Philippe, and he badly wanted to be admired. So occasionally we went to these clubs to meet them after dinner. Flattered to be included, he immediately took on their cynical tone. *"Ah, mes vieux amis,"* he'd begin. Sitting on a bentwood chair, his pale, faun-like face tilted back, he then launched into an explanation of why Nietzsche hated women, or a provocative defense of Céline's anti-Semitism.

But thinking yourself a genius or, in his case, a genius who is failing, requires constant stimulus. With no real work or purpose, his life needed to be more decadent, more intense. He started taking heroin, and at some point I took it too. Not that I liked it much—snorting up a line on the back of a tin tray, then lying back in the foul-smelling bedroom, floating in the void, pretending to mine the inner depths. Did the world seem a less-threatening place? Yes. For about an hour. Then the *lack* of worry set off alarms. With no distraction it was all distraction, and the emptiness was filled with thoughts of inadequacy or sheer terror. Still, I was willing to try anything then, to see how far I could go. I had no standards for myself—or perhaps I did, because after a few weeks, when the heroin affected my liver and I couldn't stop vomiting, I gave it up. The sickness saved me, that and my old dread of completely *letting go.* Despite my need to escape, apparently I had no desire to leave the planet. And after that, if Philippe so much as opened one of his little glassine envelopes, I ran to the toilet and threw up.

It was all exhausting. On the pretext of skipping out for a pack of Gitanes, I'd walk to the Musée Rodin on the Rue de Varenne. To stand in those airy rooms with the creaking parquet floors, the afternoon light slanting across the exquisite sculptures, was a huge relief. Or I would wander up the Rue du Bac to Deyrolle to gaze at the stuffed gazelles and polar bears. Paris was a big part of the romance. I wanted to belong to the city. In the Luxembourg Gardens, I'd sit on one of the little back-breaking chairs, trying to digest Gide. Or I'd traipse around Galeries Lafayette for hours just to buy a pair of fishnet stockings. Then every few weeks, I went back to London. And not only because I had to find a job. I was also seeing someone there—a blond, cheery English actor who was the opposite of Philippe (no subtext). I didn't feel guilty about this dual existence. In fact, when I'd recovered, when I felt safe and content, if slightly bored, I would dream up an excuse (a sudden modeling job) and get on a plane back to Paris for more.

As if I needed to keep myself in permanent suspense.

I loved France. I loved the language. With Michel, I'd learned a few rudimentary sentences, but with Philippe I learned a lot more. From the beginning, he wanted to teach me every vulgar sexual expression he knew. Things that to this day I can't repeat in public. It turned him on. "*Oh, encore!*" he'd shout. "Tell me again—*Je veux te tailler une pipe, gros cochon!*" and by then he'd be shaking with laughter, cigarette ash raining over the sheets. I had no idea what I was saying. But eventually, when we progressed to normal topics, some of it sunk in, and after six months, I was speaking French fluently. It just rolled out. It was shockingly liberating. During those long, drug-addled nights, when I'd listen to him quote from Les Lumières or Huysmans, or expound on the romantic tragedy of Rimbaud (whose untimely death his premier disciple, Philippe, would no doubt soon be emulating), or when we argued, I didn't feel the need to be defensive, or polite. I could say things without betraying my English self because French words didn't *resonate* for me in the same way. If I admitted I was confused or jealous or that I loved him (*"Je t'adore"*—always easier to say than the sober British version), or that I *didn't* love him anymore, that I was sick of it all, it was as if I were talking about someone else. And in a way, I was. My fear of giving offense was behind me. Suddenly I could throw up my hands and shout *"Tu m'emmerde! Va te faire enculer!"*—Go fuck yourself!—feeling utterly released. It was a powerful thing.

One night we were invited to dinner at Paul Gégauff's. A screenwriter who'd collaborated with Claude Chabrol on many movies, such as *Les Biches* and *Les Cousins,* he lived in a country farmhouse outside Paris with his charming—though, I suspected, long-suffering—wife, Danielle. He was noisy, garrulous. But when she spoke, she glanced too often at her husband, her smile fading. We sat at a round table with five or six other guests. There was *blanquette de veau,* plenty of red wine, and at some point talk of a friend's bad love affair. So far I'd said nothing. Then one of the men asked me what I thought about love. Ah, well— *chacqu'un à son cauchemar,* I replied—to each his own nightmare—which was greeted with peals of laughter. Then Gégauff remarked: *"Ah la petite Anglaise. Très drôle! Tres intelligent!"*

Naturally, I was happy to be thought of as droll or intelligent in any language. And being able to make a joke in French felt like a great leap forward. Though you might say it allowed me to remove myself even further from reality.

Not having enough money to live was a problem. I had to find work. Coming back from Paris, I'd find letters from my bank manager about my overdraft: *Dear Miss Maxwell Lewis* (as I was then called), *Perhaps you might inform us if funds are coming from another source.* There was no other source. So I would have to go to tea with Mr. Newcome in his wood-paneled office at Coutts—he in his tailcoat, I dressed in some provocative but financially affirming low-cut dress, suitable for a rising star. "I'm up for several jobs," I'd say, listing a few auditions. And he'd smile reassuringly and say, "Yes, yes, the precarious world of filmmaking," then advance me another fifty pounds. This would immediately be exchanged for several articles of clothing and a plane ticket. (In those days flying from London to Paris cost about fourteen pounds, a pair of shoes six pounds.)

But I could never concentrate on men *and* my career. Men always won. Acting was harder. And I only remember going for one audition during that time, arranged by Olga Horstig.

A well-know agent in Paris, Olga was famous for representing Brigitte Bardot, among others, and I'd been introduced to her by Roger

Vadim. She was a tough old bird. At our first meeting, casting her cold eye over me, she remarked to Vadim, somewhat disparagingly, "You think you can *do something* with her?"

Nevertheless, she became my French agent, and one afternoon she set up an interview with Darryl Zanuck. Still the legendary producer, having spent years running Twentieth Century Fox, he was now in residence at the George V hotel. I have no memory of the film he was casting, or even if there was a film. But one afternoon, armed with my box of photographs and my résumé, I arrived at his penthouse suite. Zanuck himself answered the door. He was wearing a silk dressing gown. Open at the front, he was naked underneath and casually holding his penis between his first two fingers, as if it were a lit cigar. "Have you ever seen anything so big?" he asked, which I instinctively knew wasn't a question. But I was floored. A wave of Englishness rose up. I couldn't utter a word. In French, I could have leveled him. Instead, I turned and headed for the elevator. "Hey, come back," he shouted. "C'mon, I was just kidding. It was a joke." So I went back in the suite and sat on the sofa. What I thought would happen, I don't know. But after five minutes of talking about my career, which he listened to with a kind of bemused indifference, he asked if I'd like to sleep with his girlfriend. When I declined, he was furious. There was a wooden box on the coffee table. He took out a few thousand francs and tossed them in front of me. "No," I said firmly, my manners still intact. In fact, I might have actually thanked him—*No, thank you very much; I don't need any money right now!*—before I walked out. As I headed for the door, he shouted, "You will *never* work in Hollywood!" Well, he was wrong about that. The girlfriend in question I'd seen only briefly. On the pretext of getting a cigarette, she had swanned across the room—a young, elegantly dressed Grace Kelly type, wearing gray flannel slacks and a white cashmere sweater.

Afterward, I hurried down the Champs-Élysées, amused by my squeamishness. How did that work? I wondered. Was it his idea or hers? And what could a beautiful girl like that possibly be doing there? Money couldn't be that important, I thought—a naive deduction based on her air of sophistication.

Philippe was annoyed. "*Ah non! Merde!* You should have taken the money."

"Oh, you think I should have fucked them both?" I was insulted. Feigning boredom, laughing, he said, "Why not?" He was practicing being a méchant.

seventeen

Château de la Vinouse.

I am exhausted. I am on my hands and knees in the bedroom, scrubbing. I've decided to try to remove the red paint from the tiles myself. In fact, I'm determined to do it because I've been told repeatedly that it can't be done. Perhaps I'm more like my mother than I think. Luckily, Celine is helping.

I asked Raymond in the shop for advice, and he suggested trying St Marc, an old-fashioned cleaning powder made from soda crystals, and strong enough to strip the skin off your hands. We have rubber gloves, scouring pads, three buckets lined up—one for the paint, two to rinse—and a pile of cut-up T-shirts. The paint is like glue, and each tile takes about five minutes of scrubbing and rinsing. Some have to be done twice. It's backbreaking work but rewarding. Not only to see the tiles emerge in their original soft pink but also because David and his father, Boudet Sr., walk in regularly to have a look. *"Ah, oui! Ça c'est du travail!"* The patronne, her face smeared with red, her hands raw, is working as hard, if not harder, than they are (no lunch break). Instead of losing their respect, I have gained it. And Celine, her dark hair sweeping the floor, has the strength of a stevedore. We have music to spur us on. Jean Sablon singing "Si Tu M'aimes," my preferred chanson of the week. As his soft, velvety voice wafts through the house it seems to render our audience, as well as us, slightly giddy. But this could be due to the heat. It's suddenly extremely hot. There is no running water upstairs, and many trips are required down the stairs to fill the buckets from the garden tap. It's draining. My fingers are numb. We have three rooms to go; I've already lost weight. And I can never remember to get to the shops to buy food.

So Celine stops at Raymond's for me in the morning to pick up a baguette and some sliced ham. I live on sandwiches. I've abandoned my gluten-free diet. I can happily eat my way through an entire loaf of bread and several pains au chocolat. When I down three glasses of rosé I don't break into hives. I've also abandoned the vitamins, the herbs, and the probiotics. They stay in their plastic bags, lined up in Kathryn's kitchen, and nothing happens. I don't keel over. In fact, I have more energy. A miracle. Could it be that simple? The physical exertion has somehow cured my neurosis? I have purged myself with hard work. And when I'm not scrubbing all day, I leave Celine to carry on while I make a run to the Zone Industriel. The ZI, as it's called. This is a depressing wasteland of corrugated hangars and cement blocks in the northern part of Montauban. Stretches of asphalt dotted with more paint, air-conditioning, and bathroom showrooms than one medium-sized French city would seem to require. Modern France. It's my least favorite destination, the antithesis of life in the countryside; but I need what they have, if in fact they have it.

I've already ordered taps, shower heads, and a farmhouse *evier* (a deep kitchen sink), and bought crates of white tiles for the bathrooms. Now I'm driving around trying to find some matching beveled edges, the finishing bits to go around a shower stall. For some reason, the French see no practical need to manufacture decorative pieces that run along or around a corner of anything in a bathroom, particularly when two ordinary pieces of tile stuck together at right angles will do. But after searching several showrooms, I find some at the more upscale Cornil. Samples of edging stuck to a demonstration board. "Yes," says a salesman, "I can get these *lentils* for you." He will order them from the company in Germany. Of course, it might take a few weeks, he adds—*chère madame*—"because it's almost May." At first I don't see the significance. May?

I am back at the house. It's Friday afternoon and the general exodus begins. In gratitude for a good week's work, I'm handing out bottles of Terre d'Ocre, the cheap pink rosé that looks more expensive. The Boudet family, M. Gomes, and M. Bruni all shout good-bye from the front door. *"Bon weekend,"* they say. "See you on Wednesday"—*À Mercredi!*

I already feel the familiar wave of Friday afternoon panic: the fear that no one will show up on Monday. But Wednesday?

"Mercredi?" I ask again, thinking I must have misheard.

Yes, says David Boudet, snapping his toolboxes shut, pulling out extension cords. "Next Tuesday is the first of May, a holiday. We're taking off Monday too. What's called *le pont"*—the bridge. Perfectly normal, he assures me, not only for them but for most of working France.

I find out there are three saint's days in May, or *jours fériés.* They fall coincidentally, or not so coincidentally, either on a Thursday or a Tuesday, allowing for their respective ponts (Friday or Monday), which leaves three working days a week. Shops are closed, or open only in the mornings. Some owners might string a few ponts together and leave for an extended vacation.

What I'm trying to learn is patience. Not my strong suit. But this is France, and the French, as M. Bruni is only too happy to remind me, when he does show up, *work to live,* not the other way around. Besides, I tell myself, there are still ten weeks left until August.

A lazy weekend. I sleep. I eat. I make lists, and lists of lists. On Monday morning, I go to the house and scrub more tiles. That evening at Kathryn's, my husband calls from Sofia. From the background voices, the tinkling Muzak, I can tell he's in the hotel Cigar Bar. Things are going better and he's having a martini to celebrate, he says. "Or maybe I'm having a martini anyway!" He's in a good mood, and he wants to know if I've spoken to the pool company. When are they coming? I'm in the kitchen, standing over the sink, soaking my red-stained hands in a mixture of hot water and paint thinner, Kathryn's portable phone jammed under my chin. When I tell him that Bainluxe has sent an estimate and that somehow the price seems to have jumped a few thousand, we launch into a familiar conversation about money. *How much is this all costing?* A math whiz, he runs through the figures, quickly going from dollars to euros and back again. At the current exchange rate, he wonders what the house will be worth when it's finished. If we can "get out." If some enterprising English or German might buy it. "Because no American in his right mind would *travel that far!*"

This is well-worn territory. Arguing is futile. Besides, my back is aching from the scrubbing. As we continue the hypothetical discussion about profit and loss, as he flirts with the notion of owning a château and at the same time panics at the idea of actually having to *go there,* I take the phone upstairs. With one hand I run a bath and get undressed. Still talking, I climb in. I relax for a moment; I manage to shave my legs (for whom? I wonder). Finally, still holding the phone, I sink back. Having failed to sell him on France as a desirable vacation spot for more than a two-week stay, I find myself defending the whole of Europe. "It's only a short plane ride to other countries," I say. "To Madrid, or to North Africa. We could travel. We could take the train and go to Rome."

"I've been to Rome," he says. "I've seen it."

He'd been there. As an experience it was finished. He loves to talk like this. Yes, he saw it, but what exactly did he see? Was he in a state of mind to connect to anything pleasurable? "That's the problem. Working all day, e-mailing, texting," I say, "you don't allow yourself to notice things, or to be inconveniently distracted by them."

"Oh. Is this your not-so-subtle way of saying I can't relax?"

"No. I get it. I'm being sympathetic."

Was I? Part of being married for a long time was knowing how far to go in the bitchy department. "It's the modern dilemma. Having to be constantly stimulated by action. When chaos feels better than calm."

That sounded a bit glib, but I'm thinking that if strolling around Piazza Navona didn't do it for him, then landing in the middle of the French countryside is going to feel as if his life is officially over.

Suddenly the phone slips. I manage to jerk myself upright, water cascading onto the floor.

"You're still in the bath?"

"Yes. I've been scrubbing tiles all day. I'm exhausted."

"Well, why can't you get other people to do that for you, at your age?"

"Other people?"

"Yes. Hire someone."

"Who would that be?" I ask, laughing. "As you've probably noticed, France is not next to Mexico. There's no cheap labor here."

"Offer them double."

"It doesn't work like that. They're artists, or say they are. As it is, France is taking a five-day vacation. I'll be lucky if anybody shows up next week. What can I do? They take advantage of me because I'm a woman."

"Oh, the woman thing again!"

I hate his voice, the supercilious tone. "You have no idea how hard this is."

"Well, you *wanted* a house in France!"

"I know. I know!" I hear myself shouting. My head hurts, I slide down in the warm water again. "Look, I'll call you later," I say, then hang up.

But I don't call him later. Later, I'm wrapped in a towel, lying on Kathryn's bed. How selfishly happy I feel to be alone at the end of the day. The air is still; the windows are open. Pink shadows move across the walls, the last rays of the sun. I have a pile of books next to me on the table: Saint-Simon's diaries, Rousseau's *Confessions,* Raymond Radiguet's *Le Bal du Comte D'Orgel*—books that I've read, and reread, and that I like to think represent some part of my self. Or, at the very least, my salvation. I need them to perpetuate the fantasy of my life in France—a France that, naturally, no longer exists but one that *in essence* I'm determined to create. Of course, in L.A. I'm also alone in a room with books, fictionalizing a more interesting world. But there I'm working. Or I convince myself I'm working, paralyzed most of the time by the idea of maintaining a career. I write to survive while not doing a very good job of either. My husband gets up at six to work on a script or a book, and he's done by nine. I stay in my office all day, laboring obsessively, correcting my corrections, filling myself up with words. Why do I go on? To find out how I feel? To uncover the truth? Or is it a hedge against a more basic fear: that without this self-imposed structure, this *busyness*, my life wouldn't be worth much at all?

Here, I'm prepared to confront the worst of my fears. *So I tell myself.* Stretched out on the bed, I feel weightless, as though I'm floating upward on currents of hot air. Who am I? What am I worth? What is success? And how do you measure happiness? What exactly do we mean when we say we want to be valued and comforted and *adored?* Are we demanding too much? Is insecurity a form of narcissism? Yes. You can't hang on to a man like a lifeboat. *Dare to be great*, as my husband would say. Well, I'm trying. Perhaps building this house will replace my sense of non-achievement. Perhaps I'll finally calm down, get the big picture, and become the woman I want to be.

Over the weekend, I e-mail him a photograph of a toilet. Not just any toilet, but the one M. Boudet has installed in the master bathroom, the first flushing water closet.

He calls as soon as he gets it.

"Well," he says, "I'll never be able to pee in it."

"Why not?"

"Because the room is too big. It would be like peeing in the middle of someone's living room."

I laugh. Though it occurs to me that I might have put it there on purpose. So he'd have to pee somewhere else.

eighteen
Marrakech—London.

Everything with Philippe turned out to be either dramatic or dangerous. And things got worse in Marrakech.

He'd arranged to rent a small house owned by an American antiques dealer. From the airport we went to pick up the keys at the old Café Glacier. The café was the place to meet, leave luggage or messages, or have a crème de menthe while you waited. A deep, dark room with high walls and ceiling fans whirring, it was empty when we arrived. At least it looked that way. Only when I went back to find a bathroom did I see them. A row of dark-faced Bedouin tribesmen, sitting in the shadows, lined up against the wall. They didn't move, just eyed me silently, and except for a flutter of a white robe or a flash of silver as one of their cutlasses caught the light, I would never have known they were there. Marrakech seemed very exotic, very Graham Greene–ish to me—the smells, the colors, the mud buildings, all of it soaked in a terra-cotta glow. I didn't know Africa then, but it was magical. And scorching hot.

Our *skiffa* was a ten-minute walk from the café, through the Medina—a maze of winding streets, most of them too narrow for a car to pass. In places the mud walls rose to twenty feet, and in the pitch-black nights it was easy to get lost. The house had no number, just an anonymous blue door opening into a small courtyard. Inside there was a small fountain, a circle of cracked Zellige tiles, and beyond that a few shabby rooms that had been tarted up recently. Each one was painted in either electric blue or lurid pink, and with matching pillows thrown across the floor the place had a kind of poovy-palacio feel to it. Of seedy romance. But the house was cheap, all I could afford. And I didn't mind paying anymore; it gave me a sense of superiority, as money often does.

Marrakech was supposed to be a break from our sybaritic life in Paris—an ironic choice, as it was obviously the place to buy cheap drugs. We found a boy the first day. Angelic, no more than ten, he strolled the back alleys, his hash cakes laid out on the lid of an old cardboard box. A plastic strap was attached to the tray, and with it strung around his neck he looked like a cigarette girl from the 1940s. We bought cakes every morning then, suitably loaded, went forth.

Philippe knew people in Marrakech; they were part of his exaggerated playboy past. I was taken to meet a rich Parisienne, a woman of a certain age, a friend of Yves Saint Laurent, who owned a grand villa in the Palmeraie. She sat us by the pool for lunch. *"Bonjour, madame. Enchanté,"* I said, with an exaggerated smile. But she wasn't having it. Though still quite beautiful, this woman was bristling under her turquoise caftan, and from her disdainful glances at me—braless in a flimsy embroidered peasant blouse, and with my electric hair—I could tell she and Philippe had once been lovers. He wanted me to see this, or for her to see me. I didn't know which. We were getting to that stage in the relationship where the drama no longer worked so well, and I'd withdrawn from him—imperceptibly, I thought, but he sensed it. In Paris, before we left, he'd been mournful and romantic: "You don't love me anymore"—*Tu ne m'aimes plus,* he said, with all the solemnity of a choirboy. Now he'd resumed his imperial air. At the skiffa, he grumbled because it took thirty minutes for the stream of dirty brown water to fill the tub: "We should have rented something more expensive!" Putting on his long-tailed shirt and black *flaneur* trousers, he'd give me one of his moody stares and say, "And I need a cup of mint tea, *chéri*!"

I ignored him and stayed in bed.

But he wanted to impress me. He took me to the famous Mamounia hotel. "It's magnificent, you'll see," he said, as we sped over in a *petit taxi*. And it was: the exotic art deco lobby, the long terrace with tables covered in stiff white cloths, the lush 200-year-old gardens. "Everyone stayed here—*tout le monde*—Churchill, Roosevelt, Rita Hayworth. Hitchcock made a film here . . ." We ordered martinis and watched the sun go down, pale purple shadows rippling across the Atlas Mountains.

We met another friend of his: a Colonel Baba. A charming, soft-spoken man with a clipped David Niven mustache and manners to match. "He commanded the Moroccan army during the border war with Sidi Ifni, you know," said Philippe airily, fanning himself with his napkin. We clinked glasses and I smiled as if I knew what that meant. After that Colonel Baba insisted on showing us the sights. We visited the Saadian Tombs, normally closed to non-Muslims. He took us in his air-conditioned Mercedes to have tea with one of the king's sons—not to the palace but to a *riad* in town. Gold chairs were lined up in the living room, baronial thrones pushed against the walls so that we sat facing each other like patients in a dentist's waiting room. I was the only woman there. Exhibit A: the loose-moraled Westerner. Or perhaps I was being offered up as a swinging London souvenir. Five other men were in attendance, besides the prince, all in spotless white robes, their Gucci loafers poking out from below the hems. The prince talked about his stables—suddenly Philippe seemed to know a lot about horse racing—while servants scuttled in and out, bringing tea, sweetmeats, and hand-rolled hash cigarettes. They were presented in little boxes, like Winstons, impeccably wrapped in gold foil.

"So how do you *know* all these people?" I asked afterward. I was incredibly impressed but didn't want to let on. "Oh, chéri, for years," he'd say, giving nothing away.

A lot of my fascination with Philippe, apart from the narcissistic cleverness, was the way he took everything in his stride. He would march forth, his shirt billowing behind him, his scuffed Chelsea boots kicking up the orange dust. "We're going to the souk. I know all the good places—" and off we'd go, down into the maze of rush-roofed lanes to find the best seller for babouches, kohl, dried rose buds, to get his tattered copy of *Iluminations* rebound in yellow leather, or to buy amber beads as big as ping-pong balls. I would rather have explored the warren of little shops by myself, but he forbade it. *"C'est dangereux, chéri!"* A few years before, an English girl on her own had been stoned to death for wearing a miniskirt, he claimed. "Oh, come on! Ha ha!" I didn't believe him. I was too enchanted by everything.

And when we went to the Place Jemaa el Fna that night, I was completely blown away. "This is where it's at," he announced. And he was right. It was like a mirage. We arrived before dusk, just as the sky was turning a deep eerie pink, and at that precise moment they appeared: the jugglers and the acrobats, the snake charmers and the monkey men. After that came the fire-eaters, the public scribes waving their big black umbrellas, the storytellers and the young transvestites—the dancing boys who pranced around bare-chested beating little tambourines. It was like a scene from *The Arabian Nights*. "Wow!" I kept saying like a demento, as Philippe dragged me through the crowd. People were pouring in from the side streets by now and the square had turned into a sea of flapping djellabas and shuffling feet. You couldn't move and the noise was incredible—throbbing drum rattles and rattatoos and high-pitched flutes.

When the sky eventually turned blue-black, strings of naked lightbulbs popped on across the top of food stands. There were warnings posted about the health hazards, but we didn't care. "Tourist stuff," said Philippe. We sat on a bench, surrounded by the din of whistles, and cymbals clashing, and ate plates of mutton and couscous served from greasy vats. Despite the noise, I felt sublimely calm and as far removed from normal life as I'd ever been. Which, of course, was the whole point.

But the euphoria didn't last.

. . .

I liked the quiet mornings when Philippe slept late. I would make myself a glass of mint tea, then go out to get the bread from a little bakery I'd discovered a few lanes away. Because the passageways looked so similar, I'd memorized the route: two lefts, one right, then left again under an archway, just past Herborista Rubio, the little herb shop. These shops were no bigger than shower stalls—narrow openings in the mud walls: a fruit and soda pop stand or a butcher shop with a few bloody goat heads strung up, crawling with flies.

But one day, I didn't go out until the late afternoon. It was still hot, but the shadows were already creeping down the lanes. I found my way to the bakery, but coming back I must have taken a wrong turn because I couldn't find the archway. I kept on walking and eventually turned into a wider mud street but stopped when I saw the warning sign: DEFENDU A NON MUSLIMS—Forbidden for Non Muslims. I had wandered into a different part of the Medina—different but looking the same: the same sandy lanes, the same wrinkled foreheads peering from the hole-in-the-wall shops, the same ancient woolly smells of camels and dog turds. Vivid, but no longer quite so intoxicating.

I was lost and it was getting dark, the shadows now reaching the tops of the walls. There was no one about. Except for two veiled women in dark robes, who stood staring at me from a doorway, muttering disapprovingly at my bare arms. I couldn't have looked more conspicuous: a blond in tight jeans and a flimsy T-shirt. "*Chéri,*" I remember Philippe warning me, with some delight, "remember, a European woman alone in the street here is considered nothing better than a whore." I ran on, down another lane, and another, then stopped at a welder's shop. A man, naked except for a loincloth, was sitting on his haunches banging a piece of metal over an open fire. A few passersby had gathered to watch. "Herborista Rubio?" I asked, trying to sound normal. The men turned to look. No one spoke. Then, behind me, I felt a hand touch my leg and someone whisper in my ear. It was a boy about twelve, barefoot, straddling a bicycle. "*Feluse, feluse,*" he said—or something like that. I didn't know what *feluse* meant but thought it couldn't be anything good.

So I quickly walked away—down another passageway, then along more snaking lanes. Finally, out of breath, I stopped at a fountain—not even a fountain, a leaky tap stuck in the wall, backed by a few blue tiles. But I felt safe because the street was quiet.

Then I heard the sound of a bicycle bell, and streaking out of an alleyway came the boy from the welder's. He'd followed me. He was wearing an open shirt and as his knees pumped up and down it flapped out behind him, showing his narrow, dark chest. Suddenly, other boys appeared out of the darkness, all on bicycles, pedaling furiously, ringing their little bells. They skidded to a stop at the fountain and formed a half-circle around me, their front wheels almost touching my knees. I remember stepping back, feeling the water from the tap soak my sandals. Then the first boy got down from his bike. Holding his crotch with one hand, he slid the other around my waist. He was grinning. The others boys were grinning too, making clicking noises in their throats and daring each other with sly winks. There still wasn't a soul around—nothing but dark mud walls and closed doors. A second boy then leaned over to touch my breast. He did it casually, his small brown fingers squeezing as if he were testing a piece of fruit. "Fuck off!" I said. And still the smiles, the row of pink gums and little white teeth.

So I started to shout. I remember the words coming out with a tremendous force, the vilest things I knew in French, every sexual insult Philippe had taught me, plus a few choice remarks about their mothers. They were shocked. Their sandy faces stared in astonishment. Still shouting I slapped the second boy's hand away—so hard I accidentally hit him in the face. He stepped back. Miraculously, then, some of the others moved their wheels—barely a foot or so but enough for me to escape. I ran. It was dark by then, the walls and sky had melted together in an inky black. As I fled, I heard their jeering voices and the tinny ringing of the bells just behind me. But I kept going, up one lane and down another, out of breath, panting, the red walls streaking past, the ting-a-lings echoing in my ears. Eventually, I caught the faint sounds of whistles and drums from the Jemaa el Fna square, and a few minutes later, I saw the

little shop and the lit-up sign: Herborista Rubio. The owner was standing in the doorway. *"Bonsoir!"* he shouted, waving as I tore past, and by
then the bells had begun to fade. When I got to our skiffa, the street door
was locked. I don't know why. Perhaps I was supposed to have a key. Still
scared that the bicycle boys might be behind me, I banged on the door
for what seemed an eternity. Finally, Philippe opened up. He wasn't in
the least sympathetic. In fact, when I blurted out the story, he looked
bored. *"Ah, non, vraiment tu exagère!"* He accused me of overreacting—as
if by complaining, or even getting myself into such a ridiculous situation,
I was profoundly uncool.

Things never end as quickly or as graciously as they should. I still have
a letter I wrote to Philippe, found in an old notebook. Four pages, full
of crossed-out lines and scribbled inserts (obviously a first draft) as I
tried to find the right words to tell him I didn't love him anymore, while
promising him I did. *We can never be happy living together in London.*
Had we planned to? But I also tell him not to give up hope: *Ne soit pas
desesperé, mon amour.* So vain. Letting him down gently while still trying
to keep my foot in the door. Either I never sent it, or he refused to accept
it, because nothing changed. I carried on, going back and forth to Paris,
arguing with Philippe, then arguing with the man I lived with in London; getting on planes with unfocused dread or exhilaration, purposely
not stopping long enough to ask myself what the hell I was doing.

Then one night I was with Philippe at Café Flore. It was around eight
o'clock. We were inside having drinks with friends. I wanted to leave, impatient as usual, so I walked out to wait on the terrace. On Boulevard St.
Germain it was raining slightly, one of those soft autumn nights when
there are misty halos over the street lamps and cars make low swishing
sounds as they pass. I was staring at the church across the street, idly
watching a group of people at the curb, waiting to cross. One of them
was Michel. I hadn't seen him for more than six years. I was shocked. I
felt a pang of—I don't know what . . . despair, panic. I didn't know he

was living in Paris now, and the mere thought that I might have passed him on the street without realizing it was almost unbearable. He was dressed as usual in one of his gray serge suits, but he looked thinner, more sophisticated. Guy was with him, and a pretty woman. She was laughing, and as they stepped off the curb, perhaps to steady herself, she took Michel's arm—just as I might have done. The scene had all the drama of a B movie: Philippe behind me, still chatting to his friends, me standing transfixed in the street, wondering why I couldn't walk over to Michel, if only to say hello. But I couldn't. I didn't have the courage. The truth was—and it only hit me the next day—it was too late. How could either of us connect to that young girl from Grenoble anymore?

It's hard to explain those feelings. It was more than the loss of my first great love. Standing there on the sidewalk, inhaling the damp air, I felt utterly bereaved, stuck with myself, my demons, and the big void.

I ended it with Philippe. I sent him another letter. But he wasn't having it. He came to London. He was staying with a journalist friend who had a house in Islington. "I have to see you," he demanded on the phone. His voice sounded pitiful, so I drove over. When he opened the door, he looked pale, more ethereally wan, but his eyes were boiling. He wanted to *tell me some things* in private, he said, and steered me into his friend's office. And as soon as he closed the door, he hit me. I can see the room now, the expensive blond wood bookshelves, the high ceiling, light streaming in the tall Georgian windows. When I fell on the parquet floor, he kicked me. *"Salope, emmerdeuse,"* he yelled, as he'd done so many times, except that now he meant it. "Fuck you! It's over, you little shit!" I screamed. So he kicked me again. I was facedown, bracing myself against the blows. But after the first few seconds, I felt nothing. It was an odd sensation; there was no pain. As if by then I'd become so good at separating myself from my emotions, I could *physically* remove myself as well. I must have been screaming, though, because his friend James had to come in and pull him off.

In some perverse way I was relieved. Maybe I wanted him to beat it out of me, to wake me from my stupor. I was humiliated, I wanted to kill him, but I couldn't blame him. And I wasn't about to complain. Exactly whom would I tell? My parents? Besides, in those days, I never thought what happened to me could be someone else's fault. Or that anyone might even be *interested*. That's a modern luxury. The fuckups, the bad trips, the sexual misadventures; back then, you were out there screwing up on your own. And as usual, my way of taking responsibility was to brace myself and move on.

After that I stayed in London, doing nothing or just reading. Books saved me. I used to hang around the Tottenham Court Road second-hand shops, looking for copies of Balzac and Céline. I developed a passion for American writers: Wolfe, Steinbeck, Miller, Bellow, always trying to catch up. But there were gaps. I was completely ignorant of Dickens or Shakespeare, and I never read female authors. No Woolf or Browning or Austen. I still couldn't identify with women, not considering them (or myself) important enough. It seems obvious now. But in those days what little I knew about the women's movement had to do with equality in the workplace, or about housewives dumping monogamy and child-bearing. Sexual freedom was supposed to be the *answer*. Of course, I'd heard about the book *The Female Eunuch*. And one day, with Victoria, we ran across Germaine Greer in a pub. She was cool and sexy, grooviness personified in her clinging minidress. She was chatting to a group about sex, promoting women warriors, explaining that men didn't realize how much women hated them. But I didn't hate men. By then, I didn't even hate Philippe. And I'd never seen him as a real villain; he was a *méchant raté*—a failed bad boy. In fact, he was more fragile than I was. He'd been crying when he rammed me with his Chelsea boot.

Twenty-two years later, in 1994, I went back to France to look for Michel. I told myself I was doing research for a story about my student days, but I took enormous pains to find him. In Grenoble, none of the university buildings looked the same; in fact the campus had been relocated to Saint-Martin-d'Hères, outside the city. Eventually I managed to track down one of my old teachers, a Mme. Faugère. An attractive brunette who I'd always admired, particularly for her collection of white pointelle blouses. She agreed to call Michel for me. I wasn't surprised she remembered him; but the fact that after all these years she had his home number made me realize she must have been one of his old lovers. "Guess who's here with me?" she said on the phone, winking at me across the administration office. Michel sounded amazed but agreed to meet the next morning at my hotel.

At the Lyon airport, I'd rented a car. But when I arrived in Grenoble, nothing seemed familiar. A few of the old cobbled streets remained, but La Maison du Café was gone. I randomly chose a hotel on the outskirts of town, a soul-destroying concrete slab overlooking a roaring highway. That night, having heard Michel's voice on the phone, the old emotions came flooding back—which seemed unnecessarily sentimental at my age. So I stayed in my claustrophobically sealed room and worked my way through a shelf of the mini bar. I didn't sleep that night. And I felt even more stupid in the morning, arriving fifteen minutes early for our rendezvous in the coffee shop downstairs. Incredibly, when Michel arrived, he looked the same. Older, a little heavier, but with the familiar cynical smile, the big, glossy hair. He was in the construction business, he said, and had made a lot of money in speculation. He told me this right away; and as if to prove it, he was wearing an expensive-looking camel hair coat. He had married an old girlfriend, someone whose name I vaguely recognized, and had two children. "But I'm divorced now," he said. "And I just broke up with my twenty-five-year-old mistress." The confession bore more than a tinge of pride; he radiated confidence. "Oh," I said gamely, "so you cheated on your wife?" He shrugged, still smiling. "Well, a little—*un peu*—a few times at Christmas and during the summer holidays." In other words, the acceptable French idea of fidelity.

We were playing around. But when I brought up our affair, he was silent. He seemed older then; the creases around his eyes had a grayish tinge. "You were the one who ended it," he said, giving me a look of wounded pride, as if it had happened yesterday. He was certain of that.

Though he might have been pressured by his parents, he added, because his father had gone broke around that time. "Do you have children?" he then asked, out of nowhere. "No," I said. "None."

I'm ashamed to say that I made him believe that not having children had something to do with the abortion (though this was partially true). "There were miscarriages—*fausses couches*," I said. He went silent again. I felt stupid then, as if I were making a passionate declaration to a man I barely knew, to see if the fire would light. What was I doing? Forcing him to admit he still loved me? Eventually, he did say, "Yes, you were the love of my life." He only had two regrets, he added, me and not sailing his boat around the world. When I suggested that one of those things might be rectified, he said, *"Le bateau?"* He hadn't lost his comic touch. But neither of us dared to go any further.

We decided to walk to the center of town. When he took my hand to cross the street, it felt perfectly natural. One of the old cafés, Le Cintra, was still there, so we went upstairs and ordered espressos. We were awkward with each other then and sat staring stupidly at the fogged-up windows. He knew I was an actress, so he asked about Hollywood: "Do you know a lot of movie stars?" I was disappointed, of course, that he seemed so taken by this. He said he'd seen me in a couple of films and thought they were *pas terrible*—which doesn't mean not terrible, but *not good*. I laughed, relieved in a way, but after that, it was impossible to get back to the all-absorbing past. Still, he wanted me to have dinner with him that night. We drove around in his Mercedes, then stopped in front of a restaurant he'd taken me to decades earlier. A fashionably somber place with wood paneling and flickering lights that in those days had an all-female orchestra—four middle-aged women in black shifts with lace collars grinding out a painfully slow "La Mer." The front was now a wall of stucco, punctuated by modern windows and a neon sign. We laughed about that. Then he bent me across the front seat and kissed me. The feeling of his face against mine was shockingly tender. I was ready to sleep with him right there. I was also on the brink of tears. "Why don't we go back to your hotel?" he said. "Okay, yes," I agreed, but

I didn't trust my feelings. After all, I was supposed to be in love with a man in California. My future husband. When we pulled up in front of the hotel's entrance, I said, "No, I can't." He didn't press me. Instead, he offered to drive me to the Lyon airport. "I've rented a car," I said, so there was nothing left to do. We kissed again. I told him to call me if he came to Los Angeles. He promised to write. But on the plane to London that night, I thought I'd made a terrible mistake by not staying. I was weak with emotion. Really? A forty-something-year-old woman playing the role of a lovesick teenage girl?

I spent an extra day in London trying to sort out my feelings. I was staying at my brother's house in Fulham and lay on his sofa in a stupor of self-pity. "Are you *all right?*" he asked—my little brother in his pinstripe suit, looking like my father and now my best friend. "Oh, just a cold," I said.

How could I tell him? How do you explain such madness?

In 1973, the idea of becoming a writer was still a secret thing. Telling someone I wanted to write was as awkward as owning up to being an actress. "Oh, you're an *ac-tress!*" some bloke would say, not wanting to appear too interested. This would then be followed by a cross-examination about my credits, which, when reluctantly rolled out, were met by a look of dismay, or worse, sheer indifference. "Ah—didn't see any of those!" By that time, the streets of London were teeming with potential stars, the model-slash-actresses. And though I was getting better and had received some decent reviews—one in particular for playing a ditsy blond in *Dr. Phibes Rises Again* with Vincent Price—it was a horror film. There were a lot of low-budget horror pictures being made then, most of them camp remakes of 1950s screamers. Somehow it was a niche I fit into well. I'd had a starring role in *Blue Blood*, a story of ritualistic sacrifice among aristocrats. It was filmed at Longleat, the seat of the Marquis of Bath. A fitting backdrop, as it turned out, most of its stately walls having been graffitied with lurid sexual tableaux by its owner, the young, though possibly unbalanced, Viscount Weymouth. It starred the Viscount's wife, myself, and Oliver Reed. Oliver was the perfect on-location companion for me. By then, I'd given up drugs but was still keeping the demons at bay with alcohol. We went to the village pub together after shooting. Oliver was a notorious show-off, a prankster. And on more than one occasion, having downed several drinks, he would climb up on the bar. There, watched by a rapt audience of astounded locals, he then proceeded to chew his way through a half dozen lightbulbs, removed from a ceiling fixture. His star turn. Incredibly, there was little blood. More incredibly, like his fans, I too, was in awe. And after that, I adopted him as my soul mate. Someone who was also bent on upholding the Englishman's inalienable right to drink himself into oblivion.

I wanted to write. But I didn't know how to start. It was years before I saw the connection between fiction and the real world, or that without it there was no point writing at all. And it never occurred to me to reveal anything about myself. What could be less interesting? But solitude forces you to have insights—if not about yourself then other people. And by 1973, I'd managed some short stories, each a few pages long. One was about two elderly women in an insane asylum. It took place on visiting day, and the character who sounds sane, who is busy berating the other for her tiresome craziness, turns out to be the one who's incarcerated. Later on, in California, a therapist naturally seized on this story. She pointed out that the subject was merely the reflection of my divided self: the extrovert actress and the privately morose writer.

I fell for anyone who knew about books. While I was shooting *Lisztomania*, I'd had a crush on the lighting cameraman simply because I saw him reading Dostoevsky between shots. Nothing came of this, but he couldn't help noticing and graciously took extra care lighting my close-ups.

I was a fan of John Osborne, whom I'd discovered one rainy afternoon watching a matinee of his play *West of Suez* at the Royal Court Theatre. Occasionally, John still worked as an actor, and around that time we did a small film together. I can't remember the title, or if it ever came out, but it was financed by a wealthy woman in Chelsea and some of the scenes were shot in her house. Every morning, John would arrive with an elegant basket of fruit and a bottle of chilled Stolichnaya and we would proceed to anesthetize ourselves against the outside world—or, more immediately, against that day's scenes, both of us being nervous actors. In between shots, we retired to a room in the attic, empty except for a few large pillows. We lay on the floor and talked about movies, about vaudeville, in particular Max Miller, the music hall comedian. Max was also one of my father's favorites. We laughed about his flowered suits, his correspondent shoes, and even managed to sing a few bars of "Mary at the Dairy," his signature tune. And naturally, we talked about books. "Have you read Céline?" "Who?" "This French writer, Louis-Ferdinand Céline. You'd love him." I gave him my only copy of *Death on the Installment Plan,* pleased that he'd never heard of it—trying as usual to be seductively smart. But John wasn't that relaxed with women. Awkwardly shy, he was still a victim of the repressed '50s, so we flirted in a kind of joking, sweaty, English way. I would have willingly thrown myself at him, but every evening he was summoned home by his wife, the actress Jill Bennett. She was famously terrifying, a woman he was bound to obey, and whom he soberly referred to as Adolf.

I met John Betjeman when we were both guests on a TV game show in Manchester. He was the poet laureate then—charming, pink-faced, a bit of a rogue, and obviously used to girls such as myself presenting themselves as aspiring writers. I left carbon copies of my typed poems for him at the hotel desk. He never mentioned them, and I didn't even dare ask if he'd read them when he took me to the pub for a drink the next day.

But there were men who helped me as a writer. And later on this brought the usual complications—feeling beholden, resentful. Weakened by sex and obligation. Roderick Mann, a London columnist, wrote for the *Daily Express.* Charming, haughty, and flirtatious, he liked to help girls and so arranged for an article of mine to be printed, a piece I'd written about *Lisztomania.* I didn't include the argument with Russell but concentrated on Roger Daltrey who, I pointed out, as Franz Liszt was parodying his own career playing the bawdy but prodigious composer. I hoped to get noticed, at least by Fleet Street. Instead, the article resulted in the paper's journalists threatening to go on strike because I wasn't a member of their union. Still, it was a start.

nineteen
Château de la Vinouse—Los Angeles.

The heat is tremendous, scorching for early June. Fabrice in shorts and work boots is trimming the front box hedges. Earlier this morning, in the spirit of creating a *jardin français,* he was up a ladder, trying to shape the bay tree into a perfect cone. Still clipping with determination, he now looks a little sheepish. "They should have marked the pegs with red flags," he says defensively.

Two days ago, M. Menard, the engineer from the pool company, Bainluxe, finally showed up. A man not happy with his work—or not happy that I was indecisive about where the pool should start or end, or how wide *la plage* (the deck) should be—he arrived with a laser measure to calibrate the pitch of the land and the depth and length of the hole. When this was determined, he stuck a dozen markers in the ground, and it was these, unfortunately, that Fabrice removed when he decided to mow the grass—what little of it existed. So I had to call M. Menard again.

He shows up the following afternoon. A small man, with a flat, shaved head and ears like ripe plums, M. Menard is even more aggravated than before. We stand in the garden and have a heated discussion about what is and what is *not* included in the price. Apparently, it's my responsibility to get someone to lay the slab of cement for the machinery. "Also," he says, "you have to arrange for someone to lay the *margelle*—the lip around the pool edge—*and* get an electrician to dig a trench so that we can run the wires up to the house. Didn't you read the contract?" he asks indignantly. I did, I say, and the small print too, although, admittedly, not all twelve pages. The final price, however, is unforgettable. I have the distinct impression, I say, that I'm getting the American price—*le prix Americain*—instead of the *prix Français*. He looks at me nonplussed, his ears growing redder. "Normally, I would have insisted on the *prix local*," I go on, "but thought it might be unreasonable as your main office is in Nice!" The joke falls flat. He's far from amused, but after another fifteen minutes of heated discussion, he concedes one point: his company will pay to lay the slab for the pool machinery. I'm surprised to win the argument—any argument at this point. Until I realize that by speaking French convincingly, forcefully, as I'd once done, I can still lose myself in the words and become, in effect, a stronger woman.

Three days later, two men arrive, one driving a bulldozer. An enormous hole is dug for the *piscine*, mountains of earth rising on each side like the Pyrenees. Then a smaller one is scooped out down the incline for the machinery. Having finished, they hand me a bill for 1,600 euros. Incredibly, it seems, the *hole* for the pool is not included in the *price* for the pool. No, they say, their company is subcontracted by Bainluxe—"Didn't you read the contract?"

This time, I'm at a loss for words.

One of Kathryn's black Arab mares stands tethered to the side of her stone barn. The local blacksmith, a portable forge grilling away in the back of his Deux Chevaux, is fitting a new shoe. Bare-chested, in shorts and a leather apron, his tanned biceps flexing as he hammers away, he's drawn an admiring crowd. Her guests can hardly believe their luck. Having just arrived from London and Los Angeles, it's everything they've been promised, dropped into the middle of France *profonde*.

Kathryn arrived three days ago and now her guests have turned up, as though spontaneously, from ports east and west. Ten adults are staying in the house, plus several children who run in a pack, wild and shoeless. Often there are more than twenty for dinner. I watch her and wonder how it's done. A modern *salonnière*, she is a cross between Mme. d'Epinay and Zsa Zsa Gabor. With her vigor and confidence, her inspired bonhomie, she commands everyone to have a good time. "We're leaving in ten minutes for the flea market; after that, lunch at a *divine* place in Gaillac, then we're going to Bruniquel, a *fabulous* medieval village founded by Queen Brunehaut." Only occasionally do I glimpse the struggle to keep her English schoolgirl insecurity at bay. The furrowed brow, the arched command—or perhaps I'm reading more into this than I should, envious that I'm not more like her. I've now spent months in her house as a lone lodger, often with barely the strength to open a can of peas at the end of

In the village of Puycelsi.

Kathryn Ireland.

the day. Not used to company, I have to pull myself together, get the brick dust out of my hair (and my underwear), and put on something halfway decent.

I feel out of place at dinner. But it doesn't take much encouragement to talk about the house: the problems with the workmen, the pool, the escalating costs, the drama. *My* drama. On this particular night, there is a couple from New York, an assorted group of English, and a Polish count with his girlfriend. The count is tall, suave, a former deb's delight, dressed in a silk shirt and linen trousers—the casual summer deshabille of the deposed nobleman. "I've already seen your house," he says, looking vaguely amused. Earlier, it seems, while I was making a quick run to Montauban, Kathryn drove everyone over to have a look. The conversation continues: the count's lineage, his stately homes (lost decades ago), his string of wicked stepmothers. Then, without missing a beat, he leans over and says to me—the words delivered in a breathy, concerned-for-the-starving-villagers voice: "Dah-ling, you have to change the pool. Just fill in the hole. It's in *completely the wrong place!*"

Suddenly, the whole table agrees. Now that the count has been brave enough to bring up the tricky subject, I hear a chorus of voices. "The pool's far too *near* the house," says Kathryn. "Better if it's out of sight, traditionally speaking. Some secluded spot at the end of a romantic pathway—" "Yes, yes, something to *discover,*" says the count, who, when it comes to the placing of swimming pools, is obviously an expert. "After all," one of the English women goes on, "you do have a lot of land. All those hectares with absolutely nothing on them!"

It's hard to defend yourself against a table of guests who claim only to want the best for you. Still, I'm taken aback. "Actually, I like it where it is. I mean, who wants to walk that far?" I say, echoing my husband, while secretly blaming him. And I'm easily influenced. As the evening continues—a spectacular electric storm, then several rounds of *poire liqueur,* after which, like refugees from Happy Valley, we dance until dawn—I finally give in, "Yes. You're right! I have to *move* it!" A few hours later, what is now early morning, I call my husband.

He is just starting his day. "I'm having breakfast," or the Bulgarian equivalent, which he says includes a particularly good goat's yogurt. In my weakened state, I blurt out the problem: Kathryn and her guests insist the pool is in the wrong place. "We just have to fill in the hole. Put it in a different place. Aesthetically it's *all wrong*." And even as I'm saying this, I realize how ridiculous I sound.

Surprisingly, he's amused. "Really?" he says. A clink of china, then the sound of him taking a swig of coffee. "Well, I want you to tell Kathryn and her guests, *whoever* they are, that if the pool is so offensive where it is—and where it's *definitely going to stay*—we'll erect a large curtain across that side of the house so that when they come to visit they won't have to look at it!"

Finally, I admit, I have to calm down.

But a few days later, things do go seriously wrong. It begins with the lunch hour. It's already scorching by noon now, and only M. Boudet Sr. and M. Gomes the plasterer go home for lunch. To save time and energy, everyone else stays at the house and David Boudet volunteers to cook. "I'll set up my barbecue outside on *la plage*"—the beach—what we now call the mountain of sand that surrounds the pool hole. He brings his own utensils, a cozy collection of plates, glasses, table, and chairs—nicely carved chairs, I notice, from where I have no idea—then arranges them in the basement. With the doors open, it's cooler there, he says, more comfortable for dining. I have no objection. But when we discuss what time he plans to stop work to *light* the barbecue, we disagree. "Eleven thirty is unreasonable," I say, too early—even though I understand the coals won't be ready until twelve. "But starting the fire," David argues, "is hardly the same as *starting* lunch." "Yes, it is!" I say. But he's offended. Eating is a serious business. So we finally agree on eleven forty-five. After that, David, Christophe, Uncle Boudet, and M. Bruni assemble downstairs every day for a three-course meal. They keep their beer and wine in a rusty old refrigerator, one that Mme. Moulin left behind. And M. Bruni contributes. He brings a noodle flan, a mysterious-looking burnt casserole, and always cuts me a slice. I'm reluctant. But in light of his hard work and his wife's reputation—who, according to him, is a "fantastic cook"—I can hardly refuse.

The weather has been odd. A hot ninety degrees one day, raining the next, then violent storms, the wind suddenly rushing across the fields, tearing through the house, doors banging. As a precaution, during the lunch hour, I check the rooms to see if the windows are closed, afraid they might slam shut, breaking the centuries-old panes.

Two days later, I'm returning from Montauban after another harrowing trip to the Zone Industriel. Despite his so-called expertise, M. Bruni has miscalculated the number of tiles needed to finish the downstairs bathroom floor, so I've had to collect another load myself. Coming back, the traffic is heavy. The car is stifling, and once again I've forgotten to bring a bottle of water. I am dehydrated, not to mention nauseated—the result, I suspect, of Mme. Bruni's spicy noodle flan. I'm also worn out from loading the tiles. Almost 200 pounds of them, which, for some illogical French reason, couldn't be delivered for at least three weeks. When I arrive at the house, the place seems empty. I can hear a radio playing, the heavy pounding of bad French disco imitating bad American disco, and the sound of raucous laughter. I go down to the basement. The boys are all there, lunch is well under way. In fact, judging from the remains of steak and potatoes, bread, cheese, salami, plus two empty wine bottles, lunch has probably been going on for more than an hour, and it's only twelve thirty. Everyone is shouting; David and Uncle Boudet are laughing, egging on M. Bruni. He's in his element. Pleased to have secured such a receptive audience, he's giving them a story about Saint-Tropez, the old days. "With my friend Sylvester Stallone." *Stallone? No kidding!* Yes. What's more, he's got proof. "Just go to Pierre's shop on the port— the famous photographer. The pictures are still on his wall—*even today!* Me and Stallone. His arm round my shoulder—"

"I need someone to help unload the tiles," I say, trying to interrupt. No one pays attention. Bruni is carrying on triumphantly now about a woman: some salacious incident involving food, dancing, and the removal of a dress. More raucous laughter. "*S'il vous plaît!*" I shout. "Can somebody please unload the tiles? The back end of my car is about to *collapse!*" Bruni swiftly holds up a hand. "Later!" he says indignantly, as if some rude heckler is trying to pitch in from the stalls. "*Plus tard! On mange!*" We're eating! And he continues with the story.

This little scene, and what follows, tells me something. As the pa-tronne, I've exhausted my capability to deal effectively with the men. It's one thing to get on your knees and scrub paint off the floor—by its very nature a female specialty. Quite another to be delivering a few hundred pounds of floor tiles like some common tradesman *and* during the sacred lunch hour. By gamely pitching in this time, I've crossed the line from benefactress to coworker.

After lunch, the argument starts downstairs. M. Bruni, volatile, un-questionably drunk, is standing in the hallway complaining loudly. He can't finish the tiling in the ground floor bathroom, he says, because the Boudets' "down pipe"—the one running from the upstairs plumbing—isn't installed correctly. "*And* it's in the wrong place!" Well, shouts Uncle Boudet from the stairwell, if he wasn't so slow in *relaying* the tiles upstairs—the ones taken up to bury the radiator pipes and now piling up in the doorways—they might have room to work in a correct man-ner! "You're holding *us* up, *vieux connard!*" M. Gomes is also upset. He emerges from the kitchen, bucket in hand, a red blush spreading across his pallid cheeks. "Look, I've got another job to go to. But I can't *fin-ish* plastering because of M. Escalet's window! It's crooked—laughable by modern building standards, and there's no *brick lip*. Just then Joseph chimes in. These days he only shows up in the afternoons, but his animal alertness senses trouble. "And how can I be expected to install any base-boards down here," he barks from the front door, "if the tile and plaster-ing *isn't done,* for God's sake?" And with a surly wave, he's off. Where is M. Boudet Sr.? I wonder desperately, always the calm mediator, but who hasn't reappeared since lunch. "He's gone to the hospital," says David. "A knee injury." By this time, everyone is standing in the hallway, swear-ing at each other: "*C'est toi! Merde! Putain!*" And Bruni is shouting the loudest. Feeling vulnerable, his star turn at lunch now forgotten, he suddenly corners me. "You know why I can't *finish*? Because you bought the *wrong* tile cement," he says vengefully. "Even though I *wrote it down* for you. And where the hell is Celine to help?"

By now, any remnant of my Anglo reserve has gone. "Look, I don't *work* for you!" I shout. "*Je ne travail pas pour vous!* I'm not your employee. I don't run errands. I'm the one paying! Overpaying, in fact! *Je suis la patronne!*" The thrill of letting go in French is too great. I feel a surge of adrenaline and start shouting at everyone else. Not only is their behavior *honteux*, I say, but in light of the drinking, *disrespecteux*. "You're unprofessional! I've had it with all of you! A bunch of amateurs! *Vous etes tous des amateurs!*" I'm racking my brains, trying to come up with the right words for "grossly taking advantage of the situation," but I can't. So I scream, "*C'est vraiment dégueulasse!*"—it's absolutely disgusting, an old Belmondo line, his dying words from *À Bout de Souffle*, although why this movie suddenly comes to mind I have no idea. But I'm finished. Waves of nausea rise from the poisonous flan, my chest heaves, and the tears well up. The men stare at me silently. I'm about to keel over. I'm also aware that the tears are fake. That I'm acting. In fact, I'm acting far better than I did when I *was* an actress. And as if swayed by my own performance, plus the suffocating heat, I do cry in earnest. A sort of hiccuppy burst, the tears streaming. So I quickly escape. Out the back door, down the stone steps, and across the lawn to the big cedar where, ducking behind it, I throw up.

While I'm hiding, the weather breaks. Black storm clouds roll in. Wind rushes through the chestnut trees, whipping up the sand from the swimming pool hole. There are hail stones (not unusual in June), punishing lumps of ice, then rain. Sheets of water that drop fiercely, horizontally, for fifteen minutes, like something out of the Old Testament, then stop.

I stay there until the workmen leave, then I go back into the house. Several windows, left open, have slammed shut, shattering the beautiful 200-year-old glass panes. I try not to think about it. Tomorrow

I'll apologize—"*Je suis désolée*"—far more effective than the English "I'm sorry." I am desolate, I will say, in order to restore peace. And then, inevitably, I will feel compelled to add some *drôle* remark about being a woman.

Then again, maybe I'll do none of these things.

That night, I call my husband. Shooting is finished in Bulgaria, and he has just arrived back in Los Angeles. I am lying on Kathryn's bed, still feeling nauseous, even though Celine came by to drop off some hot broth. "*Vieux cons*"—old farts—she said, smoked a cigarette, and left. Since then, I've downed a couple of shots of Kathryn's Fernet-Branca, the Italian digestif she keeps in the refrigerator next to the syringes of anti–snake venom serum. I go through the paces of the argument on the phone with him, calmly at first, attempting to convey the humor—a gaggle of French men trying to outshout each other, their small arms flying. After the swimming pool conversation, I want to impress him with my firm grip on the situation. But as I run through the list of grievances, I can feel my voice wavering, and when he asks, "Is it really all worth it?" I start weeping in earnest.

"It's only a house," he says.

"I know."

"Come home."

"No. I'm fine. I'm just tired." And yes, I'm extremely tired.

"I'm getting on a plane."

"No. Really. I'm fine."

"If you don't come back," he says coolly, "I'm coming to get you."

Sometimes I think he must have English blood in him. Though he can be neurotically unbalanced about day-to-day incidentals, he's extremely good in an emergency. In the very early days, I remember having an allergic reaction to a sulfur medicine I was taking. It was only ten days after we'd met, and he'd come to my Hollywood flat to pick me up for lunch. We were standing in the doorway when suddenly my throat started to close. I could barely speak. I was slipping into anaphylactic shock but somehow managed to whisper an address. He carried me down to his car, then he drove as fast as he could to the doctor in Beverly Hills who'd prescribed the drug. Bursting into his office, he grabbed this distinguished-looking man by the sleeve of his white coat (much to the alarm of the other patients) and threatened to harm him physically if he didn't save my life.

The gesture was heroic. He did save my life (the doctor merely gave me an adrenaline shot), and I barely knew him. A week later, I caught the flu, and every day he sent white roses and chicken soup. I'd never known a man who'd behaved so gallantly. And he insisted on visiting me in bed: "I want to see you at your worst." I hid in the bathroom. "You're so vain!" he shouted, laughing. "You're afraid to be yourself, scrubbed down and exposed! I *know* who you are!"

Love had never made me feel so vulnerable.

There it is, that familiar slow-boiling, back-of-the-throat taste of tarmac and exhaust fumes. I'm in Los Angeles. And compared to France, my own house seems completely alien to me, a place of stultifying order and cleanliness, like an airport hotel. But here I am. A fact that merely reminds my husband I've been gone too long. "You look tired," he tells me, glancing across the breakfast table. Naturally I'm exhausted but say, "No, really, I'm fine," trying to avoid any aspersion cast in the direction of France, my obsession, what I know is the equivalent of me having a lover. No, *worse* than a lover: a rival that's costing a small fortune and won't be going away. Still, in light of my recent breakdown about the workmen, he's trying to be understanding. I make an effort to be the woman he's so lovingly spoiled. I'm attentive and flirtatious. I wear high heels instead of sneakers. I cut roses from the garden; I put a vase on his desk. He's not buying it, though. And I can't blame him. There are the sidelong looks, then prolonged silences at dinner. "Where are you?" he asks. "Here," I say breezily. But as we both know, I'm still in France.

On Sunday afternoon, I try to relax. I sit in the garden with the *New York Times*, a newspaper I never miss in France but here read obsessively from cover to cover. It's hot. A plane drones lazily overhead. I can hear children shrieking in the swimming pool next door and the TV going upstairs—familiar noises. After flying for seventeen hours in order to spend a few intimate days with my husband "in paradise," we've slipped into our solitary weekend routine. I am outside reading; he's inside watching golf. Earlier, he asked me to watch it with him. "If you just get to know the players, you'll be interested. Come on, *indulge* me!" he says, smiling from the top of the stairs. So I do. I sit silently on the end of the bed with him. But I can't concentrate. The slowness of the game, the drone of the announcer's commentary, the hushed reverence. Still, I want to make myself interested. I look at him—the noble profile, the tanned brow. How lucky I am to have someone to love in this emotional desert, I think. We lean against each other, our shoulders nudging . . . like small animals breathing together. He gasps. "Did you see Tiger's swing?" "Yes, amazing," I say, all too meekly. "Look, you don't have to . . ." "No. I *want* to watch . . ." Isn't that the whole point of marriage, I think? To lose half yourself to another. Hand it over willingly. Get a different point of view. Most of the time I expect too much. You would have done better with a different wife, I want to say. Some gung-ho American girl who loves sports, who barbecues, organizes family seders, who's willing to listen to you talk all night. But here we are. The old married couple. I can imagine our future, toddling down to the Santa Monica cliffs in our eighties, arguing about thermostats and the high price of real estate. Earlier this morning, we tried to make love. I wanted to badly, to show him, but I was too nervous, too jet lagged, I'd been up since four. It wasn't Paris. *This isn't Paris,* I kept thinking, hating myself. Then I turned away because I couldn't face his gentle green eyes loving me, knowing me to my core. *Yes, yes, I love you, too. I will never leave.* We are doomed.

I go downstairs to make brunch, an American meal I still don't understand. Fruit *with* bacon? Really? I used to cook all the time, English dishes: shepherd's pie, lamb stews, which he pretended to like. Then he couldn't pretend anymore. He wanted American food. "Isn't it great?" I used to joke. "My husband absolutely *loathes* my cooking, so we eat out all the time. Lucky me!"

Why am I so on edge? After all, this is the life I've built, not a fantasy. I go outside. Back to reading the papers, to disappear into other people's lives: *an earthquake in Northern California; tsunami warnings along the Pacific coast; London is hit by Islamic terrorist bombings, killing fifty-two.* But it's too hot. I walk inside again. The house is cool, the rooms full of memories. The mid-century flea market furniture we bought when we didn't have much money. The Calder when we did. My outdated sets of books: Kipling, Byron, Balzac. The framed photographs: my parents on their wedding day, in drab wartime civvies; my brother at ten, grinning, pretending to smoke a cigar; an old Polaroid of my husband and me, a selfie taken in his car during one of our curbside trysts. He is smiling tentatively, as usual, self-conscious about his looks. "If you send this to your mother," he said, "don't forget to clip my *tax returns* to the back!" Funny, always perceptive. I lie on the sofa, barely able to breathe. I go over what I've been trying to say to him for weeks: *Look, maybe the point of France . . . the whole point is that I want to succeed at something on my own, to feel validated . . . nothing to do with trying to be a success, but to create something—or, rather, to recreate myself. Find out who I am. Because I'm getting old and I can't be gracious about it. I can't just join another yoga class, or go and feed the homeless. What I need you to understand is that building this house isn't a hostile act. Selfish, maybe, a last gasp, but it's not against you. Not to run away from you. . .*

But I don't tell him. I don't go upstairs. I lie on the sofa and think about France.

twenty
England—France—Los Angeles.

By 1973, the '60s were definitely over and London was depressing. The IRA bombings, the miners' strike, the collapse of the economy, then the three-day workweek. Shops were closing everywhere and there were still rolling power cuts. By this time, I was living in a small embankment flat, on fashionable Cheyne Walk. Keith Richards and Anita Pallenberg were a few houses down, and it was a stone's throw from Mick and Bianca. But the building hadn't been upgraded for decades. Damp from the Thames leaked through the walls, and at night I could hear tiny feet, the not-so-comforting sound of river shrews scuttling back and forth under my bed.

I was still acting, earning a living, although I couldn't kid myself anymore that I would ever rise above the level of the horror heroine.

That year, I did a remake of *Dracula* with Jack Palance. The cast included well-known actors such as Simon Ward and Nigel Davenport, but Palance was the visiting Hollywood star. He had historic stature; he was also the consummate method actor—a source of baffled amusement for the English-trained cast, who were suspicious of people using acting as therapy or as some expression of their own emotions. And none of us were happy standing around before a take, waiting for Palance to "warm up." He would disappear behind a tree, or retire to his trailer, at which point a series of high-pitched gurgles, or bark-like shouts, could be heard as he revved up his vocals, or simply got into the mood—usually something close to a sneering temper tantrum. In fact, he was such a devoted Stanislavski fan that during my denouement scene, when he repeatedly bit into my neck, the resident nurse had to be called. I was hauled off to first aid, bruised and bleeding.

The theater producer Michael White was a friend, and that summer he invited me to stay at director Tony Richardson's house in the South of France. Le Nid du Duc was more than a house. An old hamlet consisting of several cottages, near La Garde-Freinet, in the hills behind Saint-Tropez, it was surrounded by cork trees, sagebrush, and wild lavender. And after London, it was sheer heaven.

I didn't know Tony, but I knew his films: *Look Back In Anger*, *The Entertainer*, *The Charge of the Light Brigade*. One of the great British New Wave directors, he was famously candid and ostensibly immune to critics. After the hugely successful *Tom Jones*, when his career suffered a mild decline, he ridiculed the naysayers: "A group of intellectual eunuchs hugging their prejudices like feather boas."

This was the first of several summers I spent there, and during those hot months the guests might include Peter Hall, Jeremy Frye, the Oliviers, David Hockney, plus various children, theirs and his. It was everything I anticipated the creative life to be: sizzling days and velvety nights of genius and sloth. In reality, the atmosphere was more like a wicked holiday camp with Tony as master of ceremonies. If I was attracted to drama, Tony was famous for it. Tall and gangly, with sloping shoulders and a beaky face, he looked like a giant bird, flapping around, one eyebrow permanently raised in anticipation of the next diverting catastrophe. The persistent enemy was boredom. Mealtimes turned out to be explosions of wit and terror, with arguments intentionally provoked by him and prefaced with an exasperated, "Oh, dear me, you're all so *dreadfully sad*. . . ."

Lunch was a big affair. Trestle tables were set up under the trees, and there were often twenty or more, including local guests and some who had just arrived. An opportunity for Tony to pantomime the frantic host's dismay: "Oh, no. You weren't supposed to get here until *tomorrow!*" Or to a jet-lagged couple struggling out of a taxi from Nice airport, he would shout in shrill horror, "*Australians?* Who invited them? Everyone knows they've got *no sense of humor!*" And they would be banished to the end of the table, only to be reprieved by the time the grilled sardines arrived. Tony was fearless, mercurial, slightly terrifying, and very funny. He was also a manic organizer. Days had to be planned. There were treasure hunts, the rhyming clues stuffed into jam jars and hidden in impossible places. There were expeditions—maps laid out, cars leaving promptly at three p.m. for an educational tour of Chartreuse de la Verne, a nearby monastery founded in the twelfth century, or a trip to Ramatuelle to see the 400-year-old tree. Falling behind was scoffed at: "If you can't keep up, you'll be *left behind!*" Everything was a test of wit or skill. After dinner we played murder in the dark, purposely horrifying, or charades—referred to by Tony as *the game*, which was no game and taken very seriously. Some guests simply hid in the bathroom so they wouldn't have to play.

Director Tony Richardson.

One night, Roman Polanski was there. Natasha, Tony's actress daughter, was visiting, and a local friend, Anne Marie, an old resistance leader. At eighteen she had apparently driven a truck up and down the Midi, a bottle of rouge in one hand, a revolver in the other. Now she carried two small terriers, one called Mr. Pinkerton, the other Simpson—"named for the London store," she said. After a considerable amount to drink, we were herded indoors to play *the game*. We were in the salon, divided into two teams: some squeezed on the sofa, the rest on wooden chairs. Roman was acting out a line—something with "murder" in the title. To demonstrate the point, he took hold of Natasha and, hands clasped around her throat, deftly flipped her onto the floor. A startling move, scarily convincing—so much so that Mr. Pinkerton went wild. Ignoring Anne Marie's shouts of "No, Pinkie. *Mummy says NO!*" he bit Roman's leg then jumped on the sofa and started tearing up the cushions. It was quite a sight: feathers flying, Natasha screaming—genuinely alarmed in mid-strangulation—and Tony, his knees banging together with delight, egging everyone on. For the finale, Anne Marie stood on a chair to sing the Marseillaise. I'd never had a better time in my life.

There were expeditions to the beach for lunch, to the Aqua Club, or to a little restaurant called Chez Camille just beyond Pampelonne, where we'd sit overlooking the water eating bouillabaisse from circular tin trays. Basking in the warm air, I felt like the girl from Westcliff again, although a lot had changed since the 1950s. Rows of tables were now lined up on the sand; there were *maisons de vacances* dotting the hillsides, and the traffic was terrible. In the evening, we'd crawl along in the sweltering heat for an hour or more just to get to the Café des Arts for a Pernod before dinner. On our way, we would pass the old Hôtel Les Palmiers. I hadn't mentioned staying there as a child, and though I'd always planned to visit Mme. Guerin, somehow I never had the courage to ask Tony, or whoever was driving the car, if they'd mind stopping for a minute, in case it seemed too self-indulgent or just boring. I was still auditioning. Not as an actress but as an amusing guest.

One afternoon, we were sitting by the pool—itself famous, immortalized by David Hockney in several of his paintings. One of the guests was a voluptuous English girl who wasn't a good swimmer. She did, however, have very large breasts, and as she floundered around, I made a pointed remark about her obvious buoyancy. I only mention this because Natasha, who became a good friend, reminded me of it years later. How wounding it was for the girl. Apparently, she'd never forgotten it.

If I had no loyalty then, even to myself, it was equally impossible to value other women. And it wasn't until I left England that I even became aware that this part of me was missing.

In a way it was Tony who was responsible for me going to California. He'd left London recently and moved to Los Angeles to make movies. And the next summer at La Garde-Freinet I met an American writer who flew in to work with him on a screenplay. A young, mildly savage-looking man, with wild hair and perfect teeth who came from somewhere called Winnetka, Illinois. John was in awe of Tony's films, astonished to find himself in the beautiful South of France, and couldn't stop smiling, or saying, "Wow. This is *fantastic!*"

In those days, I didn't know about the great American capacity for optimism. But I was attracted to John and one night found myself in his room, sitting on the bed, smoking his Marlboros and drinking Bourbon. We were flirting, divulging small pieces of information about ourselves, and I mentioned one or two films I'd done. Suddenly he leapt up: "What? You did a Ken Russell movie? Wow. That's incredible, *amazing!*" It was said with such passion, I felt immediately better, as if acting might be a worthy thing to do. In England, the equivalent response from a man I'd just met would more likely have been a cringing, "Oh dear. I hear he's deranged. Hope it turned out all right."

John's enthusiasm was genuine and infectious.

He'd gone to New Trier High School, studied at NYU, and then, having written a couple of screenplays, moved to Los Angeles. "I'm part of the New New Hollywood," he said, not boastfully but with wide-eyed gusto. It was all unreal and unbelievably cool, and I was as *cute as hell*. "So why don't you come with me to California?"

Just like that? How could I? But back in London, the perennial gloom descended. It rained endlessly. The economy was in free-fall and I couldn't get a job. Most of the American money had pulled out of the British film industry, my agent informed me, "so movies are dead, dear." I tried television. Then one cold, wet morning I was driving to Elstree Studios to audition for some uninspired sitcom when my car, an old Citroën, broke down. It was the third time that month. I left it on the side of the road, the glove compartment stuffed with unpaid parking tickets. Then I got a taxi home and packed.

It's hardly an exaggeration to say that moving to Los Angeles from London was the biggest escape ever. I'd visited briefly a few years before. But I hadn't been exposed to the great California clichés, so the clichés were new to me: the bigness, the too-muchness of everything; the cars, the houses, the palm trees lining the wide boulevards; the huge billboards and the Disney-esque mock-ups straddling the fast-food joints—a giant donut or a smiling Burrito Boy. As far as I could tell L.A. wasn't real and had no intention of being real, which suited me fine. It was August 1974. Nixon had just announced his resignation and everyone looked dangerously happy or vacantly unafraid. In the stores there were toothy smiles from the saleswomen who called you "sweetie" or "honey," and outside the sun shone. For an English person, the fact that it did this almost continuously was reason enough to stay.

I loved the lushness, the heat, even the heady smell of exhaust and melting asphalt. I was happy to do nothing, or just drive up and down the Hollywood Freeway in John's old VW, Stevie Wonder's "Don't You Worry 'Bout a Thing" playing at full blast on the radio. I spent entire days watching television. It was all new to me, the *I Love Lucy* reruns, *The Honeymooners*, the canned laughter, the game-show hosts wearing orange sport coats and toupees to match. The world of understatement had been left behind. I went to Saks Fifth Avenue just to watch the Beverly Hills matrons trying on silk housecoats and swans' down slippers. Or I drove down to Venice—in those days a sinkhole of polluted canals and vagrants. But the beach was vast and beautiful, and I sat and watched the sunset misty-eyed. In the land of overkill, I felt oddly moved.

"D'you know how to make a tuna melt?" "Whaddya mean you've never heard of a Reuben sandwich?" I knew nothing. So John was going to teach me. We were happily ensconced in his West Hollywood house. A dilapidated 1920s bungalow that nevertheless had a twinkly dollhouse charm. There was a lanai at the back where he wrote his screenplays, and a porch in front where we sat in the late afternoon to drink "dive bombers"—a shot glass of whiskey dropped in a pint of beer. Then he'd toss me across his thrift store bed and we'd laugh our way through a twilight fuck. "You're adorable!" Well, so was he with his big Jimmy Cagney grin. I threw out my English clothes. I wore sneakers, torn Levi's, and cowboy hats. I ate French toast and steaks as big as hubcaps. I even started to sound like him—"No way, buddy," or, "Yeah, you don't say, pal." I was distracted, happy. But I couldn't be faithful. Not that fidelity was a requirement in those days; for the truly liberated, not sleeping with anyone you pleased was considered somewhat hypocritical. I just didn't know how to be. Still, I was trying to be serious about work. By this time, I'd done pieces for the *Times* on Rock Hudson, on Spielberg, and Milos Forman, and, as usual, John was enthusiastic: "These are great! So why don't you write screenplays too?"

Yes, why not? After all, everyone I knew was writing one, including the man in the cleaners. I set up my portable Olivetti in a backroom, overlooking the palm tree and the square of scorched lawn. But I still didn't have enough discipline to be consistent in either work or love. One day, John found a note. It was a billet-doux I'd been composing to an old boyfriend, a well-known English director who was staying at the Beverly Hills Hotel and with whom I'd spent a salacious afternoon. I must have felt guilty, as I'd left the letter on my desk for John to discover. "I can't believe you'd do this," he said quietly. Then he shut himself in the bedroom that night to play his guitar—a sober reaction that was more chastening than any argument. It was an old friend, I protested. I was doing *my thing*, wasn't I? "Aren't we free?" But my head felt like lead. So to dramatize the situation, or to validate my guilt, I took a handful of sleeping pills—not enough to kill me but enough to punish him for being so forgiving. "I've swallowed some pills," I whispered through the door. He called an ambulance and I was taken to Cedars-Sinai to have my stomach pumped. I woke up in a bright corridor, lying on a gurney with a tube sticking out of my arm. There was a man kneeling beside me. "I'm the resident psychiatrist," he said. He was handsome and serious-looking, and tender, still young enough to be genuinely moved by a girl's attempt to kill herself. "Why did you do it?" he asked, taking my hand. I felt utterly stupid then. I hadn't bothered to ask myself *why*. But lying there, parked in the Lysol-soaked corridor, a gentle stranger at my side, I wanted to tell him everything. I couldn't, of course. There was too much to say, so I faked it. "Oh, you know, I was just trying to get my boyfriend back," I chirped, with my usual British cheer. "Obviously, I failed."

Landing in L.A., I had $400 to my name. A sum that initially seemed perfectly adequate for my new hippie lifestyle. But I was only earning $200 for a full-page article in the *Times'* "Calendar" section, and now that I'd moved out of John's bungalow, I had nowhere to live. Going back to England was out of the question. So I needed to find a job.

An Italian man I'd met briefly took me to meet the producer Dino De Laurentiis. The last of the great tycoons, married to actress Silvana Mangano, Dino had made some impressive movies, including Fellini's *La Strada*, Visconti's *The Stranger*, and *Barbarella*. He had recently arrived in Hollywood from Rome, and rumors about his tax problems, about bagmen absconding across the Italian border with lira-packed suitcases, were legendary. But this only added to his flamboyant reputation.

We went to see him in his sleek 1930s offices on Canon Drive. He was smaller than I'd imagined, a diminutive, sharp-suited Il Duce, and only half visible behind an immense leather-and-mahogany desk. I stood before him in my yellow minidress and started to list my credits, but Dino wasn't the least bit interested. He wanted me to turn for him instead. *"Girate, girate,"* he said, one finger circling his pomaded head. So I did. "Now please walk back and forth." *Per favore—va, va,* he commanded. I obeyed, gliding to and fro across his Persian rug, for some reason not finding this the least bit offensive. He was slick, but also elegantly refined. After watching for a minute, he smiled, then whispered, *"Va bene!"* And that was it. I had the part.

It was the kind of role I did well. Overly dramatic, with a fake accent. *Drum* was the sequel to Dino's *Mandingo*, a cautionary tale about a slave-breeding plantation in the South. To be honest, it was terrible. Spectacularly distasteful. A movie with flourishes of sadism and depravity and something, I realized, only a person who didn't have a full grasp of the language could have made. I played a governess who becomes the plantation owner's (Warren Oates) wife. Thankfully, my scenes were limited to a few crinoline-rustling tantrums and breast heavings, or strident commands to the black help: "Go git yo masta, boy," shouted from the top of a sweeping antebellum stairway. For the finale there was the inevitable bloody slave revolt. I remember lying in a barn somewhere near Baton Rouge, at four in the morning, smeared with mud, my dress artistically ripped, while behind me, accompanied by a chorus of extras' screams, a wall of orange flames licked the sky. Dino's version of the burning of Atlanta.

There was something glorious and doomed about Tony Richardson's Hollywood house, perched above Sunset, like a setting for a Nathanael West story. The gardens were immense and lush, an exotic wonderland of palms and eucalyptus, citrus trees and orchids, flanked by winding sandy paths. Once owned by Linda Lovelace, the porn star, the house was a half Tudor, half Spanish ranch, built decades before on a steep hill, since designated as a "slide area." It had a tennis court and two swimming pools—the second one discovered after Tony removed a wall of earth blocking the bottom garden. Underneath was an Olympic-sized basin from the 1930s, with an old Buick parked in the deep end.

Lunches and dinners there were just as formidable as they were in France, with Tony presiding, hawkish and excitable as ever, and spurred on by his pet toucan who, chained to a tree branch, kept up a screaming match from the kitchen. When the bird took nips at the passing guests, which it did frequently, Tony was cheerfully indignant: "Well, don't *torment* him, then!"

Tony loved Los Angeles and hated England. He loathed everything about the British class system. And though I never thought about myself as figuring *in* the British class system, or anywhere for that matter, I was happy to be a member of the expatriate crowd—people such as Christopher Isherwood, David Mortimer, and Laurence Olivier, who came to the Sunday lunches, which were staged with Tony's usual commanding relish. For example, he would sit a young Australian porn director, a girl called Suze, next to Olivier and then command her to describe in detail the intricacies of shooting a masturbation scene: "*Go on*, tell him!" And Olivier, the famous profile erect, would listen, then turn to the table and calmly say, "Simply *fascinating*, isn't it?"

On another Sunday, there was a woman there, a slim brunette in her forties, who'd been having an affair with Henry Kissinger. "Tell us, tell us!" prompted Tony, already rigid with anticipatory glee. "What did you *say* to him?" "Well," said this woman, "I told Henry that I refused to sleep with him anymore unless he stopped the war in Vietnam, *and* brought back the troops!" Howls of laughter, bird screams, and applause. There was no mention however of Kissinger's reply, or if she stopped screwing him.

Tony had several of David Hockney's big swimming pool canvases on his living room walls. And I was a big admirer. After John and I split up, when I moved into my first L.A. apartment, a tragic one-bedroom closet in Westwood, I impulsively bought a drawing of his for $600. A fortune for me, I managed to pay it off later with the money from *Drum*.

During these lunches, Tony and David would discuss art, or argue about art. Could one compare the camera lens with the scope of human sight? Did movies portray what we really see? Yes, *of course,* according to Tony—or was Picasso's Cubist vision the true one? as David kept insisting. He would then break into one of his big, friendly Yorkshire laughs and start sketching one-eyed figures across the tablecloth. Later, I went to visit his studio on Woodrow Wilson Drive. There was a large photo of the queen on the wall. The furniture was pink and blue, and he'd put wavy blue lines on the bottom of his pool to mimic the paintings. Art imitating art. There were also hundreds of Polaroids littering the floor. He'd just started doing his photo collages—his "joiners," as he liked to call them—about which Tony would remark triumphantly, "And I thought you said photography as art was *pathetic!*"

If Tony was contentious, it was a bit of a game. He loved to fight, thrash it out, but he was also fiercely loyal. I once heard him lambast a woman for daring to criticize his dear friend the poet Stephen Spender. He told her (and the rest of us) to shut up and listen. Then he read "Elegy For Margaret" out loud and, slamming the book shut barked, "You see. A *genius!*"

So I was grateful, though slightly alarmed, to be the subject of one of these outbursts. Before I left England, I'd been cast in a Lindsay Anderson film, *O Lucky Man!* It was a coveted part and starred a host of worthy actors, including Malcolm McDowell (*A Clockwork Orange*) and Ralph Richardson. I was amazed to get the female lead. I rehearsed with Malcolm and we shot several scenes. But I wasn't brilliant. Once again, the subtle shadings of the character eluded me; I needed help. I asked Lindsay for direction, but none was forthcoming, and after ten days, I was fired. It was a humiliating blow, and I was replaced by Helen Mirren.

I hadn't talked much about acting to Tony—not mine, that is. After all, he'd been married to Vanessa Redgrave. But one night, Lindsay came to dinner. Vanessa was there, too, soliciting funds for Palestine, and a few others. Somehow the film came up, plus the fact that I'd been fired. We were sprawled in the sunken living room, with the giant Louis XV gilt commode, the Hockneys, the jungle gardens lit up outside. "What!" shrieked Tony, leaping to his feet. "*What* did you do?" Lindsay, already at a disadvantage, lying on the floor in a rubbery beanbag chair, glanced up cautiously. "Look, you know how it is, Tony. These things *happen.*" It was irresistibly lame. "You actually *fired* Fiona!" Tony steamed on. "You, who hasn't the first clue about casting, or talent, who wouldn't even *recognize* what makes a person original, actually fired her. You're a hopeless *disgrace!*" Vanessa stirred: "Hey, steady on, Tony." But it was too late, Lindsay was on his feet. Red-faced, teary-eyed, he tore up the stairs, then ran out the front door into the street. I was mortified. Flattered to be defended by Tony but sympathetic because I knew Lindsay admired Tony so much. "Look, it wasn't really his fault—" I started to say, but Tony was still revved up, arms spinning victoriously. "Oh come on. He's *pathetic!*"

It was 1976 in Hollywood, but it might just as well have been the 1930s. I was living in a three-room apartment off Franklin Avenue, a street where buildings had been designed to resemble Roman villas and miniature châteaus, complete with turrets. Mine was a tall art deco–inspired block. The doorways were crowned with Egyptian moldings, the bathroom decorated with zigzags of pearlized black and turquoise tiles. Very Norma Desmond. Very old Hollywood. In the morning, I would drive down the hill to Schwab's coffee shop, where Lana Turner had been discovered, perched on a barstool—that is, according to Betty, one of the waitresses. A working man's Lucille Ball, Betty had pink penciled eyebrows to match her pink foundation, and wore a black velvet bandeau clamped to her orange hair. To take my order, she licked the stub of a pencil like some Raymond Chandler moll. "How's it cookin' sweetheart?" she'd say. "Got any work yet?" Well, not much, as a matter of fact. By then, I was trying to write screenplays. I would stay up late at night watching old screwball comedies on TV—Jean Arthur, Rosalind Russell, Carole Lombard—then copy down their crackling dialogue: *Sorry, my friend quota is full up right now. But if one dies, or slips into a coma, I'll let you know, pal!* Perfect for my twilight world.

During the day, I worked on pieces for the *Los Angeles Times*. My entrée into journalism came about thanks to Charles Champlin, an editor at the paper. He had written an article about me when I'd first arrived in Hollywood as an actress. I'd then shown him my old poems, plus the piece on Roger Daltrey I'd done for the *Daily Express,* and, impressed, he got it reprinted in the *Times*. He thought I should do more interviews and asked the arts editor there to hire me. By this time, Charles and I were often seen together in bars, and people presumed I was sleeping with him—a rumor he made no effort to dispel and perhaps even encouraged (untrue though it was), but I didn't care. It seemed to me an acceptable bargain in order to become a legitimate writer.

I did many pieces for the paper's Sunday "Arts" section after that. The editor refused to hire me (he'd heard the salacious rumors about Charles and me), so I worked on a freelance basis. Unschooled in the professional approach, I would simply look in the *Hollywood Reporter* to see what movies were shooting. I'd then call up the studio publicity department to inform them that the *Times* wanted to do an interview with, say, Milos Forman, then call the *Times* and pretend the studio had *asked* me to do the piece.

I was still astonished I'd become a writer, that I was taken seriously, or seriously enough to be published. Even so, I remember more than once a man sidling up to me at a party, barely able to conceal his bafflement. "Did you *really* write that?" he'd say. "Or did your friend Charles write it for you?"

The old cliché. I didn't look like a writer. I didn't dress like one. I dressed like an actress, and I still wore too much makeup. Using your looks as currency, or thinking you might not have much value without them, is a hard habit to break. Then, ironically, when I decided to wear plainer clothes and no eye makeup, and had enough confidence to say "I'm a writer," I noticed that men started talking to me in a different tone of voice—soberly, as if I'd suddenly gained some objectionable power. A revelation, albeit one just as obnoxious. I studied the *New York Review of Books* to become a better journalist. I carried Martha Gellhorn's *The*

Face of War around like a good-luck charm. I was happy working in my apartment all day, tortured by every sentence.

But going out to interview an actor or a director was trickier. I was still self-conscious in my new role. I also knew that conversations on the lot, between takes, were hardly conducive to revealing truths about an artist's work, or the real business of making movies. And the subjects weren't always so willing. I remember Truman Capote scolding me because I had the audacity to bring a tape recorder with me to his trailer. We were on the set of *Murder by Death*, a movie he was reluctantly acting in at the time. "A real journalist," he whined, "uses a pad and pencil," as he had done, he reminded me, while researching *In Cold Blood*. He was wearing one yellow and one green shoe that I wasn't altogether sure were part of his wardrobe, and took frequent sips of "water" from a thermos that obviously contained booze. But he was full of twinkly charm. "I've read your pieces. They're good," he said. Encouraged, I asked him to tell me about his scandalous *Answered Prayers*, the only thing I was really interested in. But he wouldn't—"No, honey. Not that." Nor did he want to talk about anything else. Instead he dragged me, not unwilling, to a dive across the road from Warner Brothers, an empty rib joint with Halloween masks looped over the bar, where we got smashed on whiskey sours. We talked about love, the great tormentor. "Do you think it's the *only* thing worthwhile?" he asked. "Well, it's always disappointing," I said, because I really hadn't a clue. Flush-faced, he took my hand. "Oh, honey," he whispered, "I'll say. It's the impossible dream."

On a very hot day, I flew down to Durango to interview Jack Nicholson, who was shooting *Goin' South,* his directorial debut. I had to wait until four in the morning to get his thoughts and then, blinded on coke, made a dash to the airport to catch a seven a.m. plane back to Los Angeles. I sat with Jeff Bridges in his trailer during a night shoot for *King Kong,* too polite to turn down his invitation for a hearty smoke— some ferocious backyard weed—and in the morning, having lost my notebook, struggled to make up the story.

I was compliant, still trying too hard to please. And often, my professionalism was challenged. One time, in particular, when I was interviewing Richard Burton. I knew Burton, I'd worked with him at Shepperton Studios on the movie *Villain*, and now he was shooting a film in Burbank. Charismatic, as self-deprecating as ever, he was by this time sober—or rather, only drinking beer, which obviously didn't count. A few years before, on *The Klansman*, he'd apparently been so drunk that many of the scenes had to be shot with him seated, or lying down, so he could deliver his lines coherently. Now he spoke lyrically about Wales and his early roles on the stage. We were reminiscing about London, about Elizabeth and the *Kalizima*, their luxurious yacht, moored on the Thames, which I'd visited, when suddenly he made a lunge at me across the dressing room couch. An awkward moment only interrupted by a polite, and fortunately indifferent, assistant director. I was honestly shocked. Burton was always charming, but he wasn't lecherous. Was I flirting with him, still trading on my charm to get ahead? Had I become my own bad habit? I had to start taking myself seriously. If I didn't, how could I expect anyone else to?

Sex and work and love: the big mysteries.

It seemed to me that American women had a better sense of themselves. They were bold but not overtly coquettish. They were hospitable, gregarious—undeniably so—though I admit this seemed alarming at first. A few months after I'd arrived in Los Angeles, I remember being at a cocktail party (the verb *to party* was new) when a woman I'd never met walked over and put her arm round me. "You're so pretty," she whispered, and proceeded to stroke my hair. *Oh, shit*, I thought. *Is she making a pass?* They loved my accent and my clothes: A man's suit? *So original!* They were positive and affectionate, and when they smiled, they had fabulous teeth.

Normally, my prepared reply to a simple "How are you?" tailored primarily for men, would be, "Not great, but nothing another drink won't cure!"—that kind of thing, still trying to be amusing. But it seemed that women in America genuinely wanted to know. It took me a while to get used to their geniality. One summer my parents were visiting, and a girl

I knew from New York came to lunch. More than once she jumped up to hug my mother, telling her what a "great friend" I was, until eventually my mother, exasperated, turned to me and whispered, "Who *is* that woman?" But I was grateful to them. I admired their sense of self-worth, their insistence that women were valuable. Also their genuine desire to be helpful. They knew where to find the *best* dry cleaners, plumbers, gardeners, masseurs, shrinks, and gynecologists. And they talked about sex as if it had nothing to do with men. Nobody I knew in London, including my friend Victoria, would have sidled up to a woman at a party to ask: *What kind of contraception do you use? Diaphragm or the coil? And do you use a vibrator?* Not without a nudge and a laugh, that is. In America, these were serious issues.

I was intrigued by these women, but I still felt like a loner. And I missed Victoria. I missed her cynical English wit, her dark truisms, her barking laugh. Most of all, I missed her intimacy. I was always looking for a version of her, or a version of my secret self: a strong girl with an aching heart.

One night, I went with a friend to a party at Susanna Moore's house on Outpost Drive. It was before she'd written her first book, when she was married to the art director Dick Sylbert, then running Paramount Studios. She lived in a big Spanish house, and as we walked in from the garden through the French doors, I saw her sitting on a sofa with four other women. She had a cool, luminous beauty, her head tipped back, a hibiscus in her hair, and she was laughing, telling a story about the Hawaii of her childhood. The camaraderie of these women as they listened to her, their heads close together, struck me because it seemed such a comfortable bond, exclusive only in its congeniality. I was envious.

But later Susanna and I became good friends. She had a sophisticated wackiness, but she was also serious about writing and gave me books to read: Elizabeth Bowen, Djuna Barnes, Jane Bowles, and Joan Didion. Didion was one of the few female authors I had read. I'd met her at Tony's not long after *Play It as It Lays* was published. In my naive enthusiasm, I remember asking her how on earth you started a book. But she was encouraging. "Begin with very short chapters," she said. "In any order. It doesn't matter. Just get it down."

Though from different backgrounds, Susanna and I were similar. She hadn't had much formal education, she had graduated from model to actress and appeared in some pretty dreadful films. We were roughly the same age. We still suffered from the same insecurities as other women brought up in the '50s and early '60s. And it was she who would say years later, in her astute, witty way, "I can't wait to get to an age when I can stop *bluffing*." By then, we were in our late forties.

Around this time I also became friends with Lynne Giler. A big, noisy redhead, Lynne took me under her wing and we started writing scripts together. She had a genuine flair for comedy. Her father had been a screenwriter, and she knew how to pitch a story. There were few women executives in Hollywood then, and no female studio heads, so this could be a daunting process. Like performing stand-up in a bar full of men who'd been expecting pole dancing. "If an executive tries to kiss you at the end of a meeting, you can be pretty sure you didn't get the job," she'd say, laughing. She lived in a 1940s Spanish apartment a few blocks from me on Fountain Avenue. In the afternoon, we'd lie on her bed to watch *All About Eve*, *Bringing up Baby*, or *The Front Page*, trying to think up ways to modernize these heroines. But by the mid-'70s things had changed. Even if women were starting to be featured as stronger types in films, the acceptable female protagonist was more likely to be portrayed as either stunningly earnest or, if witty, charmingly dumb. Lynne was a genuine old-fashioned dame, and we both wanted our leading ladies to be fighters to the core. She took me to the Santa Anita racetrack so we could soak up the "ambiance." We went to Musso and Frank's. She knew all the waiters there and would charm one of them into delivering a script we'd written to some unsuspecting producer having lunch in a back booth. At night, we went with her brother to the Seven Seas, a 1930s club on Hollywood Boulevard that featured lava rocks and a "rain forest"—full thunder-and-lightning sound effects—where, both of us laughing hysterically, she would drag me onstage to leap around with the tiki warriors. Our screenplays were rejected (old-fashioned, too much dialogue). But on many days, Lynne saved me from myself.

But my relationships with men weren't getting better. And my next affair was also with a writer. My attraction to writers was obvious. I was a fan. I was also under the misguided notion that any truths discovered about human nature, insights about love or life as seen through Bellow or Roth—or whomever I was obsessed with at that moment—would also be present in the writer himself. Any writer.

Walter was older, Jewish, though he'd chosen a professional name that was not. He belonged to that era. He was a successful screenwriter and actor, and when I met him one Sunday at Tony's, he had a rolled-up copy of the *New York Review of Books* in his jacket pocket. Something that a few years later would make me run in the other direction. Back then it merely confirmed his appeal as an intellectual. I was still drawn to anyone with a good education, meaning that I chose to ignore unsavory character flaws, many of which matched my own: the inability to be truthful, for example, or intimate. But I *went after* these men. The pursuit of sex was still secondary, the almighty orgasm something that struck only occasionally. Heart-stopping but just a jolt. As for the much-touted multiple orgasm: fiction, I presumed.

Walter was witty, smart, and loved politics. Sitting in his atrium-like hilltop house in Hollywood, we relived Watergate every night on television: Erlichman and Haldeman, the break-in, and the missing eighteen minutes of tape. And when Nixon finally leaned in to the camera to say, "I can't bear to see other people cry," we started screaming and laughing at the television. It was fun. But it was intimacy at arm's length. And there was a certain meanness in the way Walter doled out affection. He would threaten me with security, buy me gifts, then take great pleasure correcting me about modern art or current events. The kind of man who bullies a woman under the guise of generosity. And his aversion to female paraphernalia was extreme. I would make a point of leaving my underwear strewn across his bedroom floor just to see him wince.

There was a lot of talk in the '70s about men who were afraid to be intimate, or who refused to grow up, and this was true. Things were moving so fast. All the old rules were gone (even if they weren't), and there were women who talked seriously about being celibate, excluding men altogether as a viable option. This was hardly realistic, I thought. After all, if men didn't change too, we'd all be lost. But I wasn't capable of changing them, or myself. I had the same difficulties with Walter that I'd had with men in the past. Nothing had much meaning emotionally, or had too much meaning because nothing was being said. I needed romance, or at the very least a declaration of romance because the effort of concealing my feelings was exhausting. Love in America was easy. Love was an industry, a universe. Relationships were still tricky.

Walter often had to go to New York for work, and at some point, I found out he was having an affair. I'd recently turned down an offer to do a Mexican film, a low-budget version of *Jaws*, but feeling wounded, I decided to take it. *Tintorera* was filmed on Isla Mujeres—the Island of Women (encouraging, I thought)—a slither of tropical land opposite Cancun. But the shooting was slow, the script terrible, translated from Spanish in what seemed like fits and starts: "I go now. You go too." I was aggravated by the director, the actors, the insects. *Oh look, a tarantula!* And I was drinking too much. During a scene near the end—an interminable afternoon when I had to handstand upside down in the ocean, my legs waving in the air to simulate my own demise—I remember thinking, *Well, this might as well be the real thing.*

The darkness was there, circumventing the truth. And I would write *that* in a notebook. Because most of the time, I was just being dramatic. After all, I lived a charmed life. I was earning money, doing anything I wanted. There were girls I knew who were still stuck in Westcliff, married with children, trying to figure out what the '70s had to do with them. If I hadn't yet learned how to choose between myself and pleasing men, if I couldn't get love right, then at least I'd learned to value women.

twenty-one

France 2005.

My father, leaning back in his wicker chair—the chair lopsided, the cushion under him a lump of faded chintz—looks triumphant, if a little overwhelmed to be back in France. It's been a long time. My brother is here too, and we're having lunch with the De La Falaises—new friends of mine—Louisa and her son, Daniel, who are renting a small stone house near the village of Castelsarrasin, a place with creeping vines and a misty view over Gaillac. There are quail eggs for lunch, figs, salad, three kinds of asparagus—all prepared by Daniel, a former London chef. The garden, something Louisa has hacked out of the stony ground, is a small, magical plot, like something out of a fairy tale: clouds of roses, wallflowers, and marigolds, banks of rosemary, plus an old tractor seat balanced on a tree stump so that visitors can sit and admire the view. Slim and fairylike herself, she urges my father to "Please go on!" Not that he needs prodding. Having spent the winter by himself in a leaky English house, he's happy to be back in the limelight. He's on his favorite subject: the navy days, World War II. The best years of his life, he admits, mainly because he wasn't wounded. For dramatic purposes, however, there were near-misses. They were attacked by U-boats; several times the ship caught fire. It was also freezing cold and the food was dreadful. "American sailors couldn't believe the terrible conditions. Compared to us, they lived like gods. And of course the English women *loved* them." Laughing now, he shoots off the old line, singing, *Overpaid, oversexed and over here!* Followed by, "Have you heard the one about the new utility knickers? One Yank and they're off!" which always gets a good laugh.

He rattles on, his face lit up, one elbow raised, a glass of rosé on the tilt. There's no stopping him. I've heard it all before, of course: stories that for years were tedious and which I now tolerate—no, *love*. My brother is gentle with him too, despite their old arguments, when he was failing the bar, trying *not* to be a lawyer, desperate to be anything else. "The idiot boy!" my father would say, laughing. He never realized how wounding his remarks were. In fact, he's still amazed when something he says offends people. Why don't they get the joke? After so many years of isolated self-interest, he's incapable of imagining himself in someone else's shoes.

But the stories are his way of staying alive. Talking about himself is his prerogative because he's beaten the odds. Bladder cancer, a stroke, several heart attacks—he's survived them all. That and being on his own now. My mother died a year ago, and at the advanced age of eighty-eight, his determination *not to go* is suddenly reinforced by being in France.

During the 1950s, he always talked about buying a house here. It was his ongoing fantasy, something that got him through those impenetrable English winters, kneeling on our living room floor, the Michelin map spread across the carpet. And one summer in St Tropez, he took us to see a place near Ramatuelle. A low, whitewashed cottage, with tall trees and a stream running through the garden. We loved it, but my mother was against it. There was some question about a farmer's right of way across the property. Besides, she said, we'd be *obliged* to go there every year—meaning, of course, more housework and cooking. This untenable burden was the decisive blow; we didn't get it. Something my father talked about for years, his voice tinged with wonder and regret: "Only five thousand pounds!"

· · ·

My father at the château.

From the airport we had driven straight to the château, and my father had fallen in love with it immediately. "Magnificent!" he shouted, moving quickly, despite his walking stick, to inspect the ground floor: the two large salons that would eventually be opened up to something as big as—well, perhaps a small ballroom. "Incredible!" The classic corridor, the double doors at each end that reminded him of a hotel in Saint-Malo where he'd stayed with my mother after the war: "Amazing!" And the floorboards: "Where would you find planks that *wide* these days?" The ruined upstairs, the basement—everything explored in a rush of excitement. Then outside, his feet poised precariously at the edge of the pool hole, gazing across the valley: "Look at that. What a view! Who would have thought it possible? A house in France. Miraculous! I can't believe you did it!" And seeing it through his eyes, I couldn't quite believe it myself.

He then added, his Scottish thriftiness rearing its head, "God knows how much it's all costing. You're bloody lucky to have such an understanding husband!" Which immediately sent me into paroxysms of guilt.

· · ·

After lunch with the La Falaise's, we return to the glorious ruin and my brother sets up a chair for him under the chestnuts; he wants to sit and face the view. I then go into the house to resume my daily battle with the workmen.

M. Gomes, busy plastering the hall ceiling, tells me that M. Bruni has left for the hospital, complaining about his hand. About a week ago, he had an accident with his sander. He was working on the staircase, the only section of the hallway downstairs that hadn't been done. The old paint was difficult—dark and thick—and he was having a hard time in the corners. Bent over in his flyless shorts, his black Speedo pants underneath, he was going at it with such tremendous force that his sander had suddenly jammed or accelerated—I'm not sure which—the wheel spinning off and cutting him. *"Putain de merde!"* he shouted. Blood spurted everywhere. For a moment I thought he'd cut off his whole hand. His leg was bleeding too. There was no first-aid box, and no one else was around. Panicked, I got a bottle of vodka from the kitchen, poured some over his fingers, then over his leg. I ripped an old towel into strips, slitting the ends as I'd done in the Girl Guides, then bandaged his hand. When he dropped his pants and hiked up his Speedos so that I could wrap his thigh, I thought perhaps now might be the time to stop using the formal *vous* and find out his Christian name. But he was swearing too much. I offered to drive him to the hospital. He waved me off. "I'll be back to-morrow." "Are you sure?" I asked. "Of course," he said, raising his bloody fist. "*Je suis Bruni!*"

He had come back the next day. He'd driven over with his one good hand, the bad one bandaged professionally at the clinic. I was genuinely touched. But he didn't look well, his eyes swimmier than usual. And these days he'd been coughing a lot, complaining about a lump in his throat—a recent development after inhaling vast quantities of cement dust. But what could I say about the cheroot smoking, the cough, or the open bottle of wine on the back seat of his car? At least I couldn't *keep on* saying it. Besides, when he does show up, he manages to do in an hour what it takes Joseph, for example, two days to accomplish—that's if he does anything at all.

I'm trying to avoid Joseph. When I do catch sight of him, skulking down the corridor, or eyeing me with his fixed bayonet stare, I walk the other way. I'm not in the mood to hear what a lucky girl I am, or what a bargain I'm getting for twenty-five euros an hour instead of the usual thirty-five.

Then yesterday there had been another setback. It was eleven o'clock, I was just getting back from Montauban and saw M. Boudet Sr. and Uncle walking out the door. David was already in the truck, loading up the tool-boxes. *"Au revoir!"* they announced happily. "See you in two weeks."

"Two weeks?"

"Yes," said M. Boudet Sr. "I told you about it a couple of months ago. Remember?"

No, I didn't. I felt the familiar surge of panic. Neither the electricity nor the plumbing was close to being finished. No sinks or tubs or showers had been installed, wires were still hanging out of the walls, and it was almost July. "We have a deadline," I said. "Guests are arriving in *August*—remember?" In the old days, I would throw out the word August like a religious zealot, as though heralding the Second Coming, ready to drop to my knees and beg for mercy. Now I was more cynical. "Taking a little holiday, are we? *Les vacances?*" I said to Boudet Sr., not bothering to hide my suspicion. "Oh, no, no," he replied, looking unusually contrite. "I have to honor a job with another client. But don't worry. *Pas de souci!* Everything will be finished in time. I *promise!*"

Since my little breakdown, I'm given a wide berth. No one raises his voice, and sometimes I feel like Olivia de Havilland in *The Snake Pit*—a role I am only too happy to play, if it works. *"Au revoir! À bientôt!"* they say cautiously, backing off toward their white vans.

I don't mention these setbacks to my father. But he's seen the sign I staked to the ancient box hedges, a warning not to throw any paint or chemicals there—S'IL VOUS PLAIT, NE JETER RIEN ICI. LES BUIS ONT 200 ANS—erected after the first bucket of M. Gomes's plaster slops was tossed in this direction. This was also meant as an appeal to the French sensibility regarding beauty. "I bet they don't take any notice," my father says. But they do. At least they do now. No one wants to antagonize the patronne these days. *La femme affolée* who is in danger of erupting.

But my brother's calm overrides any potential hysteria. I can step back, relinquish my responsibilities, and become the girl from Westcliff again. Because that's where my father is; everything in France reminds him of the old days in Saint-Tropez.

I have booked rooms in the Hôtel le Pré Vert, in Rabastens, another ancient town, twenty minutes away, its red brick houses rising majestically from the banks of the Tarn. The hotel is an old nineteenth century *maison particulier*, with a rambling garden in the back. We used to stop at places like this on our way south; family-owned hotels with geraniums on the window sills, blistered shutters, and a metal stand in the street advertising the *plat du jour*. Such dilapidated charm reminds my father of Les Palmiers, and before we've parked the car he is reminiscing: "Remember Madame Geurin and her husband, Sailor . . . remember La Dorade? You always had the fish soup."

I take them to the summer night market in Monclar, the Marché de Nuit, the stalls and sideshows lit with Chinese lanterns and offering everything from candyfloss to Panama hats or a game of Shoot the Ducks. The evenings are blissfully warm, and we sit at trestle tables under the plane trees, elbow to elbow with the locals. There is a feeling of airiness, of disembodied calm. Yes, we say, *this is how it was*. Bettina, who owns the local café with her husband, Joel, carries over *moules frites*, the plates lined up on her forearms. On the next lap she arrives with carafes of rouge and blanc. A saxophone player belts out a blues number to a playback, and a young girl with a microphone wanders through the crowd singing "Smoke Gets in Your Eyes."

In the summer, there are fairs like this in every village. On Friday night, we drive over to Lisle-sur-Tarn to see a fireworks display. Traffic jams the roads, and so we leave the car in a field and walk, moving en masse with the crowds—a long trek for my father, so we find the first patch of grass near the lake and collapse. The fireworks are dazzling. It's like Bastille Day, showers of reflected gold and red and orange bursting overhead. As they shoot up, my father ducks down, hands on his head in mock terror, laughing like a boy: *Incredible!* Later, we manage to grab a table at the café in the village square. A band is set up under the arches. A four-piece combo with trumpet and accordion, they play old French songs, war songs, turn-of-the-century waltzes, sambas, and foxtrots. Couples stream out to dance, most of them middle-aged or older. The women in their best flowered dresses, the men in fancy suits, with pointed shoes and slicked-back hair, showing off the moves they learned as boys. "Look," says my father. "None of them know how to do the steps *properly!*" And he pulls me up to dance, something we haven't done for thirty years. He steers me across the cobblestones in a waltz, suddenly light on his feet, my hero again, and I feel the tears come. Everything is so intoxicatingly reminiscent: the bobbing lights, the band, people laughing, drinking cognacs and Pernod. "Remember," he says, "the Citadel bar in St. Trop?" "Remind me," I say, though I know the story well. "Your mother and I used to go there after hours. The waiters locked the doors, then a few of us climbed in through a back window. There was an old pianola, and we danced around the tables for hours."

In a way, France has come too late. He's already dreading going back to face another wet English summer. He doesn't sleep well anymore. "Although if I imagine myself in the navy, rocking in a hammock, I can sometimes doze off." He takes a lot of medication and travels with a plastic box, divided into sections, each compartment containing six or seven pills. He checks his blood and injects himself twice a day with insulin, which he regards as a "damn nuisance." He is preoccupied with his health. Another one of his big topics. And it's no good reminding him that he's lucky, that other people have been through worse, that at his age he can still walk and read the newspaper. "Yes," he says, "I know, I know. But what good is that to me? I can't *think like that.*" He wants to keep his diseases in focus: read the literature, talk about them, as if by paying due diligence, by checking his vital signs every five minutes, he can keep the worst at bay. My mother couldn't stand his self-obsession. Childishly frightened of injections, or pain, he nevertheless delivered himself to the hospital with relief—to be "*properly* cared for." During one of his stays he accidentally defecated in the bed. He was mortified, but as the nurses had been so kind, he wanted to reward them. "Bring in the checkbook," he told my mother. The idea of financially rewarding these twenty-year-olds, however, after her own tireless care, when she was often in too much pain herself to cook or even listen— but nevertheless did—was the last straw. Or the last of many. No checkbook was brought in. He is tortured now by the idea that he didn't appreciate her. And of course he didn't. But then I'm not sure I did either, so I'm tortured in my own way.

Every summer, I would go back to Paglesham for a couple of weeks or more, particularly when they were older. Most of the time, I hung around with my father. We still lived in a world of mutual admiration, going for walks, trudging arm in arm across the marshy fields, talking about books. Or we'd take nostalgic drives to the Westcliff seafront, past the old pier. "Do you remember when you were eleven and a man *exposed* himself to you here? I had to call the police!" (Yes, I did. And the sight of that wrinkled chicken-neck penis had been stamped on my mind for eternity.) We'd stop at the Leigh sheds to get a pint of prawns and a cockle tea. He would often look mournful then, sitting on a bench, staring out to sea. He wasn't so good at hiding his fragility anymore, not when it came to the arguments with my mother. Her constant nagging about his reading, his daydreaming, his not helping in the kitchen. She'd even told him she never really liked going to the cinema. "Imagine, after all these years, saying she didn't like *films!*" Bewildered, he'd add, "I'm not sure she even likes *me.*" So I'd take his hand and we'd sit there for another ten minutes, in silence, listening to the seagulls screaming. Then we'd trudge back to the car.

I tried to keep the peace between them. I made an effort with my mother, although by now my sunny nature had become a bit of a put-on. I could smile through my teeth at anything. "Well, dear, you're here!" We hugged tentatively in the hallway: the blue eyes, the cigarette-lined face, the frail child-woman weighing all of ninety-five pounds but still *managing*. I wanted to help. I shopped for groceries, peeled vegetables, made endless cups of terrible Nescafé. I stood in the kitchen to keep her company, leaning against our pine dresser, clutching my glass of vodka, while she trussed a bird for dinner. "Is that a pheasant?" "No, dear. Cornish game hen. Safeway's. They're very good. You can get everything now. Mozzarella. Brie." We were both tamed and trained. I could listen to her chat about the upcoming village produce show, or my brother's unsuitable marriage to a half-Chinese girl, without feeling I had to take a quick turn around the garden or bolt upstairs to my room. Perhaps I wasn't trying so hard to be loved. I was still sensitive to her moods, though in the same way I might be attuned to the hum of distant traffic. Because the old grievances were still there. If I made a passing reference to Westcliff, for example, she might suddenly blurt out, "You know, when I was nine months pregnant with you, your father made me *walk* to the Meteor nursing home. He refused to call a taxi, because he said it was only three streets away!"—the remark said while the inconsiderate husband was in earshot, but nevertheless directed at me, the baby who was "overdue, enormous" and who apparently "refused to be born!"

"Well, I think you're stuck with both of us now," I would say, laughing.

Nostalgia ate away at my soul. I spent afternoons going through our old photo albums, falling to pieces, many of the black-and-white snaps jammed haphazardly in the spine. Photographs I'd been staring at for years: the Austin Atlantic, Seymour Road, an increasing number of prams, small legs straddling bicycles. What was I looking for? There was one of my mother in the garden. Slim and pretty in a gingham sunsuit, her blond hair swept up like Betty Grable and balancing my baby brother on one hip. Tiny versions of my sister and me are by her side and she's smiling, tightly holding my hand. Why didn't I remember *that*?

Why didn't I remember her saying, "My lovely pink-and-white baby," meaning me, not my brother. Well, I did now.

Sometimes I think there is a deep, dark part in children that is unchangeable, a small central hollow that, no matter how many things get stuffed inside, will not close. But I wanted it to. I looked for a way back in. And there were missed opportunities.

It was the autumn of 2002. By now, I was a woman close to middle age and my mother a frail eighty-six. More birdlike than ever, she had crippling osteoporosis and walked badly, even with a stick. But she still clung relentlessly to her daily routine. Every morning, after she'd made my father's breakfast (he was incapable, she thought, of preparing a boiled egg or a piece of toast by himself), she hobbled back upstairs to get ready for the day. Though the chances of her leaving the house were close to zero, she'd put on her famous red lipstick, then dress in a tweed suit and her pearls, come down again, if only to sit on the sofa.

On this particular morning, I was leaving to go back to Los Angeles. I'd been there a week, and a car was waiting outside to take me to Heathrow, three hours away. I came into the drawing room to say good-bye. She was sitting, dressed, as usual, her legs in black stockings now to cover the purpura, the dark bruises that appeared at the slightest pressure. When I leaned over the sofa to kiss her cheek, she suddenly grabbed my arm. "No, don't go. Don't go!" she blurted out. " Please don't GO!" She was close to tears. I didn't know what to do. So I slid around and sat next to her on the sofa. "Of course, I'll stay," I said. But I wasn't used to her needing me, and the words sounded shallow. We sat silently, me awkwardly holding her hand. Then, embarrassed by her outburst, she whispered, "It's okay, dear. Go on, get your plane." Again I offered to stay, but she wasn't having it. And I didn't say, "No. I *am staying.*" I wasn't insistent. I didn't cancel the car. In fact, when she said, "It's all right, I'm perfectly *fine,*" laughing now like a young girl, wiping her eyes as if she was amazed by her own foolishness, I got up and left. I can't think of anything I have regretted more in my life. On the way to Heathrow, I sat staring at the miserable wet asphalt speeding past and wept. *How dare she do this to me now!* I told myself. *How dare she need me.* Then, a moment later *Forgive me, forgive me!*—because what if she died. What if this was my last chance to tell her I loved her? Or show that I loved her? It wasn't, but I hated myself then. I hated our English reticence. Our brave misery. For eleven hours on the plane, I barely spoke. How tragic, I thought, that at this late stage in life neither of us had the courage to say how we felt.

But it's easy to have regrets.

I am in the kitchen, the phone line pulled taut from the salon, talking to *Bainluxe.* I am having another unsatisfying conversation with the woman there, trying to find out when they might be coming to finish—or, rather, *start*—the pool. About the mountain of sand, *la montagne de sable*, that has been untouched now for more than a month. "We'll let you know, madame," is all she will say. "*Bientôt!*"

Through the window, I see my father sitting exactly where we left him, under the chestnuts. To please him, about an hour ago, I put on Django Reinhardt and Stephane Grappelli's "It Don't Mean a Thing (If It Ain't Got That Swing)." When he heard the music wafting from the house, he shouted, "Do you remember seeing him in Saint-Tropez? In front of Senequier? Grappelli—right there on the port, playing his violin?"

"Yes, I remember."

"Imagine! And none of those French even took any *notice!* Poor fellow. He must have been hard up!" He was shaking his head in wonder, as he always did telling the tale, indignant at this great man's comedown.

But he looks fragile now. Legs that used to be athletically strong are spindly under the baggy cotton shorts. His long arms hang down by his sides and his head is slumped on his chest. Is he breathing? Panicked, I think he's dead. I call my brother, who is somewhere in the garden, and together we run over. But he's merely fallen asleep. He wakes up, disoriented at first, then takes in the view.

"Magnificent," he says. "Pity your mother isn't here to see it."

twenty-two
Los Angeles 1978.

I thought I would be saved by marriage. Admittedly not a very original idea. It was 1978. We were in New York, having lunch in one of those small places off Madison Avenue with the cream-colored walls and the tables pushed too close together. Nancy "Slim" Keith was telling me that the first time she caught sight of my new husband, Bill Hayward, whom she referred to affectionately as "my darling boy," was on the platform of the Biarritz train station. He was sixteen years old, and as he climbed down from the train dressed, she said, rather amusingly for a holiday in France with his father and new stepmother, in a beret and sporting a cane, she immediately fell in love with him. "I thought, How could I *ever* let this boy out of my sight again?"

I didn't know much about Bill's childhood then, or his father, the late Leland Hayward, a respected agent and film producer; about his father's near-marriage to Katharine Hepburn, his subsequent marriage to the actress Margaret Sullavan, then to Slim Keith, ex-wife of the director Howard Hawks, then to Pamela Harriman, ex-wife of Randolph Churchill and later ambassador to France. I also didn't know that Slim was a famous socialite, reputed to be the model for Lady Coolbirth in Truman Capote's *Answered Prayers*. Sophisticated, slightly intimidating with her scraped-back hair and slash of red mouth, she had a lot to say about her successor, Pamela, perhaps for my benefit, or perhaps as a warm-up for her memoirs. She was talking into a tape recorder every day, she said. There was the story about "the pearls," for example. The Hayward pearls, famously large, unquestionably rare, that had been inherited by Bill's sister, Brooke.

Apparently, after Leland's death the pearls had been "taken away" by stepmother Pamela for "safekeeping"—along with a Modigliani and various other treasures that were then passed on to Pamela's son, young Winston Churchill—never to be seen again. "She probably sold them, or they were broken up," Slim said. "After all, you can't trace pearls!"

An awful woman, Slim admitted. But extraordinary. Apparently men fell over themselves to get close to her, despite the fact that she wasn't particularly beautiful. Once Slim asked one of Pamela's "very grand lovers" (Gianni Agnelli, Bill thought) what her secret was. Sex? "No," this grand person said. "She was definitely *not* a great lay. But she made every man feel like he was the best, the *most* intelligent." Also, before screwing a man, Slim said, Pamela had Tiffany engrave the prospective lover's name on the inside of a gold cigarette case. A postcoital surprise that was then presented to him the next morning at breakfast.

If there was any jealousy, Slim didn't show it. Instead, perhaps to show she was no slacker herself when it came to men, she told us about her romance with Hemingway. The many love letters he'd sent her. "When a phone was finally installed in the house in Cuba, I was the *first person* he called." As I said, I felt a lot of this information was for my benefit. The newlywed actress from Los Angeles (though I could hardly compare myself to her old pal Lauren Bacall, whose character in *To Have and Have Not* had been based on Slim). There was, for instance, a tip about how *not* to behave with a man. Her married daughter, Slim said, had made the irreversible blunder of telling her husband the truth about an affair she was having. "A typically modern mistake," Slim pointed out, referring to the '70s preoccupation with coming clean about everything. She turned to me then, her face pleasantly flushed, her eyes raised over a glass of Sancerre. "Never," she said, *never admit to anything* when you're married."

Which I didn't.

Bill Hayward's pedigree was impressive. Before Leland, his mother, Margaret Sullavan, had been married to director Walter Wanger, then to Henry Fonda. His childhood friends were the sons and daughters of Hollywood royalty: the Mankiewiczes, the Lubitcshes, Robert Mitchum's children, Jennifer Jones's boys. But apart from Bill's sartorial originality—progressing from the French beret in Biarritz to the hospital greens he liked to wear around the house, and sometimes out to dinner—he had inherited none of the facility or drive needed to be a success in Hollywood, or perhaps anywhere, the weight of his parents' fame engendering instead a paralyzing fear of failure.

Saying that, it wasn't obvious at first, because he had produced movies, the most successful being *Easy Rider* with Peter Fonda. Peter was his best friend. They were both motorcycle fanatics, they had a production company together, and there were other films. But by the end of the '70s, Hollywood was emerging from its hip decade and Bill, a gentle soul, didn't possess the required ruthlessness to survive. Although he tried.

Our first meeting was like a scene out of a 1940s comedy. I was still living in the art deco building in West Hollywood and Bill had the apartment two floors above. We'd never met. Then one day, I walked into the elevator and there he was. Tall with wavy blond hair and startling gray-blue eyes, he looked like the young Joseph Cotten in *The Magnificent Ambersons*. I was on my way to the airport, carrying an expensive suitcase. It wasn't mine, but on loan from my old writer boyfriend Walter and unreturned since our break-up. I had no idea the case actually belonged to *his* previous girlfriend who, coincidentally, happened to be Bill's sister, Brooke. During our silent three-floor descent, I saw Bill eyeing it, then eyeing me. "Where did you get that suitcase?" he said, finally, feigning indignation. "It happens to be my sister's!"

We were married three weeks later. He kept asking and, flattered, I finally said yes. I said yes with all the logic of someone convinced that if I didn't do it quickly, I wouldn't do it at all.

Did I see the hint of looniness in those beautiful eyes? No, I was more fascinated with Bill's cultivated eccentricity: the delicate East Coast manners, the discreet tattoos, the fact that he could make a perfect soufflé *and* rebuild a Harley-Davidson. What's more, unlike my former boyfriends who'd been odd-looking—what I'd considered "intellectual" types—he was handsome. Just the kind of man my mother would have approved of. But I didn't invite my parents to the wedding. In fact, I forbade them to come, the reason being that by taking the marriage seriously, I would have had to ask myself what the fuck I was doing.

I was trying to ground myself. And I think Bill was too. In those early days, I didn't know about his childhood suffering. Back in the '50s, when psychoanalysis became the miracle cure, Bill had been sent to the New York shrink Dr. Lawrence Kubie, who had then packed him off to the Menninger Clinic in Topeka, Kansas. A sixteen-year-old locked up in a mental institution after a minor infraction at boarding school: ducking out to meet a girl. Apparently, the famous Kubie had arranged for quite a few "unmanageable children" to be taken away so that parents, or studios, could get on with the business of making movies. "Gene Tierney was one of the inmates," Bill said. "And *everyone* was in love with her!" The windows and doors were bolted; heavy medication and cold packs— being rolled in iced bed sheets—were standard.

One day, Bill managed to escape, skipping the drugs then forcing open an upstairs window. "I only had six cents to my name, so I stole a car and drove to Mexico." His father chased after him. He begged not to be put back, but Leland wanted to teach him a lesson. "He thought I should be grateful. He kept saying, 'It's so expensive—and not even a *tax deduction!*'" By this time, Bill would be laughing. He had a big laugh, head thrown back, his shoulders shaking, and at first I mistook the cheerfulness for a great inner strength. Like other sad memories, Menninger had become a good tale. But not everything could be buried. One night, we were sitting up late with Peter Fonda and Chris Mankiewicz—son of screenwriter/director Joe Mankiewicz—also a patient of the ruthless Kubie and who had narrowly missed being sent to Menninger himself. They were reminiscing about their childhoods, about the big houses, the elaborate birthday parties with magicians and circus ponies and elephants, when suddenly Peter said: "Don't you think it's a coincidence that *all* our mothers committed suicide?"

For the wedding, I wore a peach-colored voile dress and, Titania-like, a gardenia in my hair, and floated around Connie Wald's living room. Connie, a well-known socialite and dear friend of Bill's parents, lived in a pretty Dutch Colonial–style house on Beverly Drive. The guests included my brother, who happened to be visiting from England, Peter Fonda (the best man), Larry Hagman, and the actress Joanna Cassidy. I was petrified, fairly drunk, enough so that the judge finally took me aside: "You have to put down your glass of champagne, so we can get on with the ceremony." Bill's sister Brooke was also there. We didn't like each other much. I found her superficial, a snob. And she knew I saw right through her loathing smile. She arrived late, dressed defiantly in white, then during the vows kept whispering, "How can we *stop* this!" One of the few people who didn't think we were an ideal couple. Perhaps we weren't. But we were similar.

By then, Bill was seeing a shrink in Beverly Hills and on several medications, lithium being one, and he drank a lot. And if I didn't notice he was an alcoholic, it was because I was drinking too.

I was thirty-two. Having promised myself I would never become domesticated like my mother, I went about creating a home as if I had just landed the leading role in *Mrs. Miniver*. I repainted the walls of our old Spanish house, I baked, I planted tea roses and geraniums. For dinner parties, I laid out the Baccarat crystal and porcelain, determined to make things normal. And for the first time, I wanted to get pregnant. Bill already had two children from his first marriage. He rarely saw them—or couldn't bear to after the guilt of abandoning them. Perhaps he'd never left his childhood long enough to face being a father. He certainly didn't want any more.

Bill Hayward and me on our wedding day.

Not that he ever said it. But these were tricky subjects, and if I brought up the idea of getting pregnant, he retreated into his safe, non-intimate world. "What's wrong?" I'd ask. "Nothing!" "I love you." "*I love you too*," he'd murmur, skipping out of the room with a goofy smile, going off to do his thing: his carpentry, his cooking, his kayaking. Sitting in our Mexican-tiled breakfast nook, he'd pore over brochures for Native American rugs or steam-bent Eskimo chairs; or he'd mark pages in army surplus catalogs, circling binoculars and guns. He kept a small arsenal under the bed. "Here's how you load it," he'd say, calmly ramming in a magazine. "In case you're alone one day and someone breaks in." He had the loner's fixation regarding danger. Quick and fearless. Yet to me he was the least violent man I knew. A vulnerability that was endangering his soul. And mine too. Sometimes we would lie in bed clinging to each other. But in those tender moments, if I made a move sexually, he would freeze. Or jump up and lock himself in the bathroom. I wasn't perceptive enough to know why. "What did I *do*?" I'd scream through the door, in tears. Like most women, I presumed it must be my fault. Sometimes I'd force him to make love, or try to when he was loaded, half comatose, the beautiful gray eyes drifting. I'd kiss his neck, his stomach, his feet, crawling over his perfect body like an impatient child, pleading, "Come on, *come on* . . ." I'd take his cock and work it with my mouth for hours, to show him I wasn't giving up, then finally flop back, exhausted. Now and again it worked. After all, sex was survival, and part of him was just as desperate as I was to make the connection. Eventually, I did get pregnant. It seemed like a miracle. I remember standing in the dry cleaners one afternoon, mesmerized by the hangers whirring around, thinking, *Oh my God, I've made it. I'm finally grown up!*

I was euphoric. I stopped drinking and smoking. I exercised. Then one day, I fainted in Tony Richardson's garden. He was giving a Sunday brunch for Jocelyn Herbert, the costume designer he'd worked with since *Tom Jones*. It was a big affair, Tony flitting nervously across the front lawn between Anjelica Huston and Christopher Isherwood. Suddenly, in slow motion, I sank into the rose bushes at Jean Vallely's feet—a new friend of mine, another strong, independent American woman who was Tony's girlfriend then. When I came to, a concerned crowd was staring down at me; everyone, that is, except my husband. I caught sight of him across the lawn, laughing, talking with a man, oblivious—or not so oblivious. Having a baby terrified him.

Then at five and a half months, I lost it.

"Possibly due to a damaged cervix," said my doctor. (When I first arrived in L.A., I'd been fitted with an IUD, something called a Copper T, an excruciatingly painful procedure and a device that later became infected.)

I was in the kitchen with Bill one afternoon when my water broke. He drove me to Cedars-Sinai hospital, but the baby left me. I can remember the brightly lit cubicle, the pained look on the nurse's face, and a terrible feeling of emptiness. I buried my face in the pillow, trying to push back the misery. I have no idea how long he lived. (I was told it was a boy.) An hour, perhaps. Long enough that, according to hospital rules, he had to have a proper burial. Bill refused to come with me to the cemetery. "I can't face it," he said, which by that time seemed a perfectly normal response. Instead, I asked my friend Susanna.

That day remains vague. We are driving somewhere in the San Fernando Valley. It's unbearably hot, but I insist on opening a window because the air-conditioning is too punishing. A continual shock of authenticity. Then we are in a dark office. Strips of yellow light leak though the venetian blinds and I'm standing with Susanna and her eight-year-old daughter, Lulu, facing an anonymous man in a dark suit and a greasy tie. He is sitting behind a desk, expressionless. Eventually, he slides over some official-looking papers. "Sign here, please," he says. So I do. I manage a wobbly signature, conscious that behind him, on a long table, is a stunningly small coffin.

Our social life was a way of keeping things going. Los Angeles was a small town then, a suburban paradise. People rode horses down Rodeo Drive; Southern Pacific's freight trains clattered slowly along Santa Monica Boulevard's center divide. We went to the old haunts: the Brown Derby, the Luau—famous for its mai tais and the clam-shaped urinals in the men's room, to Cyrano's on Sunset and the peach-walled Perino's, where Bill's father had dined and where Cole Porter had supposedly scribbled a hit or two on the back of his menu.

I looked respectable. I had a collection of demure black cocktail dresses. I had Bill's mother's pearl-and-diamond bracelet with the sprig of lucky heather attached in a gold locket. It didn't work for me, nor for her. She had died taking an overdose of sleeping pills. His sister Bridget had done the same. And Bill felt doomed to follow. But we carried on; we drank our fears down.

There were dinners at Connie Wald's with Jimmy and Gloria Stewart and Audrey Hepburn, or Gore Vidal and Billy Wilder—where old Hollywood glamour, if a touch ancient, still reigned. Audrey, Billy's wife, was a pale-faced beauty, an ethereal-looking Louise Brooks with dark cropped hair. She had big, luminous eyes, though often they seemed to be drifting elsewhere. One night, leaning across the veal in aspic, she said, "Would you like to see my jewels?" "Love to," I replied. I had the feeling I was the only one who hadn't. She was wearing a black Chanel suit that had secret pockets sewn into the lining. Reaching inside, she fished out a handful of stones—one an enormous emerald—then rolled them across the tablecloth. "I never leave home without them," she whispered.

Bill felt comfortable among his parents' friends. He was still the darling boy, even if he occasionally passed out at the table. Eyes fluttering, he would pitch forward, his chin grazing the cutlery. It wasn't inelegantly done. Rather than blame it on the last fatal Negroni, I would say, "I think he might have a touch of flu," then ask the butler to help me put him in the car. No one commented. In fact, some of the guests were completely gone themselves. In an old journal I found, I'd noted: *Mrs. Jules Stein fell over twice, as if in slow motion. She fell again in the hallway, almost dragging Gloria Stewart with her. A dead weight with all those diamond doggie brooches . . .*

When we got home, there were arguments, ferocious battles. About his drinking—not mine; I was getting just as plastered, of course, but could handle it better. And I wanted to get drunk, to get down to the grisly depths. Not that I ever went deep enough. Some little corner of my brain was always lit up, fizzling like a neon sign: *Save Yourself You're Dying Here!* And I resented Bill because he managed to wipe the slate clean every night. He'd be laughing when I pushed him up the staircase to our bedroom, deliriously happy when I peeled off his trousers, yanked at his shoes. And I gave him hell. "I should never have married you. You're *hopeless*," I'd shout furiously. "You're not even capable of getting a *job*. And when was the last time we had sex? I'm leaving you! *Do you hear me?* I'm leaving you!"

But he was already comatose. There I'd be ranting like a madwoman, screaming into the void, because I couldn't do it when we were sober. And in the morning, we'd move gingerly around each other. "Did I pass out last night?" he'd ask, squeezing past me in the bathroom. "Yes." "Oh, shit. *Sorry.*" His movements were exaggeratedly precise, slipping on his loafers, buttoning his flannel shirt. Trying to resume his fragile dignity. I felt empty, bereaved. He remembered nothing. Or if he did, he wouldn't say.

He wasn't working much then. Peter Fonda was doing projects on his own, Bill was waiting for things to materialize. He did crossword puzzles. He was very intelligent. He read feverishly and spent the afternoons devouring *Scientific American* or the *New Yorker*. "You must read this piece about cultivating hydroponic tomatoes," he'd say, or, "Fascinating stuff about Augusto Pinochet . . ." It was his way of not falling apart. But on hot summer nights, the humidity dripping off the walls, I would lie awake, full of despair.

I tried to work. There was a small room in the basement, what had originally been the chauffeur's quarters, next to the garage. I wrote there compulsively, sometimes eight hours a day. Or I escaped to my friend Lynne's apartment. I was closer to her than ever and would talk endlessly about my problems with Bill. For a long time she indulged me then, finally, with her usual comic flair, said, "Let's face it, honey. You gotta get that first marriage out of the way!"

Work was the only real distraction. I wrote four screenplays during this time—ironically, all of them romantic comedies. I wrote on spec, or I got development deals, happy to be earning money, even if none of them got made. For meetings I dressed in tailored business suits. I wore flat shoes and glasses. But it wasn't easy to convince people I'd switched careers—I wasn't even sure I'd convinced myself. One day, walking out of a meeting at MGM, I overheard one of the vice presidents say, "After all, she's only an *actress*." I was shocked. But the comment wasn't completely wrong. I was still trying too hard to be liked. I hadn't grasped how different it was auditioning for a job in America. The old British standby of downplaying your abilities, undervaluing yourself as a sign of modesty, didn't work. A bold declaration of status was required. Anything less was looked on as suspiciously amateur.

And I was still an actress. I'd just finished *The Fury*, directed by Brian De Palma: a flashy terrorist yarn involving scenes of psychic horror and buckets of blood. I played a doctor, a by-the-book, white-coat role, with some gratuitous sex thrown in. At first, I'd turned it down, but Sue Mengers, a powerful agent at the time, called me in a rage. "Don't you *want* to be a star?" she shouted. "You're English, Fiona; you can't get *fucking arrested*. And this is Brian De Palma!" It was hard, however, to think that such a hackneyed role would finally propel me to stardom. I remember one day being on the set with John Cassavetes. It was the lunch hour. The rest of the cast and crew had left, but as we'd been shooting a gory scene, both of us were soaked in fake blood, we had to stay behind to eat our sandwiches. Sitting in the semidarkness, dripping like pieces of raw meat, John said, "Aren't you glad you didn't bother going to acting class for *this?*" I also endured, in what seemed a perverse amount of takes, a violent rape scene with the young actor Andrew Stevens.

Fortunately, it was considered too disturbing for a normal family audience and was eventually cut. (I think a late thank-you to the kind editor is in order here.)

In the summer of 1981, Tony Richardson invited us down to La Garde-Freinet. In France, my malaise lifted. The lazy breakfasts with bowls of café au lait, the big outdoor lunches, Natasha in the kitchen making vichyssoise and big pans of rosemary chicken.

As usual, Tony organized our days and nights. He had brought a movie camera to make a short film. Bill was the cameraman. Tony and I wrote the script, and everyone participated, including Natasha and her sister, Joely Richardson; the actress Joan Plowright, Laurence Olivier's wife; and their son, Dickie. For four days we ran around laughing, tripping over our thrown-together costumes of scarves and beach towels. Tony was in his element. The circus maestro. And he kept a punishing work schedule. One afternoon, when we abandoned shooting to watch Charles and Diana's wedding on Anne Marie's television, Tony, the staunch anti-royalist, stood in the driveway shouting as we drove off:

"You are all *pathetically sentimental.*" There were excursions to the beach and shopping in Saint-Tropez. We were invited to dinner on Sam Spiegel's yacht. That night, the port was packed, literally throbbing with people. Late for dinner, we ran through the crowds. Senequier and L'Escale were lit up, and with the cars honking, the sound of waves slapping against the boats, I felt the old rush, the magic.

Spiegel had produced, among other films, *On The Waterfront* and *Lawrence of Arabia*, and Leland Hayward had given him his first job. I hadn't told Bill or, in fact, anyone that years before I had spent a weekend with Sam in Paris at the George V. I had agreed to go during one of my usual lapses of good sense, unable to say no. But I'd insisted we have separate rooms, and much to Sam's annoyance, nothing happened. That night on the boat, however, he greeted me warmly. He was delighted that I was married to Bill, and in front of the other guests (Jack Nicholson and several anonymous beauties), he announced that I was "a very good girl," presumably as a reward for not sleeping with him. At dinner, he kept putting his arm around Bill, like a proud father. "Can you *believe* it?" he croaked, in his thick Mittel-European accent. "I gave this boy his twenty-first birthday party!"

I'd never seen Bill so relaxed. And Tony loved him. He loved his eccentricity, his esoteric knowledge. He encouraged him to talk about vintage motorcycles, about trawling for tuna in Alaska (Bill had once owned a fishing boat) and, naturally, about Hollywood, the old glory days of Ben Hecht and Charles MacArthur. They'd been clients of Leland's, and as a teenager, Bill had been taken to meet them, lying around their pool with a bevy of naked girls. "Oh, you *poor* boy, ha ha! *Go on.*" There were stories about Leland's affairs—in particular the one with Katharine Hepburn. In the mid-1930s, Leland and Hepburn were living together in Los Angeles. At the same time, he was also having an affair with his actress client Margaret Sullavan, who lived in New York. When she told him she was pregnant, he decided to do the gentlemanly thing. He flew back to Los Angeles—he had his own plane—to give Katharine the bad news. But once there, halfway up their driveway in his Hispano-Suiza, he couldn't face it. So without saying a word to the waiting Hepburn, he turned around and headed back to New York. Apparently, Hepburn never got over it, though the official version was that she refused to marry him because she was too "focused on her career."

Sometimes you can look at a man, the person you're living with, and see him objectively, as a stranger would. At Le Nid du Duc, I watched Bill across the lunch table, talking and laughing, head thrown back, his large hands clasped, feeling I would burst with love and sadness and guilt. More connected to him than ever.

On the set of *Wanda Nevada*, Grand Canyon, 1978.

We drove in the hills behind Ramatuelle to look at a property for sale. Val Verdun it was called, a broken-down stone farmhouse with a garden of old oak trees, their silver trunks shimmering in the afternoon light. "Let's buy it," he said. "Could we?" I shouted, already excited, running through the long grass, though I knew we didn't have the money. But I thought about it all the way on the train to Paris. We were treating ourselves to a night at the Ritz. A nostalgic stopover as Bill had spent time there as a boy when Leland was shooting *The Spirit of St. Louis*. It was full, but they knew his name and somehow we were given a suite— two large rooms, the ceilings and walls decorated with pink and gold plaster swirls. That night, lying in the hotel's marble-edged bath, listening to the BBC on the piped-in radio, I felt desperate, suicidal. I wanted to sink under the water and stay there. I am so homesick, I thought. Meaning for England not Los Angeles. I was dreading going back to the stifling house and the arguments. But the next day, I recovered, as one does. We ate lunch (Sole César Ritz) in the hotel's elegant dining room—the maître d' graciously loaning Bill a tie to go with his Hawaiian shirt and motorcycle jacket. Then, afterward, walking through the lobby, a clerk at reception recognized Bill from his youth. He had loved Leland. "A man of great class," he said, with the sobriety of someone appalled by the present state of anarchy. "I made all his luncheon reservations." He told Bill he'd say a little prayer that we would come back very soon.

But we never did. And in Los Angeles, we slid into our old ways.

I started seeing a therapist. A terrifyingly austere Argentine woman who had an office in Westwood. Twice a week, I parked myself in one of Dr. Spencer's backbreaking Danish chairs to stare at her dark walls, unsoothingly hung with African masks. I felt entombed. I'd never been to a shrink before. Aside from my English skepticism, it was hard to imagine revealing any deep truths to this icy woman in the big dirndl skirt and Earth shoes. She was impressed by my husband, his Hollywood connections—too much, I thought. And she obviously disapproved of me. Of course, I disapproved of myself just as much.

We talked about the lost baby; I went on about the hopelessness of my marriage. She didn't agree. "If you could just get pregnant again," she said in her commanding voice, "I think your problems would be solved." When I pointed out that since our sex life was now nonexistent this seemed highly doubtful, she suggested I "look for someone with Bill's coloring."

That summer was scorching hot. There were brushfires in the hills, and fierce, dry winds with cinders raining down. In the mornings, white soot dusted the cars. On the news were urgent reports about a large hole discovered in the ozone layer over Antarctica, about more people dying of AIDS. It felt like the end of the world. I was at my lowest point. I couldn't sleep. I took too many pills. I had rashes and bad headaches. Occasionally, I would make the effort to go out with Bill to a party, hoist myself up into cheerfulness. One night, we were at Joan Didion and John Dunne's house in Brentwood. It was after dinner and I was standing in the den with another woman. She was wearing a chic green taffeta dress, I remember, and matching shoes, and we were chatting, laughing about something—Ronald Reagan, I think. "Fiona," she said, "you are always *such fun!*" Smiling, I quickly walked out of the room, went upstairs to find an empty bathroom, sat down, and wept.

Bill and I agreed we should separate. Or, rather, one morning, I said, "I *have* to go," and he didn't disagree. We had exhausted each other. Neither of us had been loved like we wanted to be. But I was trembling. It was like wading through mud, strolling around our living room, pretending to be sensible about dividing up the furniture. "Would you mind if I took the sideboard, one of the Donghia sofas and the spare bed?" No, he didn't mind. "Put a sticker on them, so I remember. Where are you going to live?" "Oh, I've found a place in Hollywood for now, with Lynne Giler." I was moving out. We agreed to talk about the rest later. But I could see the pain in his eyes. And when the removal truck came, our good-bye kiss was heartbreakingly sad.

twenty-three
France 2005.

I now look at my life as a kind of time-lapse repetition, without the usual progression of chapters: babies, diapers, children's birthday parties, prom queens. The same, the same, starring the monotonous me with male shadows drifting through like ghosts. But I am at peace here. The romance of solitude. The evenings are long, the earth shimmers with heat. I sit on the back step watching M. Moulin's sunflowers turn deep orange in the fading light and think, *Yes, France will save me.*

But there are the usual problems.

I can't find M. Bruni. Now that his hand is healed, he's supposed to be here tiling the master bathroom. And it's a big job. At five feet by four, the shower is larger than anything we have in Santa Monica and designed, naturally, with my husband in mind. My attempt to make up for everything lacking out here *in the middle of nowhere.*

Bruni started the job two days ago. That is, he arrived early but left well before noon. *"Dejeuner"*—lunch, he said needlessly, getting into his beat-up Renault. "And I've got a dentist's appointment this afternoon. But I'll be back tomorrow, nine sharp!" When I checked the bathroom, I saw four white tiles had been laid along the bottom of the shower pan. *Four!* He didn't show up the next day, or the next. I called his house several times. It rang endlessly, then the line was busy. When I got hold of the operator, she told me his phone was out of order.

Today, for some reason, no other workmen have turned up either. It's not a national holiday or a pont. I can't find Nicola. And I've just had another incomprehensible exchange with the woman at Bainluxe about the pool. I am careful to be polite now, hoping to appeal to some sense of logic that I'm almost certain she does not possess. "I realize you're very busy"—*débordé*—I say. "But as you may remember I was promised a pool by August—" she stops me with a laugh. "No, madame," she says, "not *by* but *during. Dans le mois d'Aout.* You have confused your prepositions!" Then she hangs up.

Frustrated, I wander around the house. Hot and empty, the stillness somehow magnifies the wreckage: loose wires hanging down, scattered lumps of brick and plaster and the same blitz-like holes in the walls. But when I go upstairs, I see a brand-new doorframe. A piece of triple-edged molding that has somehow, miraculously, been installed around the entrance to the master bedroom. Who could have built it? Surely not Joseph?

An hour later, M. Elbou arrives. A round-faced man with an air of calm sobriety to match his professional smile. "*Bonjour, madame,*" he says, one hand extended, the other clutching a spirit level. Nicola has engaged him, he tells me, to build the new double doors to the bedroom, one to the bathroom, and another downstairs. Well, good for Nicola.

That afternoon, Joseph shows up. I catch a fleeting glimpse of him, shoulders braced, tousled head thrown back, as he ducks into the salon on the fly. I presume he's come to work on the baseboards—I presume, although it's impossible to know if he is doing anything because, as usual, the hammering is worryingly sporadic. M. Elbou, however, seems refreshingly normal. Obviously more than qualified to do the work, which means I can fire Joseph.

I am upstairs, pacing the corridor, wondering exactly how to do this, when I hear the argument downstairs: Joseph's sarcastic whine—"*Ah, merde, enfin. Tu exagére!*"—followed by M. Elbou's more civilized,

"Menteur, menteur!"—Liar, liar! Suddenly, the accusations are flying and I hear M. Elbou shouting over the din: *"Non, non, je ne supporte pas!"*—I will not tolerate this! I run downstairs just as he is walking out the front door. "I can't work if this man—*cet homme*—is here," he says, heading for his white van. "Why?" I ask, following, trying to catch up. Finally, he turns, his face crimson. *"C'est personnel!"* is all he will say. It's personal.

Later that evening, I get the details from Nicola, who heard it from M. Boudet—and, for all I know, half of southwest France. It seems that Joseph either A) once made a pass at M. Elbou's wife or, more curiously, B) has been overheard impersonating M. Elbou, a much-respected carpenter in the region, trying to secure a date with a woman in a nightclub.

Before driving off, M. Elbou told me that though he was willing to finish the bedroom doors at home, he would only install them when Joseph was not in the house. Normally this little episode would have sent me to the magic circle to lie down, but I feel surprisingly levelheaded. I'm looking forward to my next run-in with Joseph: a confrontation, then the triumphal firing.

But when I get to the house the next morning, Joseph is already there working. With unprecedented speed, it seems, he has finished the baseboards in the kitchen and is now halfway through installing them in the salon. *Fee-onn-aa*, he shouts as I come in, altogether too familiar and looking suspiciously buoyant. I was expecting a defensive attack, some surly reference to M. Elbou. Instead, he holds up a plank of wood. "Feel this," he says suggestively, *"touche."* And taking my hand, he guides it across the surface. "Yes, very smooth." *"Oui, très lisse,"* I say, too unnerved to be anything but enthusiastic. But he won't let go of my hand. Instead, moving closer, as if to divulge some burning secret, he says, "So I'll start on the shutters next week." Initially—that is, a *long*, long time ago—I'd mentioned building four sets of new shutters. But Joseph's quote, I remember, was ridiculously high. Now he's going on enthusiastically about types of wood, as well as hinges and casings. He's also standing too close, giving me one of his combative leers. A good time to bring up the problem with M. Elbou, I think. Also, to mention his high estimate *and* my lack of money—a lead-in to firing him. Nothing personal, of course, I will say. I am way over budget and what with the sinking dollar, the climbing euro, the prohibitive exchange rate—when it comes to fiscal belt-tightening, I now defer to my husband, the mystery man in America: *"Mon mari ne veut pas."* (Here, at least, the truth.) But before I can utter a word, he says, "Now that the baseboards are almost done, can you pay me?" his top lip curling in another lascivious smirk. *"Fee-onna, tu peut me payer?* By the end of the week? Cash?"

The money, as usual. I hesitate. Then, realizing this will be the *final* payment, I say, *"D'accord"*—okay. So he hugs me. He grabs my shoulders and presses them against his shirt, flattening my breasts. My head slams into his neck. I can feel the stubble of his oily, two-day-old shave, the briny shirt odor rising again. *"Vendredi?"* he whispers. Then he kisses me. A rough, thoroughly penetrating kiss on the lips. And instead of shoving him away, or fainting from nausea, I feel weak and small.

"Friday," I say. No subtext. Vendredi. Yes, I think, less confrontational. Besides, I can hardly fire him this minute. I will simply write a note and include it with the cash. Then I add stupidly, "I'm married." As if he didn't know.

Ten minutes later, I am in the kitchen sweeping up plaster dust. I attack the mounds of brick ends and wood chips like a *boniche*, a scullery maid, or a madwoman. A kiss as a reward for money? Really? Hardly original. I feel ridiculous. More unsettling is the fact that I'm enjoying the sensation—though *enjoying* may not be the right word. More stupefied that I could be attracted to a man who is so utterly dislikable.

I call my husband. I lie on the floor in the salon. The paint-spattered phone, a relic of engineering, balanced on my lap. "What's wrong?" he asks. It's early in L.A. Just after six a.m.

"Nothing. Sorry, I didn't mean to wake you."

"That's okay. But you sound annoyed. Why did you call?"

"Because I miss you."

"Missed telling me how difficult I am?"

"No. I feel bad that you're there alone."

"Don't. I'm fine."

"Well, I *do* feel bad," I protest. "And yes, I miss you." But I can already hear the edge to my voice. Do I miss him? Why am I calling? To say what? *Stop me from making a fool of myself!* The truth is our phone calls haven't been so friendly lately. We argue all the time. If he's agreeable, I'm the one who's sulking. If I fight back, he'll say, "Look, no one has to win. Life isn't a *competition*." His coolness kills me. And the jokes don't work so well. The last time we talked, I tried to explain, once again, that being in France might actually make America work for me—"After all," I said, "I'm a *European*."

"Well, I'm from Kiev," he replied, "and I have no intention of going back."

And instead of laughing, we both sank into silence.

I go to Kathryn's to take a shower. I think about Joseph, about my body, the part of me I'd decided, with great relief, *not* to think about anymore, but here it is again, resurrected from the dead. I think about sex, about a man (this man)—his shoulders, his tight ass and strong legs. Then there's me. Sitting on the edge of the tub, looking in the mirror, I see a pink-faced, startled-looking older woman with a freckled forehead and gray roots growing in at the temples. Who is she? In the harsh afternoon light, the physical deterioration seems shocking. As if my memory has tricked me and I had a totally different person in mind.

Just how is a woman supposed to adapt to the nothingness of old age? What exactly are the advantages? And please let's not have any talk about being *wiser*. Recently, in California, a woman in her twenties asked what my worst fear was about aging—no doubt expecting some insightful reply. "Standing in front of a three-way mirror, naked," I said, and we both had a good laugh. But I was dead serious. Obviously nakedness isn't the fun thing it used to be. Gone are the days of plunging neckline, the slit skirt, the golden thigh. In her wisdom, Catherine Deneuve once said that at a certain point you have to choose between your face and your ass. Thank God for humor. Except that underneath I'm still full of vanity and self-pity. Beauty is a shaky foundation. Having relied on my looks for so long, there's always the fear that without them I have no value at all. And without the normal distractions (children), it still feels as if I'm not properly *grounded* in real life. For years, I used to look longingly at babies. Then, after fifty, I stopped. A worrying cloud that suddenly lifted. What a relief! Self-interest had replaced the hormonal need. I was free to do anything I liked. But then I missed the longing. The weight of what I understood being a mother was all about: the unconditional love, the need to care about someone other than myself.

Who are these modern heroines who get it all right—juggling the kids, the cooking, creating start-up companies, running marathons? The American goddesses. I used to visit a friend who had four young boys, and every time I saw those small, beautiful upturned faces, beings who relied on her completely, I felt like an alien. I still do. You have to stay busy to fill the void. So I threw myself into work. Then, a few years ago, my second novel was refused by my publisher, and no one else was interested. It was a crushing blow. And not only because of the five years I thought I'd wasted. Sitting in the Safeway parking lot one afternoon, I suddenly found myself sobbing. I couldn't stop and I couldn't get out of the car. I was not going to be a success. I was not going to be a *different* person. *This was it.* I hated myself for not having learned to be a woman earlier, but then I hated myself more for being so ungrateful for what I had.

The next morning, I try M. Bruni again. Surprisingly, his wife answers. *"Excusez-moi de vous déranger, madame,"* I say politely, feeling exactly the opposite. "Where might your husband be?" Coolly she tells me that he was expecting to hear from me two days ago. But I didn't call. Well, I say, actually I *did* call—at least I tried to, but her phone was out of order. "Yes, it was," she admits—a fascinating though not unfamiliar reply that defies all logic. "Well, where is M. Bruni right now?" "The dentist," she says. "And tomorrow?" "I really don't know." I'm getting aggravated now. "Laying four tiles can hardly be called a week's work, *madame!*" I say, wondering if I should also mention Bruni's empty beer bottles strewn inartistically across the bathroom floor. A defensive pause. Then she says, her voice bristling with authority, "My husband has taken another job"— *une obligation*. An obligation to honor a client. "Madame," I shout, all reserves of politeness gone, "I AM A CLIENT, TOO!"

There's no winning here. I've forgotten the rules: coercion, humor, endurance, and a certain determined *légèreté*. The way the French conduct a conversation is like something out of a Feydeau farce. Time is of no consequence, detail is metered out only as a ploy, and logic, obviously, takes second place to staying power. Frankly, I'm in awe.

It's Friday afternoon. Almost six. I am sitting downstairs on the hall-way floor waiting for Joseph to come get his money. The house is boil-ing. Bright green geckos dart across the walls. The telephone rings. It's Joseph. He tells me he can't come. Could I meet him at the church in Nègrepelisse? I know this is a test, some macho, try-it-on-for-size move. But I agree. "Why not?" I say, as if I'm daring myself to go. After all, I've written the letter, I have the envelope of cash; it's time to get rid of him. So I get in the car. Because of the heat, I don't bother to change out of my work shorts and T-shirt—at least this is the reason I give myself. I'm also not wearing makeup because I've noticed—and, presumably, Joseph has noticed too—that on days when I expect him to show up, I appear with enough eyeliner to audition for a circus act. So I'm going au naturel. A mature decision that fills me with anxiety.

With the windows open, I drive fast to catch the breeze. But by the time I get to Nègrepelisse, it's still red hot and the small town is sizzling. I wait by the church, now annoyed at myself for coming. Then I see him, sauntering down the street. He's wearing his old, faded jeans, but for once, I notice, a clean shirt. "Ah, *Feeoona*," he says, taking my arm. "Why don't you come and have a drink?"—"*Boire un verre?*" "*Non, merci*," I say, and hold up the envelope. But he's already shoving me up the narrow cobbled street.

He stops at a plain-looking door to a basement. Inside, a few steps down and we're in a modern kitchen. A room with white refrigerator, white stove, and white table. A bright, boiling cube. A woman is sitting at the table. "My wife," says Joseph, giving me a look. I smile, my face, already crimson from the heat, getting hotter. His wife is wearing a pair of skimpy shorts and a halter top. She is surprisingly large, fleshy, and with her big, white calves slung carelessly across the Formica and her bleached hair cut unflatteringly short, she's hardly the match I'd imagined for our nightclub Lothario. What's more, she's all business. She is holding out her hand, so I give her the envelope of cash. *"L'argent, madame,"* I say, my eyes on the door, already anticipating my escape. But now she wants to count it. She makes little piles of fifty euro notes on the table. Then reshuffling them, her fingers working like a Las Vegas croupier, she counts them and makes the piles all over again.

Instead of watching her, Joseph is watching me. He's leaning against the wall, the slow gears of his face working their way into a smile. He is fabulously pleased with himself. The man who has made the American woman drive eighteen kilometers to deliver his money. I feel idiotic. At the same time, I wish I *had* put on some makeup. Apart from his wife's large thighs and the bad dye job, we don't look that dissimilar. *"Un verre?"* he asks, pulling an open bottle of wine from the refrigerator. "No, thank you, I must get back," I say, dying to get back. But he wants to talk about the price for doing the shutters, *les volets*. His wife, the accountant, looks up, also interested in the shutters. She gives me back the empty envelope—empty, that is, *except* for the note. I can't bring myself to hand it back to her, or to Joseph. Instead, I say I have a dinner I must go to and, with a polite *"Bonsoir,"* duck out. I leave the envelope on the dresser by the kitchen door, praying Joseph will find it over the weekend.

I drive too fast on the way home, feeling utterly stupid. The temperamental outbursts, the ambiguous flirtation—I'm beginning to think the drama was all mine. Why couldn't I just say: "You're fired"? Because his wife was there? Or because by thinking he's attracted to me, I feel some girlish obligation to be charming back? In Monclar, I stop at Le Vieux Fut. There are a couple of locals inside, red-faced workmen in overalls who eye me silently, their chairs pushed against the sweating cream walls. A fan whirrs behind the bar. Grateful, I sit and order a Pernod, drinking it too fast. Then I have another.

By the time I get back to Kathryn's house it's dusk. The phone is ringing, as it has been for some minutes. I heard it from the car.

"Hello?"

"Where were you? I've been calling for ages." My husband's concerned voice.

"I went to deliver some money to Joseph—one of the workmen."

"*You're* delivering money? Why can't they come and get it? You're so polite. And could you please get a cell phone so I can find you? I know they have them in France," he says. "Step into the twenty-first century."

"Actually, I was perfectly happy in the last."

"And who's Joseph? You've never mentioned him before," he says. "Some local boyfriend?"

"Ha ha. Well I *did* mention him."

"Don't think so."

"He's the carpenter. A nightmare, basically," I say, trying not to sound too vulnerable. "Full of himself, the tortured artist—you know the type. Temperamental, manipulative, cunning"—exaggerating his faults to absolve myself (of what exactly?) until I sound unhinged. "Like some character out of Stendhal. You know, *Le Rouge et le Noir*?

A pause. "You think I don't know who Stendhal is? Just because I don't speak *French*? You underestimate me, as usual. I did spend a few years at Berkeley."

"I know. Look, I'm just tired. It's been a hectic week."

"It's always a hectic week when I call."

"Yes. Well it *is* always hectic. I'm *sorry*."

"And don't apologize if you don't mean it."

"Okay, I won't."

I slide sideways onto the sofa. My eyes close. My head feels like lead.

"Have you had a drink?"

"Absolutely *not*," I say, giving myself away.

"Because you sound . . . Look, stop the drama. Don't be a *victim*. You're behaving as if the rest of your life is nothing without this house. As if it amounts to nothing. Because you have it pretty good, you know. I don't think you realize how *great* things are."

"I hate the way you say that, as if I don't know what my life is. You've been doing this for twenty years. Telling me how lucky I am. Because I'm attractive, *for my age*. As if I can just float through life. The carefree shiksa—how could I have any real problems? My life must be fucking perfect."

Silence. Then, "All I said was, don't be a victim."

"I heard you."

"Do you miss me?"

"Right now?" My mind is slipping back and forth as it always does after drinking on an empty stomach.

"All I ever wanted was to make you happy," he says testily.

"Thank you. But you use that as a weapon. The St. Bernard of Hollywood."

I'm being an asshole. I have to stop. I hear the swish of an e-mail being sent. When he comes back, he sounds calmer, distracted. "So what's happening about the Internet?" he asks. I tell him I'm trying to work it out with France Telecom. Apparently we're in a bad area. "I'm going to see how much it would cost to put a dish on the roof."

"Jesus, I can't believe I'm doing this."

"What?" As if I didn't know.

"*Coming there.*"

And with that he launches into his familiar list of complaints— what's so inconveniently wrong with travel, with the countryside, with *France* in general: jet lag (severe), the language (impossible), his allergies, the heat, the insects, the lack of air-conditioning, and now, no Internet connection. The fact that the house is, of course, *stranded in the middle of fucking nowhere.*

"You're right. You shouldn't come."

"You don't want me to come?"

"No."

"Look, if you really don't want me to come, just *say so*. I won't be angry. Just be honest."

"Okay. I will be honest. I don't want the responsibility of things going wrong. I don't want to feel guilty. I don't want to be grateful for every penny spent, or anxious that you won't have a good time. Or worry about how to please you every second. We *keep* having this conversation. So don't come. Or come another time. I don't care. No, actually, I'd rather be alone. Let's face it, we have nothing in common."

"We have enough."

"No. Really. We don't. We need a break."

"You want to *separate?*"

"Yes."

"Seriously?"

"Yes."

Long after I hang up, I stay on the sofa with my eyes closed. The buzzing noise in my head from a recent bout of tinnitus is back, only louder. The systems are shutting down. I can feel part of me disintegrating. Age. Cell collapse. Cosmic fade-out . . .

The next morning, I go over to the château early, before the workmen arrive. It is quiet, beautiful. The sun streams though the high windows; outside, the chestnuts are in full bloom. Green against turquoise blue. It's for the best, I tell myself. It was a long time coming. I am relieved, even happy . . . *the unfocused optimism of the believer, the self-delusion that allows us to survive.* Well, not happy in an oblivious way, but unafraid and free. Finally, I have told him what I want. I will repossess my life, have confidence in my own worth. *Finish the house.*

The following week things speed up. The Boudets manage to install three sinks, a bidet, and two toilets. Radiators are lined up in the hall. Taps turn, water flows, baths are hooked up. Even the Bainluxe team arrives. One morning, without warning, a large white truck pulls up and four muscular men jump out. They leap into the pool hole like acrobats.

In bathing shorts and with T-shirts wrapped turban-style around their heads against the heat, they work furiously, egged on by M. Menard, the foreman, who paces up and down like a ringmaster. Their speed is amazing. The iron scaffolding, a multilayered skeleton of pipes and struts, is erected so quickly that everyone stops work to come outside to look. David and M. Boudet Sr. and M. Gomes walk gingerly around the edge. *Ah! La Piscine Americaine!* I walk over to remind M. Menard about the steps. I want them running the *length* of the shallow end, I say. And when exactly will they be back to pour the cement? But he either doesn't hear or pretends not to. *"Madame,"* he says with a wave, "call the office!"

Sebastien Gastaldi arrives to install the finished balcony. He comes with a small crane and with his friend Leon to help. The structure is beautiful, a work of art. Shyly pleased, Sebastien shows me the wrought-iron rosettes he's made to match the original design on the back balustrade. Something that might have graced a window at Versailles. Not that I'd dare mention this to Sebastien, who, bearing the sickly pallor of the dedicated artist, even in mid-July still reeks of *commune* restraint. He works the crane while Leon guides the iron bolts into the brickwork. It takes all day to fit the balcony, and if Leon looks a little starry-eyed (obviously stoned), I only admire the precision more.

That afternoon, Joseph calls. He's found the note. He can't believe it. *"Mais ce n'est pas possible!* It's not possible," he says, his voice a petulant whine. "Don't you know I'd do anything for you, *Fee-onn-aa*?" I'm sure he would, I say, unmoved. But my decision is final. "Besides," I add, only trembling slightly, "you are *completely* unreliable and far too expensive."

I walk around in a daze of relief. But at the end of the day, the misery rolls in. The conversation with my husband fills my mind. Over and over it I go, like I'm auditioning for a play: cynical, defensive, then furious. All those times I tried to leave—so many times—but didn't. Is there a woman on earth who hasn't apologized to a man out of cowardice and exhaustion? To keep the peace? *It's my fault. I am so sorry, forgive me,* etc. I don't sleep. When I do for a moment, I dream instantly, deeply. And the nightmare comes. It's a familiar one from my childhood. I am in a dark field, alone. It's cold. In the distance, I see a faceless man wearing a long overcoat and a bowler hat. One minute he's standing, the next he's disappearing into the ground, silently, smoothly, as if riding a down escalator. He looks back to warn me. Of what? I run toward him, but it's too late. He sinks into the blackness, the earth closing over his head. I am grief-stricken. Grief is inexplicable, disorderly. I can barely catch my breath. I wake up sweating, exhausted. My stomach aches. But I have to get up. I have to go to the château to check on the workmen, to keep things moving. Stay in the present, as my husband would say. Well, *this* is the present.

And there's a lot to do.

M. Bruni finally shows up. It's two in the afternoon and I'm at the back of the house, exhausting myself by stacking old bricks. I'm ready to give him hell. But he looks miserable. He walks down the steps, his head bent. "Look, I am really sorry," he starts, his usual rapid-fire delivery conspicuously absent, "but my other client happens to be my doctor . . ." And he stresses the word *docteur* to lay on the gravitas. It's a complicated story. Something about promising to finish this man's patio, waiting for tiles to arrive, sitting around, losing money—"How will I eat!" But if he could carry on there then come to me in the *afternoon*, he'll even skip lunch to work late. He looks at me expectantly. We are now standing by the fig tree. Almost twenty feet high, in full bloom, its branches are heavy with bright green fruit. "Have you tried them?" Bruni asks, breaking into a goofy smile. "I took a few home. They're delicious! Thank God you didn't tell Fabrice to cut this one down too!"

His humor restored, we go upstairs to the master bathroom. He strips off his shirt, mixes some grout for the tiles, then kneels down in the shower. "I can finish this in three days. Easy! Nothing to it!" Then, veering off, he says, "So what do you think of my wife?"—a common point of interest, he presumes, now that we've chatted on the phone. "Do you want to hear how we met?"

I don't. It's stifling, the sun bouncing off the newly plastered walls.

I want to go downstairs to lie down. But I stay to make sure he keeps working.

"She was something else," he says. "Beautiful. It was a *coup de foudre*. I was doing my military service. I had this terrible haircut—did I tell you I used to be a barber in the army?"

"Could you please talk *and work* at the same time? *Parlez et travaillez en même temps?*"

"Anyway, the hair grew and I got her! We've been together forty-five years. I go home. The place is spotless. Dinner is ready on the table. I'm a god! In heaven! Because despite my little indiscretions, despite the *flirting*—" and saying this, he drops his trowel and steps out of the shower. Hands on his hips to demonstrate his irresistible allure, he starts parading around the bathroom. It's quite a sight, his bare chest stuck out, the old knees working up and down. "Because what does that mean in the end? Flirting? It's nothing! *C'est rien!*" He stops prancing and leans on the cracked mantelpiece. "No," he says seriously. "You see, *that's* what marriage is. It's having breakfast, lunch, dinner. The same thing every day. *Every* day. Trust. Fidelity, sheer boredom. *La grande ennui!* I'm so lucky!"

I turn away. I can feel the tears coming. A big wave of grief. So I launch into my usual tirade: "Look, not only does this shower need to be finished," I say, "but there's the guest bathroom to do. Plus the shower downstairs. Boudet can't install the taps and sinks until you're *finished*. We're halfway through July. I'm paying you by the day. Time is running out. Not to mention money. *My money!*" While I'm ranting, Bruni picks up the roll of toilet paper sitting on top of M. Boudet's new WC. Tearing off a strip, he dabs dramatically at his eyes. "Stop, stop!" he begs, "you're making me cry!"

He is laughing but finally glances over. "What's the matter with *you?*" By this time I'm trembling, my cheeks damp with tears. He looks baffled. Then, rolling his eyes, he tears off a couple more sheets and hands them over.

Admittedly, the evenings are difficult. I go to bed early. That is, I drink too much to exhaust myself and to avoid answering the phone, which might start ringing, and does in fact ring twice one night. I don't answer. But I can't help thinking. Going back. There are too many memories, and the nostalgia rolls in. The early days when I would laugh at my husband, his charming eccentricities: his fear of insects, his refusal to park underground, his sudoku marathons, his cream (not white) cashmere socks—days when I was grateful for his toughness. When, for instance, I was sitting in the Safeway parking lot sobbing uncontrollably about my career and he took me home and sat me gently on the bed. "Anyone can manage success," he said, stroking my head like a child. "It's how you deal with the hurdles in life that counts." His maxims. His brutal truths. I bury my head in the pillow. *I have to do this, I have to see it through.*

Some mornings I skip going to the house and drive around, up through the cool winding lanes to medieval Bruniquel, or to the church in Puycelsi, where I sit and stare at its magnificent purple-and-gold vaulted ceiling. The desire to see beautiful things. On Sunday, I distract myself at the Toulouse brocante. I wander through the stalls in the Allées Jules Guesde, under gently fluttering plane trees, to search for things I need. Or think I need. I get embroidered sheets, more forks, more glasses. I find a peach-colored damask screen, a relic from a duchess's house in Biarritz, then a Restoration sofa—or, rather, a worn 1920s copy from M. Richard Pascal. I only know M. Pascal by sight, but when I hand over my Crédit Agricole check, he recognizes my name. "Ah," he says, his weathered frame listing my way, "Polanski. *Le Bal des Vampires!*" He tells me he couldn't sleep the night before and had watched the movie on TV. I fake a look of humble surprise, flattered and equally dismayed, imagining my young breasts stirring the vanities of insomniacs across France. But the camaraderie is welcome. I need to talk, to distract myself. I chat with other vendors. I buy a Napoleonic crumb tray, more sheets. Then hidden at the back of one booth, I see a painting. A five-foot-tall oil of a dark-eyed chevalier in a shoulder-length Charles II wig. Streaked with dirt, a large hole in one corner, it is still expensive: 750 euros. Normally, I would call my husband—not to ask his permission . . . or perhaps, *yes,* to ask his permission, knowing he likes to be asked, to be acknowledged for his generosity, at the same time allowing him to mock my sense of fair play. The mistress/wife, the game player. The old me. But I don't. I just buy it.

And by the time I get back to the house it's almost four p.m.

As I come down the driveway, I see the white Bainluxe truck in front of the house. As usual, no one from the office called to say they were coming. Another truck is parked below the chestnuts, this one larger, vibrating loudly and with a fat plastic hose snaking out the back. Down in the hole, one of the men is maneuvering the hose, shooting cement at the scaffolding. It comes out with a tremendous force, and the others follow quickly behind, scraping and molding the cement to smooth it down Again the operation is astonishingly fast. The shallow end is already finished, and so are the steps. Too late, I see. They're not the steps I'd asked for: narrower, they also look dangerously steep.

I call out to M. Menard, who is joking with the boys, handing down beers to spur them on. "Monsieur Menard!" I shout over the din. "The steps—*les marches*—you remember? I told you I wanted them wide, running the *width of the pool*." He still can't hear me, or he chooses not to. Instead, he comes over, then launches in about the cement. "It has to be watered down," he says, "*deux fois par jour*. Twice a day, soaked from the top. Otherwise it'll crack in the heat." "Fine," I say, still preoccupied with the steps. But it's too late now; I can see the top one drying as we speak. "And what about the *plage*?" he goes on smugly. The deck. "Who's going to lay the cement for that?" Is he joking? Obviously not. "I'd presumed it would be you," I say. But I'm wrong. Naturally. I'm the woman who didn't read the contract, the woman who has arrived late, complaining, in her dust-streaked jeans. "The plage is separate from the pool," he says, "which is also different from the margelle—the lip that runs around the *edge* of the pool." What am I doing about that? And *when* am I going to get my electricians to run the wires up to the house? I feel dizzy, my throat closing. I scan the horizon, looking for some assurance that I'm not losing my fucking mind. Then I hear the phone ringing inside the house. I know it's my husband, and I know I can't possibly make it up the back steps in time to answer it. And now I badly want to talk to him. I feel exhausted, and once again, the tears are coming. Menard looks startled. "Okay, okay," he says. "We might be able to do the *plage* for you. But you know it will be—"

"I know," I say, choking. *"Extra."*

Things don't go well that night, or the following day. Not least among the problems is that I talk to my husband. From the beginning, the conversation is strained. "I understand that you'll be staying in France to finish the house. But how long is that? Exactly?" His voice is edgy, removed. *"Exactly?"* "Well, is it going to be a month or six months or—?" "Who knows?" I say. From the various responses I could have come up with, this is the bad one, implying that it might be *never*, when in fact I wanted to say *not that long*, or even *I'm sorry*, although I'm not really sure how sorry I feel. "Do what you want. That's your prerogative. That's what you do. You're a *writer*, you live in your isolated world. Stay there forever if you want," he says bitterly, and after that we veer off into familiar territory. He reminds me that we have "nothing in common," and I agree. I hate sports, the movie business; he hates to travel, go to museums, *read fiction*. "Thank you. But I have lousy scripts to read all day!" The recriminations go back and forth until we're both so angry and exhausted we can't imagine spending one more day in each other's presence.

I don't go back to Kathryn's. I lie curled up in the salon on one of the worker's paint-smeared coats that smells of tobacco and urine. Down into the tunnel of darkness I go. I am doomed. No, I am better off . . . better to be alone, not *lonely*. Yes, but then how *to be loved?* I barely sleep. At dawn, I wander out into the garden. A low mist drifts in the valley, but it's already hot. A steamy quietness. I turn on the hose and then drag it out to the pool where, following M. Menard's instructions, I start to soak the gray cement. I watch the dark rivulets of water trickle down into the hole. I refuse to even glance at the ugly steps. Instead, I look back at the house and admire the balcony. That at least, I think, is a job well-done.

Then I see something odd: both kitchen French doors are open, but the left one seems to be jammed against the iron balustrade. An optical illusion? The sun's reflection across the panes? No. The balcony is off-center. And it's tilted. I'm going to have to call Sebastien. I'm going to have to get him to take it out, realign it, then *cement it back in again*.

Well, I deserve this. I deserve the problems, the fuckups, because I am not my mother. I'm the difficult woman who's getting what she wants.

Then again, if I do need to complain, I can always talk to Bruni. He works late these days. Not surprisingly, four days to finish the shower was a big understatement, so we sit in the kitchen to have a drink at the end of the day. I put on B.B. King's "The Thrill Is Gone"—mournful, to suit my mood, but not so tragic that I actually fall apart. I pour two small glasses of rosé, careful not to overindulge him, and we take turns. I complain about the pool, money, *finishing the house*; he sounds off on taxes or his latest peeve: a neighbor who continually parks a truck in his driveway. *"Le salaud!"* he says. The bastard! I avoid discussing my marriage, but if I look rattled, or worn out, he tells me. "Still, not bad for your age!" he says. He admits he sneaked a look at my California driver's license when I left my wallet open one day. So he knows. "And I know about the Botox too. *Mais oui!*" he says, pointing to my forehead. Did I think he hadn't noticed? Well, I'd hoped no one had. It must be wearing off.

He crinkles his eyes so that his crows'-feet resemble mine. "I'm thinking of getting it done myself. I used to be extremely good-looking. Did I tell you?"

"Many times."

"You should go to my optometrist's office," he says. And he's leaning across the kitchen table now, clearly about to divulge some sensational piece of information. "My eye doctor. He does it. And he does the stuff they put in the lips, too. *Oui!* He's got a sign in his office. It says, IF YOU CAN'T SEE THE WRINKLES, I CAN FIX IT. IF YOU CAN SEE THE WRINKLES, I CAN FIX THAT TOO!" He laughs, throwing his big hands into the air. "The secret is to do very little."

"Yes," I say, thinking I must do more.

At that point the phone rings. I refuse to answer. It stops ringing but then immediately starts again. M. Bruni jerks his head, *"Eh, téléphone!"* Reluctantly, I go to the salon to pick up. It's my sister.

"You better get on a plane," she says.

twenty-four
Westcliff 2005.

It is two in the morning. I'm in a dark ward, or in an empty room between wards. It's hard to tell. The ceiling lights buzz quietly and cast an
eerie glow. Occasionally, I can hear the rhythmic squeak of rubber on
linoleum in the corridor as someone walks by. Apart from that, nothing.
My father, seemingly abandoned, is propped up on a gurney. He can't get
comfortable. In a paper-thin gown, he keeps slipping south on the bare
Naugahyde, but he's not allowed to lie flat in case his lungs fill up with
water again. Apparently, there are no beds available yet. And he has no
pillow.

A while ago, I went to find the nurses' station—one left, two rights,
then down a long corridor. The Southend hospital is a century old. I
was here decades ago to have my tonsils removed, and the connecting
passages still have the same thick tramlines of pipes snaking around the
corners. "Any chance of getting a pillow for my father?" I asked the nurse
on duty. She looked up, a half-eaten sandwich at her elbow. "Sorry, no
pillows." "*No?*" I said, thinking perhaps she'd misunderstood. "But my
father is eighty-nine. He's just had a heart attack. His neck hurts. If you
don't have a bed yet, surely you have a *pillow*! After all, aren't *pillows and
beds what you do here?* Isn't this a *hospital?*" The young nurse stared back

at me, her dark, round features immovable. "I'll see about a bed," she said.

I sit anxiously by my father, holding his hand. He is pale and drawn, exhausted, but not nearly as annoyed as I am. He's a firm believer in the National Health Service, whose friendly services he has enjoyed for many decades. After all, he remembers when there was nothing. Eventually, he dozes off. I try to curl up on a plastic chair, a molded orange bucket—no doubt a medal winner in contemporary hospital design—but it is impossible to sit, let alone sleep, on.

He was here in this hospital only ten days ago. Standing in the bathroom at South Hall, he started bleeding from his penis—to such an extent, the housekeeper said, she had to wipe down the walls. "An abattoir," was my father's cynical assessment. The diagnosis was a flare-up from his bladder cancer five years before, a wound caused by the radiation. After two days, he was released. Though he'd lost a considerable amount of blood, he was only given a few iron tablets for anemia.

It is now five a.m. The nurse comes by to check. Everything is satisfactory, she says. He's stable. However, as there are still no beds available, she suggests I go home.

It's been thirty years since I've spent a night alone in my parents' house. In my bedroom, the same rose-patterned curtains, the matching bedspread, the drawers stuffed with old jumpers and gymkhana rosettes and school reports: *Fiona could do better if only she would pay attention.* On the dressing table, old paperbacks: Rod McKuen, T.S. Eliot, Kipling, my 1958 Royal College of Art certificate: "Commended." Then a blue spiral notebook, its pages crammed with large round-handed words, thoughts from a sincere young heart that I can't bear to look at. But I can't sleep either. So I wander around. Downstairs, in my father's study, I see the evidence of his loneliness: the newspapers and jazz records littered across the floor, the desk piled with unpaid bills. On the drawing room mantelpiece are pictures of my mother. It's crowded with them. Old black-and-white photos from the 1940s, '50s, '60s—on the beach, in her sheared beaver coat, wearing her homemade dresses in Viareggio, Paris, Saint-Tropez, Washington. Some of the pictures are torn, others curling at the edges, stuck fanlike into the edge of the big gilt mirror. A shrine. Her ashes, still in the box room near the cellar, are balanced on top of a stack of garden chairs because my father can't decide what to do with them. As if to bury them or scatter them would make her disappear altogether.

I was here the morning she died. I'd come to London with my husband, who was talking to some financiers about a new film, and the trip coincided with her birthday. She was already ill. She had stopped the morphine patch because it made her hallucinate, and was taking a variety of pain pills instead. Even so, she insisted on going out to celebrate. She put on her red suit, her patent heels and pearls, but at the restaurant she couldn't eat. A sliver of bread. A prawn. Twice she vomited into her handkerchief, so we took her home. After that, the nurses came every day. When she'd first heard about the cancer, she said stoically, "Well, you have to die of something," then, without missing a beat: "I think I'll have a drink."

I stayed and my husband went on to Rome for business. A week later the vomiting stopped, but the pain grew worse. Too weak to get out of bed, she still religiously took her medicines. In a little black book, she wrote down the exact time and dosage of everything, just as she'd written down her shopping lists and daily memos in order to run the house efficiently. Now there wasn't much left to manage. But she was determined to keep up appearances. She brushed her hair, dabbed on lipstick. She worried that my father wasn't getting his proper meals. If he walked into the bedroom, however, looking, as he often did now, completely lost, wandering around in a robe at ten in the morning, she would say curtly, "*Still* not dressed, I see."

To which he would reply, as he headed swiftly back downstairs, "Still *feisty!*" as if nothing in their life had changed.

Eventually, the medicine didn't work—or worked too much. She slept on and off all day and no longer bothered with the makeup. I was still shy with her. We didn't say much. I was careful not to jar her body when I set down the breakfast tray, aware that the pain from the osteoporosis—her bones now riddled with it—was unbearable. Then one morning I was bending over her and she looked up at me and smiled. "You have my eyes," she said, out of nowhere. "Mine. Not deep-set like Daddy's." "I know," I said, "I'm lucky." It was as if by giving me *her eyes*, taking something away from my father, she had reclaimed me. "But look at this body," she said, meaning her own. She pulled down the covers and showed me her arms. Poking out from her nightgown were thin sticks, the skin hanging off them. She was like a skeleton inside a loose paper bag, and her legs were covered in bruises. "Look," she said sadly, "ruined." "But your face is beautiful," I said, and cupped her chin in my hands. She smiled back shyly, as if no one had told her this in years. Maybe no one had. And she did look beautiful: her skin smooth, the wrinkles miraculously gone. She was like a tiny dove. Even her hands, always large compared to the rest of her, seemed graceful lying on the bedcover, the fingers slender and pale. "I love you," I said. "I love you too," she replied quietly. A difficult thing for her to say, but she managed it.

The next morning I slept late. When I woke up, I felt a vague sense of urgency. I told myself to get up and get ready—for what? I had no idea. I showered, washed my hair, then as I was winding a towel around my head, I heard knocking. I realized it was my mother rapping on the wall with her walking stick. I ran into her room. She couldn't speak; she was slurring her words, but I understood that she wanted to go to the bathroom. So I lifted her up from the bed to her wheelchair—her arms, those little sticks, were still amazingly strong. I got her on the toilet then waited by the door. But she was having difficulty; the drugs had made her constipated. Suddenly she lurched forward. Her arms shot out, her fingers clawed the air, and her whole body shuddered in agony. I dragged in the canister of oxygen, then shouted downstairs for my sister. By then she was doubled over, gasping for breath. "Lie down," she managed to whisper, so I lifted her back into the wheelchair. As I did, I felt her go heavy in my arms. Her face brushed my cheek as she slumped back in the chair, and her feet were like lead. By this time, my sister was standing at the bedroom door. She couldn't bear to come in. I told her to get our father, but I knew it was too late.

Later, I walked out to the garden. It was a magnificent day. Clear blue skies, the pink cherry and white apple blossoms blazing in the orchard, the lawn a brilliant green. It seemed surreally bright—a Technicolor day in April. I was bursting. So full of love, I could barely catch my breath and felt an inexplicable sense of relief wash over me, as though my mother were passing through me, floating up into the unusually blue sky, and I was going with her, liberated, out of pain. Not only couldn't I cry, I felt embarrassingly elated, something to this day I find hard to explain.

My father stayed upstairs, stunned, inconsolable. When the undertakers came, equipped with their terrifyingly sober-looking plastic bag, he asked if they might leave her another day so he could spend one more night with her. Better not, the chap said.

My husband came from Rome. He brought an expensive picnic lunch from Harrods, then stood awkwardly in the drawing room, squeezing my arm, wondering what to say about a woman he had barely known. At the local florist we picked out wreaths. I chose white; my father wanted yellow roses and freesias. He'd never been a religious man. Years before, when I'd broached the subject of the "hereafter," he said, with a laugh, "I don't believe there's anything *after.* Once you're gone, that's it." Nevertheless, when it came to writing the card, he put, "Til we meet again."

The next morning, I go back to the hospital. It had taken until seven a.m. to find my father a bed, but still no pillow. And by the time I arrive, he's been moved again, upstairs to the heart ward, a room with five other men, the beds pushed close together. Compared to American hospitals, it feels like a school dorm: the tawdriness of the furniture, dressing gowns thrown haplessly over chairs. I can tell my father hasn't slept. His face is gaunt and he's having trouble talking to a nurse. She wants his full medical history. In a raspy voice he tries to explain that only an hour ago he gave the *same details* to a different nurse downstairs. But apparently there's no system of cross-referencing between wards, so he has to start all over again: the cancer, the stroke, the diabetes, the previous heart attacks, the ulcer . . . then he lists the drugs. He's very thorough—a lawyer first, a patient second. I stand behind the nurse, waiting. "Is it possible that my father's anemia had something to do with the heart attack?" I ask, annoyed that after the bleeding penis incident, no one thought to give him a blood transfusion. He's obviously so weak. "Well," she says, barely glancing my way, "we've read the enzymes. It wasn't strictly a heart attack. It was angina."

A few minutes later, the doctor arrives, escorted by a bevy of first-year students, ballpoint pens at the ready. The cheerful embodiment of old-school superiority. "Well, you've had a heart attack!" he tells my father, as if he is announcing the winner of the local playwright competition. My father actually looks pleased. Finally a professional opinion. And nothing less than he expected. Moreover, because he's spent every day since the last attack worrying about the *next* one, now that it's happened and he made it to the hospital in time, he can relax. But I'm not satisfied. "Why wasn't my father given a blood transfusion when he was here the last time?" I ask. "Couldn't his untreated anemia, plus the diabetes, have *contributed* to his heart attack?" I get a raised eyebrow, a condescending smile, and behind him I see his minions wincing at my effrontery. I don't care. "*Possibly?* Couldn't it?" I shout, looking for someone to blame. "Well, possibly," he concedes, and that's it. He sweeps on to the next bed.

But that night my father is given two pints of blood, and the next day, he looks better. He is sitting up, chatting with the patient opposite him. I perch on the edge of his bed, as hard as iron, relieved to see him so relaxed, almost happy. And he feels safe with the nurses. Better here than at home, where he has to face the loneliness of life without my mother.

That afternoon, my sister arrives. We are much closer now but still greet each other shyly, as if trying to add forgiveness to our lost love. We go up to the ward together, where the nurse on duty tells us that visiting hours are over. I'm ready to do as I'm told and come back the next morning, but my sister takes charge. After the awkwardness of her childhood, by some cathartic leap I realize she's become a stunningly efficient woman. Particularly when it comes to hospitals. All that revved-up energy has found a place to land, something worthwhile to set alight: the British Health Service. She also believes, unlike her skeptical sister, in the doctors' and nurses' ability to put things right. Earlier, my father said to me, "You are so good to me," but the truth is, I'm the intruder, the other daughter who only visits sporadically, bringing her confrontational California ways and her new age theories about traditional medicine, too ready to question the staff's judgment or to criticize the terrible food. My guilt for living on another continent.

But my sister understands the system. She knows the staff is overworked, burdened. She deals with the paperwork, the medications; she creates a chummy partnership and gets things done while I sit by his bedside and worry. I am too emotional, already imagining his final days. I see his vulnerability, his fears—*my* fears. Earlier, he said, "How's your better half?" as if he'd just realized I had a grown-up life. "Fine," I said, and felt the tears coming. For my father, my marriage, or for myself—I had no idea. He sighs wistfully now. He runs through my mother's many talents, and I indulge him. When he marvels at how immaculately neat she kept the house, I don't remind him how he complained continually about "the bloody Hoover." When he reminisces about our trip to the undertakers, standing together by the open casket—I, shocked to see that a wax dummy had been dressed in my mother's red suit, her spirit clearly gone, and he, stroking her head, saying repeatedly, "Such beautiful hair"—I don't chastise him for continually making fun of it when she was alive. Her bouffant "do" that reminded him of the queen. I feel guilty, but I still can't help taking his side.

He is constantly surprised by his emotions. They assault him. How did it happen? My mother gone; that dashing fellow in the Jaguar XK120 long gone. He sinks into sadness. What's left? A few months ago, he called me in Los Angeles in a panic. "Something terrible has happened," he said. "What?" I asked, imagining the worst, ready to jump on a plane. "I looked in the mirror this morning," he said, "and I'm *losing my looks!*"

You're eighty-nine ears old, I wanted say. What do you expect? *Focus on something else!* But what else was there? Only worse to come. He worries he'll have another stroke and end up a vegetable, that he won't be able to walk—or worse, *travel*. Last night, when we were waiting for a bed, he said, tears in his eyes, "I don't think I'll ever see France again."

France had been keeping him going. I didn't realize it until then. Or perhaps I did. If my obsession about the house is because I think it will save me (whatever that means), I also think it will save him too.

twenty-five
France 2005.

Kathryn is back. She also has a house full of guests from London, so I move in with Louise Fletcher, another friend from Los Angeles. She owns a house just ten minutes away, an old barn painstakingly rebuilt from what was no more than a pile of old stones. A movie star, Louise was the famously scary Nurse Ratched in *One Flew Over the Cuckoo's Nest*, though she couldn't be less threatening. She takes care of me like a mother—my romantic ideal of motherhood, that is. She cooks for me but also listens to my endless moaning: the house, my husband, *me*, my marriage. She is the dispenser of calm logic. And when I drone on too long, sitting on her terrace, next to her clematis and climbing roses, she leans over and says gently, "I think you must *stop*, though, now."

But I can't. I lie upstairs in her guest room with its soothing dove-gray walls, hot and unsoothable, unable to sleep, thinking about my husband, arguing with myself, going over the same one-sided conversation: *Look, all I ever wanted was for you to say that France was magical, that you didn't absolutely hate it. That you could love what I loved. I wanted to show you what I was made of. Prove that building a house was a valid project. So you wouldn't dismiss it as frivolous, as a whim, a ridiculous obsession, or just*

a woman's thing—and yes, you know how to do that, how to make women feel
they are something men have to endure . . .

After which I feel better, or feel better feeling worse. Because here's
the question, the old question. Am I in fact someone who is happy being
unhappy, or unhappy being *happy*? There's a certain dramatic appeal to
that, the tragic sense of self.

I decide, once again, to concentrate on the work. M. Gomes's men have
finished plastering all three rooms upstairs, leaving a few sculpted ripples
for authenticity; the painters are just about done there too. The Boudets are installing the claw-foot tub in the master bathroom. They have
moved it three times on my instruction (an attempt to line it up with the
marble fireplace), and every morning they indulge me with a leery smile.
"You see, everything will be finished in time for August!"

I don't tell them that August means nothing to me now. That there is
no deadline. That I plan to sail through this sizzling summer on my own.
Still, I'm relieved that the end is in sight and walk through the rooms
thanking the workmen—*merci, merci*—feeling better than I have in weeks.

That is until the floor man arrives. I dislike him on sight. Something
about the waxed mustache, the high forehead, the know-it-all air: more
English than French. "What color stain do you want, madame? Water
or oil finish?" M. Andreu asks. Well, I've spent a lot of time thinking
about this. What I want is a light golden brown with no red in it. I am
clear about the *no red* part and show him a sample of a honey-colored
stain on a piece of wood. "Can you match that?" I ask. "Of course!" "Exactly?" I peel back the plastic sheeting to show him M. Bruni's pristine
planks underneath. "Are you absolutely sure?" M. Andreu smiles, then
gives me *that look*. After all, he says, he's an expert. "*Un expert!*" He arrives
the next day with three four-gallon cans. He works swiftly to apply the
stain, skating down the corridor, pushing a cloth-covered broom like a
one-man curling team. When he's finished, the wet planks look good,
perhaps a little dark. Two hours later, they dry to a deep *mahogany red*.

I can live with it. This is what I say to myself. Nothing is perfect. It will do. But it won't do, of course. I'm going to have to sand the floors and *stain them again.* Still, I refuse to panic. Whatever happens now, I tell myself, I can handle it.

In the afternoon, I make calls: to Sebastien about reattaching the balcony, to the shipping office to ask how long the container—sent months ago from Los Angeles and now sitting in the Marseille port—will be detained by customs and to Bainluxe. I have been calling regularly, of course, insistent, begging, trying to find out when they're coming to finish the final pool plastering. Now I call again. "Well," she says, before I can even start, "I see there's an outstanding bill to pay. We haven't received a check." "Yes, I know," I say coolly. "The check is right here." Silence. Twenty seconds go by, then she comes back on line. "They'll be there on Wednesday. *Mercredi.* At ten."

It's Tuesday morning. I am in Montauban to pick up the last sink, to buy a discount stove, to rent a dumpster from Bruges et Co., to get cash for the crew. When I arrive at the château, I see the big Bainluxe truck parked under the chestnuts, its body vibrating noisily. The men are already in the hole, stripped down, as usual. One of them, his arms swirling with tattoos, maneuvers the big-nozzled hose, shooting plaster at the cement while the others scurry behind, making big sweeps with their trowels. Any brief thrill I might have felt from this vision of efficiency, or the unprecedented fact that they've shown up a day *early,* is cut short when I see the color of the plaster. Instead of a pristine white, it's a streaky beige. "The plaster was supposed to be *white,*" I shout to M. Menard, who is standing in the shade of the cypress, draining a beer. As usual, he looks sublimely unconcerned. "No," he says, "you ordered beige." "White!" I say, walking over. "*Blanc, comme une piscine Americaine!* Tell them to stop." "I can't" he says, "it's too late." And like the steps, I know it's too late. "Besides," he adds, "most people prefer beige. It looks more natural in the countryside."

He looks at me, his head set back, his shoulders taut, like a bird of prey. I stare back at him. No tears this time. "Yes," I say, smiling defiantly, "maybe beige is better."

. . .

To complain is useless. And no doubt if I fell sobbing to the floor, M. Bruni would drag me to my feet and tell me to get back out there. He would, that is, if he were here. But he's not. I've made several calls to his wife, but he's mysteriously absent—gone to the dentist as early as seven a.m. Finally, during the lunch hour, I get Mme. Bruni on the phone. Her husband, she says, is "coming right over."

He looks terrible. Thin and pale. Even his hair looks whiter although, as he once admitted to dyeing it, this could be the real color. But there's something else: an air of defeat. "I've been to the hospital for the lump in my throat," he tells me grimly. And it's much, *much* worse. All that cement dust. "My doctor insists I take a vacation." That's it, he has to go. Obviously there's no point in arguing. Besides, I feel too guilty about the lump, not to mention his hand. He walks me into the guest bathroom. There are two shower walls left to do here, as well as another upstairs.

By the way, he says, you'll have to order more white tiles. More? "Yes. I've miscalculated," he says. *Malcalculé.* "Another four square meters should do it." I'm too disturbed to take this in. He's sorry, he says, but he's off to stay with his daughter in the mountains. "After all," he admits, cracking a smile, "it's August!" *"Ah, les vacances!"* I say, not having the heart to remind him that it's only July 23. We shake hands awkwardly. Then I grab him to give him a tearful hug.

I am overcome with sadness. My old friend has gone. I am alone in my beautiful house. The beautiful house that may kill me. I wander around the garden. I walk through the maze of shrubs and old lilacs. I look out over the stubbled fields, the hills rising away, now dotted with cartoon-like yellow haystacks, the familiar lines of trees. I love this view. I know it by heart. But I feel swimmy with emptiness.

More often now, I drive to Puycelsi, to sit in the little fifteenth-century church Saint Corneille with the gold-and-indigo ceiling and the magical stained-glass windows. I haven't spent much time praying in my life—though Christianity, life as a boiling pit of snakes and demons, is something I understand. But I do feel more spiritual now. Back in the '70s, when the enlightened were heading off to India with their gurus to make peace with the world, I had a hard time grasping the idea of being reborn, that my soul would live on and on, eternally on track like a toy train. How many revolutions would it take to get it right? And who decided *what* was right?

But here I'm beginning to see that it doesn't matter if things don't make sense. I'm ready to embrace what I don't know—especially what I don't know. And it's comforting to think there might be someone out there. Not a traditional God, delivering benediction or almighty fury, but a divine being. A guardian angel. Unlike my mother, I'm not superstitious about opening an umbrella indoors, or putting new shoes on the kitchen table. But these days I turn to her for help—something I was incapable of doing when she was alive. Oddly enough, I feel her here with me.

The first time this happened was back in the spring. I was standing at Kathryn's stove boiling eggs for breakfast when I felt a chill. A sudden whoosh of air, the smell of her perfume, Guerlain's L'Heure Bleu. I walked into the corridor to take a look, but of course there was nothing. A few weeks later, I was at the château. It was a bad day—one more building catastrophe—so to escape the chaos, I went to the magic circle. I was lying there, staring at the sky, murmuring *help* (to no one, or anyone) when I saw a large hawk. I'd noticed it before, gliding on thermal currents high over M. Moulin's fields. It was circling directly above me and kept on circling for another five minutes. The next morning, driving down the hill, the hawk came with me. Flying low, almost parallel to the car window, it came close enough for me to see the glint in its yellow eye. Then, just before the road disappeared into the woods, it swooped across the hood, banked, and soared away. Every day it would startle me like that, until I began to expect it. To imagine that my mother is the hawk doesn't seem in any way odd or fanciful. I like to think she's come to watch over me, to pass on her strength and, yes, even to *exonerate* me. Because as trifling as it may sound in the great scheme of things, attaching this much emotion to rebuilding a house—the sheer luxury, after all, of being able to say that I'm drooping with worry about the pool or the unfinished bathrooms, or agonizing over how to deal with the badly stained floors—I know my mother would understand: "If a thing's worth doing, dear, it's worth doing well!"

The truth is, I miss her. I call my father. Recovered, he is back at home, installed, as I always imagine him, in his big chintz armchair, surrounded by a pile of library books and the Sunday newspapers. "Do you miss her?" I ask tentatively. Yes, he does. Though, coincidentally, he says, he often sees her now sitting on the sofa across the drawing room, particularly during the six o'clock news. "I'm planting a rose bush for her," I say. A sunny spot near the magic circle where I will scatter her ashes. "Plant one for me," he says wistfully, his voice frail, "with a decent view!"

It's July 28. The days are trickling down to zero. I am upstairs in the master bedroom, balanced on a stool. Wasps are swarming. They've been nesting in the wooden eaves all summer and are now inside, dotting the walls like black-and-yellow confetti. I spent a good ten minutes blasting them with a can of *anti-guêpe* spray. Then, as I'm closing the windows, I hear someone at the front door. I go down. It's Lillian, our local postwoman. She's holding a box. "It's from *America*," she tells me, as if I couldn't tell. Inside is a pair of portable iPod speakers, tennis shoes, a bathing suit, suntan lotion, underwater goggles, eyewash, and jet-lag pills. The postage date is illegible, the parcel damaged—badly retaped by customs—and could have been mailed weeks ago. In other words, there's no way to tell if my husband sent it before or after our last argument.

"What do you think?" I ask Louise that night. She is packing, leaving to go to California for a few weeks. By now, she's had to listen to every woeful beat of my marriage, as I eat my way through her rosemary chickens, her exquisite *tartes aux pommes*. "Well," she says, with cosmic cool, "you could *ask* him."

But I can't. I don't want to know.

It's July 30. The whole country is about to shut down. I call the woman in Marseille to ask about the container. "It's still held up in customs," she says. "Do the customs men work during August?" I ask. She thinks for a second. "Unlikely," she says.

Sebastien comes with his crane and his coworker, Leon, to pull the balcony out of the wall, drill new holes, and reinsert it. They work silently, embarrassed. It's hot, and feeling sympathetic, I hand them glasses of Chablis through the kitchen window. David and Uncle Boudet arrive to install the light fixtures, my art deco flea market finds. Uncle Boudet, crouched in the attic, yanks on the flexes, shouting "Less? More?"— *Moins? Plus?*—as David secures them to the bedroom ceilings. In the salon, I prop the oil painting of the unsmiling cavalier on the mantelpiece. He looms magnificently, one ruffled sleeve to the fore, his gaze following me around the empty room. Later, Romuald, one of my friendly antiques dealers, delivers the huge Louis Philippe wardrobe. We carry the big pieces upstairs to the master bedroom, where he reassembles them, slotting the old chevrons back into place. Magnificent, it practically touches the ceiling. The doors, cut from whole planks of walnut, *noyer entière,* creak on their hinges. Set against the pale walls, the last rays of sun streaming in, the wood gleams like amber. When Romuald has gone, I stand and stare at it, astonished. How could a piece of furniture be so moving?

That evening, I get an e-mail from my husband. He says he's coming on the third of August for four days. The message states his flight number and time of arrival. Nothing more.

I am panicked, cripplingly so. The next day, I don't go over to the house until late afternoon. Fabrice is there. He's planting small trees on either side of the front door to distract from the mess on the front lawn, the potholes and tire tracks left by workmen's trucks. "*Bonjour,*" he says, grinning. I can barely answer. I go upstairs to the bedroom. Now that the wasps are dead, I open the window to let in some air. A heavenly breeze. At dusk, I stretch out on the floor and let my body melt into the cool, scrubbed tiles. It's quiet. I feel better. I close my eyes. I am drifting, climbing the hills above Pampelonne beach, wandering among whispering pines, the Mediterranean crashing below. I hear another sound. A whooshing noise. Am I dreaming? I open my eyes. The room is full of fluttering wings. A flock of birds swooping in circles around the room, though their high-pitched whine sounds odd. It takes me a second or two, then I realize they're not birds but bats. Small, dark, oily looking creatures, about fifteen of them, whirring close to my head. I jump up, get a towel from the bathroom, and try to guide them back outside. But they circle and dive around the room with amazing speed. Can I kill them? What do the French think about killing bats? Are bats, like the rabbits who are tunneling great holes under the box hedges, protected, only to be officially rounded up by the *chasseurs*? Fabrice would definitely disapprove. But I want to kill them. I want to kill *something*. So I leap around, twirling my weapon with all the pent-up fury of a maniac. Some escape; the unlucky ones are felled with a sharp flick. Two land on top of the wardrobe, where they stay. *To haunt my dreams.*

My husband arrives on the afternoon flight from Paris. He is sheepishly bad-tempered but trying to put on a good face. His sophisticated traveler's face, the set mouth, the green-tinted shades, the two-day growth of beard. Fashionably unkempt in his creased seersucker jacket and carrying expensive hand luggage. Though he's been training himself for this moment, the horror exceeds all expectations. The temperature is ferocious: summer in the South of France, except that it's freakishly hot this year. His misery is palpable, matching mine. Walking across the airport parking lot, the heavy fumes assault us, as do the fiery plastic seats when we heave ourselves into the rental Peugeot, a blue metallic number with a tricky gearbox. The automatic Mercedes I'd booked was unavailable—"August, madame!"

The view from the freeway, normally a welcoming expanse of green, is a runway of burnt yellow. A furnace. And things get worse when we get to Louise's. Though I have vacuumed every room to expel all traces of her cats, one must have sat on every chair. Silently my husband downs two Allegra with a glass of wine. After a bad first night, we move to Kathryn's, who makes room for us in her *pigeonnier*. But the allergies, compounded by his jet lag and a crippling headache, mean another sleepless night that no amount of pills or glasses of rosé can cure.

"I'm sorry," I say, resentful, hating him. Why did he come? "You don't have to stay."

"I *know*."

Late the next morning, we quickly visit the house, then go to Montauban to find him a decent espresso, to buy a plug adapter for his iPhone, to pick out a plasma TV. He's exhausted but insists on driving, even though he doesn't know the way. "Don't just *point*," he says, "you have to *say* left or right!" Coming back, I suggest we take a side road to avoid the traffic. He drives fast, as he always does, sixty-five up the narrow lane, tearing around corners, challenging any local idiot who might get in his way. When a truck appears, shooting out of a dirt road, he rolls down the window and curses the moron for making him brake and swerve. *Fucking French drivers!* "Yes," I say, agreeing. I agree with everything, I am accommodating. I want to die. But at least he slows down. We drive through wheat fields, past rows of poplars, then come to a small château. It has a tower, an ancient stone terrace, its walls banked with huge blue hydrangeas. "Look," I say, "how beautiful." He pulls in near the entranceway and parks under a *pin parasol*. The espresso has worn off, he's exhausted again. Adjusting the seat, he leans back and closes his eyes. "It's three in the morning in Los Angeles," he says. I watch him, head thrown back, boyishly rumpled, murderously annoying. Vulnerable. How I used to love him. "I just need to sleep five minutes. Don't be aggravated. I can *feel* you being aggravated."

I say nothing.

"Because I adore you," he murmurs. "You don't think I'd put up with this shit otherwise, do you?"

"Oh, this shit. You mean *France?*"

"Yes."

"Well, both the country and I are enormously grateful."

I open the car door to let in some air. I stick out my legs, then kick off my sandals and let my feet touch the cool grass. My head falls back, grazing his thigh. He bends over and pulls up my shirt. He kisses my bare stomach—a stomach that hasn't seen full sun or the front seat of a car for some decades. "Beautiful," he says. The power of one simple word. *God, you are such a girl,* I think. But no, I won't do this. It's not that simple. I sit up. He gets out of the car and climbs in my side. *You are beautiful. And I love you.* I'm crying a little. He pushes me back. He struggles to pull off my jeans, my underwear. I wedge my ass in the least painful position against the gearshift and we fuck on the hot seats, awkwardly, silently. I feel like the cheating housewife after a couple of lunchtime cocktails, one leg acrobatically raised, my foot pressed against the windshield. I go for it frantically, desperately, scared shitless that someone will see us. But behind us the château's blue peeling shutters are closed, the garden empty. "There's *no one,*" he says, kissing my cheek. "Miss Prim." Except that there is. My fear has willed it to happen: out of nowhere a police van comes tearing around the bend. *Police?* On a deserted back lane? We duck out of sight, except that my foot is left behind, still glued to the windshield like some anthropological specimen. We freeze, stifling our laughter, but they roar past. Of course, it's after twelve. They're late for lunch. Either that or it's too incredible to imagine a couple of our advanced age screwing on the front seat of a car, in *broad daylight.*

So far, he's said nothing about the house. And I don't ask.

The container arrives two days later. A miracle. Naturally, there was no warning from Marseille. Raymond calls me from the shop to say the big articulated truck is stuck in the village; it can't manage a sharp turn. So at the last minute, I have to hire a smaller truck to ferry the goods to the house. Guy Moulin, Fabrice, and Celine come to help us unload. It takes three hours to carry in the sofa, tables, rugs, towels, sheets, pillows, then set up a bed in the master bedroom. That night, the weather breaks. A storm rolls in. The wind rips through the cypress tree, its big branches heaving, then roars down the corridors upstairs, whistling through the gaps under the doors. The electricity goes out and for some reason the water shuts off, probably because I've left the hose on outside to fill the pool, using up my quota from the village. Mercifully, I find candles, then discover there are no matches. My husband is amused, even charmed. "Don't worry," he says, "it's just what I expected, out here in the middle of fucking nowhere!" But by the next morning, everything is calm. There's a cool breeze and the fields are shimmering as far as the horizon. The pool is full. My stepson drives down from Paris with a girlfriend, turning up seven hours late, via Lyon. He wasn't aware that France was this large, he says; he just aimed his rental car south. Brian, an English friend arrives by train from Saint-Tropez. We have our first meal in the otherwise wrecked kitchen, lunch à la campagne. I lay the table with an old damask cloth, with the flea market silver, blue-patterned hotel plates, and a set of mismatched 1920s tumblers. "Ah, your make-believe life," jokes my husband, words that for a moment pierce my unforgiving core. *No*, I think, *not now.*

I open a jar of Raymond's thick, pink foie gras. Kathryn arrives with her three sons, a quiche, and several bottles of wine. We toast to France, we take pictures and get stupidly drunk. After lunch, my husband swims in the pool, his goggles, insect repellent, and sunblock forgotten on the kitchen table. He glides idly back and forth, not noticing that the plaster is beige, that the water is green instead of California blue, or that there is no *plage*. At the deep end, he rests his elbows on the edge to contemplate the view. "Simply stunning," he shouts. No irony.

Later, when everyone has gone, we're still outside, sitting together on the back stone steps. It's past ten. The light is fading, the air soft. Billie Holiday's voice crackles from the iPod, the speakers balanced on the window ledge: *In my solitude, you haunt meee . . .*

"You were right to drag me here."

"Somehow that doesn't make me feel as good as it should."

"The house is beautiful. You've done an incredible job. But I know you're going to punish me either way."

"You're an asshole," I say, laughing.

"You don't have to be so tough. You're not invincible."

"I want to be," I say, turning away.

"No you don't. In the end, you have to trust someone," he says, taking my hand. "Marriage is difficult. But when it's good, you have to treasure it. Trust what we have. You have to stop thinking that an *uneventful* marriage is less interesting than a bad one. You're always too ready to throw everything away."

Nailing it on the head, as usual. What a bitch life is—trust, security, *freedom*. If you believe in it, you're screwed either way.

In my solitude, you taunt me, Billy sings on . . . *I sit in my chair, and filled with despair* . . .

"Look, I know you want me to be an adventurer like you," he goes on. "And I can *try*. But I just wasn't brought up like that. I remember when I was young, walking with my mother down Hollywood Boulevard, and someone was coming toward us with a dog. 'Dogs bite!' she said, then yanked me away. *That's* how I was prepared for the rest of my scary life!" He's looking at me, his green eyes filled with tenderness and sadness—and fear. He rarely shows it. My protector, my best friend, the man who saved me from my childhood, from myself, the anchor who gave me the confidence to go on being a writer, someone I've loved for more than half my adult life. I am overwhelmed—and scared shitless because I have what I want.

"I love you," I say, at the same time thinking there should be several words for love, like the Eskimos have for snow. Words that embody pain and tolerance and fear.

"And I *adore* you," he says. "I always will. Whether you like it or not."

It's almost dark now, the branches of the cedar tree spread out like inky wings against the pink sky. The music is like a drug. The anxiety seeps out through my pores. I feel the house around me, the weight of every brick. I *am* the house. The house is me. And so is this man. But he's not finished. He's giving me his *let me just sum this up* look, in case I've got the wrong idea. "The truth is, I'm not sure if I'll ever really *get* France. I mean, I can't say how often I'll come here, or if I'll even *stay*. After all, I have to make a living. But one thing I do know—"

"What?"

"Where you are is never as important as *who* you're with."

"No, but *where* often helps."

"Clarence Darrow. Always an answer."

"God, we'll be fighting to the end."

He kisses me on the top of my head. "If we're lucky."

He stayed for ten days. By his standards, with no working Internet, an eternity. I'm here for at least another month. At night, I sit under the cedar and sink my feet into the grass. I don't want to say I've come full circle because that would be over-romanticizing my life. But I do feel connected to the earth here. The night sky is blue-black, blazing with stars. Far from making me feel insignificant, it fills me with strength—the joy of being able to look *out* instead of in. Perhaps it takes a lifetime to learn how to become a woman. A late bloomer, I'm beginning again.

The château, 2017, above, my husband and me, left.

acknowledgments

First of all, I would like to thank Judith Regan for her bold enthusiasm and resolution.

Kathy Huck, for her tireless guidance throughout the editing process, her keen eye, clear logic, and endless patience. Without her, I would have buckled. To Richard Ljoenes, Hillary Schupf, Nancy Singer, and everyone on the team at Regan Arts, and the copyeditor, Laine Morreau. Lisa Bankoff, for seeing what the book could become and pointing me in the right direction. Thanks also to John Burnham, and Julie Meisionczek—with much appreciation for her swift pen.

SPECIAL THANKS TO:

Susanna Moore, for her impeccable taste and talent, and who ploughed through countless drafts over the years and kept me on track. Kathryn Ireland, for her hospitality and inspirational *joie de vivre*, and Louise Fletcher whose support and *tartes aux pommes* sustained me. To Katie Arnoldi, for her sound wisdom and logic, always available to lift my spirits. Ursula Brooks and Liv Ballard, for their true friendship, guidance, and unflagging zeal. David Mamet, Rebecca Pidgeon, Charles Arnoldi, Rita and David Milch who encouraged me from the beginning. Much gratitude to my friend Jean Graham who has been a solid ally for years. And a particular thanks to Kate Betts, for her generosity and for appreciating the value of a woman's story.

Also to:

Lynda, who, unlike me, remembered names. Cameron, for his humor, support and expert attention to the minutiae. Max and Tony, with much belated love and without whom there is no story. And Michael Zabell, John and Jennifer, Ian La Frenais, Jaqueline Bisset, Victoria Getty, Rachel, Bee, Sally, Buck, Jonathan LaP., Naomi Watts, Robbie R., Mitch and Kelly, Nick and Stephanie, Lyndall, James Fox, Valerie, the de la Falaise family, Jean and Claude P, Fabrice F., Fabrice H., Christian B., Sabastien B., the Boudets, and the Moulins. All lovers lost or dead.

And most of all, to my husband for his unique perspective, his wit, his intelligence, and his enduring patience and love.

I am grateful to the photographers Eva Sereny and to Norman Eales—permission kindly given by Paul Mc Beth and Debbie Condon, managers of Eales' estate. And to Guy Webster.